The Origins and Foundations of Music Education

Also available from Continuum

Musical Development and Learning, David J. Hargreaves and Adrian North

Music Education with Digital Technology, John Finney and Pamela Burnard

The Origins and Foundations of Music Education

Cross-cultural historical studies of music in compulsory schooling

Edited by Gordon Cox and Robin Stevens

Continuum Studies in Educational Research

continuum

Continuum International Publishing Group

The Tower Building
11 York Road
London
SE1 7NX

80 Maiden Lane,
Suite 704
New York
NY 10038

www.continuumbooks.com

First published 2010
This paperback edition published 2011

British Library Cataloguing-in-Publication Data
A catalogue record for this book is available from the British Library.

ISBN: 978-1-8470-6207-9 (hardcover)
　　　978-1-4411-2888-1 (paperback)

Library of Congress Cataloging-in-Publication Data
The origins and foundations of music education : cross-cultural historical studies of music in compulsory schooling / edited by Gordon Cox and Robin Stevens.
　　p. cm. – (Continuum studies in educational research)
Includes bibliographical references and index.
ISBN 978-1-4411-2888-1 (pbk.)
1. Music–Instruction and study. 2. Music–Instruction and study–History. I. Cox, Gordon, 1942– II. Stevens, Robin Sydney. III. Title. IV. Series.

MT1.O75 2011
780.71–dc22

2011016504

Typeset by BookEns, Royston, Herts.
Printed and bound in Great Britain

Contents

List of Figures and Tables   vii
List of Contributors   viii
Foreword by *Håkan Lundström*, Past-President,   xiii
    International Society for Music Education
Acknowledgements   xiv

1   Introduction   1
    Gordon Cox and Robin Stevens

Part 1: Europe

2   Britain: Towards 'a long overdue renaissance'?   15
    Gordon Cox

3   France: An uncertain and unequal combat   29
    François Madurell

4   Germany: Educational goals, curricular structure,   45
    political principles
    Wilfried Gruhn

5   Ireland: Curriculum development in troubled times   61
    Marie McCarthy

6   Norway: Educational progress or stasis on the outskirts of Europe? 77
    Fred Ola Bjørnstad and Magne Espeland

7   Spain: A journey from a nominal towards a universally 91
    implemented curriculum
    Gabriel Rusinek and Susana Sarfson

Part 2: The Americas

A North America

8 Canada: Diverse developments across the decades   109
Nancy Vogan

9 United States of America: Reflections on the development   121
and effectiveness of compulsory music education
Jere T. Humphreys

B Latin America

10 Argentina: From 'música vocal' to 'educación artística: Música'   139
Ana Lucía Frega, with Alicia de Couve and Claudia Dal Pino

11 Cuba: Music education and revolution   153
Lisa M. Lorenzino

Part 3: Africa and Asia-Pacific

12 Australia: Recurring problems and unresolved issues   171
Robin Stevens and Jane Southcott

13 China: Socio-political constructions of school music   189
Wai-Chung Ho

14 Japan: Music as a tool for moral education?   205
Masafumi Ogawa

15 South Africa: Indigenous roots, cultural imposition and an   221
uncertain future
Robin Stevens and Eric Akrofi

Index   236

List of Figures and Tables

Figures

Figure 4.1   Latin school (*Lateinschule*) in the sixteenth century   46
Figure 4.2   *Antikes Schulwesen* (cartoon by J. Nussbiegel)   47
Figure 4.3   'Der Herr Cantor'   48
Figure 4.4   Notation with numbers   50
Figure 4.5   King Friedrich Wilhem I of Prussia visits a typical
                 village school   51
Figure 12.1 Empire Day, Mount Templeton School, South Australia   180
Figure 12.2 Alexander Clark and the Thousand Voices Choir   181
Figure 12.3 'Tale of the Bellbirds'   183
Figure 12.4 Sturt Street School Band (South Australia)   184
Figure 15.1 Map of the Provinces of South Africa (1910)   224

Tables

Table 10.1   History of school music education in Argentina   149
Table 13.1   Teaching content and hours of music lessons as
                 suggested by the Ministry of Education, China   199

List of Contributors

Eric Akrofi holds an EdD degree in music education from the University of Illinois at Urbana-Champaign, USA, and was most recently Professor of Music Education at Walter Sisulu University, Mthatha, South Africa. He has spent over thirty years teaching in universities in Ghana and South Africa. His areas of scholarly research include music analysis and theory, music and arts education in Africa, African music and cultural identity. Aside numerous conference presentations and published articles, he is the author of *Sharing knowledge and experience: A profile of Kwabena Nketia, scholar and music educator* (2002) and was one of three co-editors of *Music and Identity: Transformation and Negotiation* (2007).

Fred Ola Bjørnstad is Lecturer in Music and Education at Stord/ Haugesund University College (Norway). He works in the field of music teacher education and his main interests include music in the classroom, choral conducting and folk music. He has published numerous articles on Norwegian folk music. Currently he is leading *Ideoskosa*, a national inter-institutional project about ideas and ideologies in Norwegian songbooks for schools from 1814 onwards.

Alicia Cristina de Couve graduated as a music educator from the National Conservatory of Music (Argentina), and as 'Professor of Pedagogy' from the John F. Kennedy University. She also holds a Licentiate in history from the Argentine Catholic University. She is Professor of Educational Policy, Didactics and Teaching Practice at the Higher Conservatory of Music of the City of Buenos Aires 'Astor Piazzolla'. Her publications include co-authored research reports and articles published in *The Bulletin of Historical Research in Music Education*, *Arts Education Policy Review*, *International Journal of Music Education* and *Boletín de Investigación Educativo-Musical* (CIEM, Buenos Aires).

Gordon Cox formerly Senior Lecturer in Music Education, Institute of Education, University of Reading, has written extensively on the history of music education, and his books include *A History of Music Education in England 1872–1928* (1993) and *Living Music in Schools 1923–1999* (2002). He is a past co-editor of the *British Journal of Music Education* and is a member of the History Standing Committee of the International Society for Music Education.

Magne Espeland is Professor of Music and Education at Stord/Haugesund University College (HSH) in Western Norway. His specialities include curriculum studies, music methodology for the general classroom, and research methodology for arts education. Professor Espeland is currently the Project Chair of the research programme 'Culture, Arts and Creativity in Education' at HSH. Internationally he has presented papers at conferences on several continents, including a keynote in April 2009 at the Research in Music Education Conference at the University of Exeter. He was the Chair for the International Society for Music Education's 25th World Conference in Music Education, which took place in August 2002, in Bergen, Norway.

Ana Lucía Frega is a life-long Argentinian music educator, with a doctorate in music with a special focus on education. She has taught at all levels of the general and artistic education system. Dr Frega was Head of the School of Performing Arts at the Teatro Colón de Buenos Aires for ten years. She is currently teaching at the University CAECE, where she leads the master's progamme in music education, the first such course in Argentina. She has published over 55 books, and is an Honorary Life Member of the International Society for Music Education (ISME). She currently serves on the History Standing Committee of ISME.

Wilfried Gruhn is Professor Emeritus of Music Education at the University of Music (*Musikhochschule*), Freiburg, Germany. From 1972 he taught at the Music Academies in Saarbruecken and Essen, and from 1977 until 2003 in Freiburg, Germany. Dr Gruhn has been co-editor of several journals for music education, President of the International Research Alliance of Institutes for Music Education (1995–1997), an ISME Board Member (2000–2004), and Director of the Gordon-Institute for Early Childhood Music Learning, Freiburg (2003–2009). His research areas include historical and empirical research in music education, particularly in relation to developmental learning theory and the neurobiology of music learning.

Wai-Chung Ho completed her DPhil in music education at the Institute of Education, University of London in 1996. She joined the Department of Music, Hong Kong Baptist University in September 1996 where she lectures in music education. She has published extensively in such top-ranking journals as the *British Journal of Music Education*, *British Journal of Educational Technology*, *International Journal of Music Education*, *Music Education Research*, *Popular Music* and *Social History*. Her main research areas are the sociology of music, the music education curriculum, values education, and the comparative study of East Asian music education.

Jere Humphreys is a professor at Arizona State University, USA. An historical and quantitative researcher, he has authored more than 100 publications, and presented and taught in 28 countries. He has served on the editorial committees of thirteen scholarly journals and as editor for the *Journal of Historical Research in Music Education*. He has been nominated for or won several awards for teaching, research, and service, including the highest (lifetime) research award from MENC: The National Association for Music Education. He is a Senior Fulbright Scholar and the contributing editor for music education for the second edition of the *New Grove Dictionary of American Music* (Oxford).

Lisa Lorenzino currently serves as Area Chair for Music Education at the Schulich School of Music, McGill University in Montreal, Canada where she teaches on the graduate and undergraduate programmes. Dr. Lorenzino's doctoral studies fueled her interest in Cuban music pedagogy, an area of research that she continues to develop in her academic career. Her other areas of research interest include jazz education, gender studies, and music teacher retention. A fifteen-year veteran high school band, choir, and guitar teacher, Dr Lorenzino is also an avid jazz flutist and composer.

François Madurell is a researcher and teacher at the University Paris-Sorbonne (Paris IV) in the Department of Musicology. He is the head of the research group MUSECO within the Observatoire Musical Français. This group was founded in 2006, and is devoted to studying the relationships between music, cognition and musical instruction, and the musicological, sociological and educational implications of their connections. In addition he is the Director of the *Journal de Recherche en Education Musicale*. His fields of research include musicology and cognitive sciences, and music education.

Marie McCarthy is Professor and Chair of Music Education at the University of Michigan. Her research studies have focused on the historical, social, and cultural foundations of music education. Publications include two books, *Passing It On: The Transmission of Music in Irish Culture* (1999) and *Toward a Global Community: The International Society for Music Education, 1953–2003* (2004). Dr McCarthy is Chair of the History Standing Committee of the International Society for Music Education.

Masafumi Ogawa completed undergraduate and graduate degrees at the Tokyo National University of Fine Arts and Music and holds a DME degree from Indiana University. He is presently Professor of Music Education at Yokohama National University, Japan. His areas of scholarly interest include comparative studies of music education curricula, philosophy of music education, the applications of movable sol-fa in education, and choral conducting. He has published in several international journals including

International Journal of Music Education, Philosophy of Music Education Review and *The Bulletin of Historical Research in Music Education.*

Claudia Dal Pino is Professor of Planning and Evaluation in the Master in Didactics of Music course at CAECE University; Professor of Research Methodology at the National University Institute of Arts; and Professor of Educational Policy, Didactics and Teaching Practice at the Higher Conservatory of Music of the City of Buenos Aires 'Astor Piazzolla'. Her publications include co-authored research reports and articles that have been published in *The Bulletin of Historical Research in Music Education, Arts Education Policy Review, International Journal of Music Education* and *Boletín de Investigación Educativo-Musical* (CIEM, Buenos Aires).

Gabriel Rusinek teaches undergraduate and graduate courses at the Universidad Complutense de Madrid where he also coordinates a doctoral programme in music education and convenes an annual research seminar (SCIEM). He has published in Spanish journals and international journals, and has contributed to the *International Handbook of Research in Arts Education* (Bresler, 2007). Dr Rusinek is a member of the advisory boards of the *International Journal of Education and the Arts* and *Music Education Research*. He is co-editor of the peer-reviewed open-access research journal *Revista Electrónica Complutense de Investigación en Educación Musical* (www.ucm.es/info/reciem).

Susana Sarfson teaches at the Universidad de Zaragoza, Spain. Born in Buenos Aires (Argentina), she studied the piano, harpsichord and Hispanic philology, and then gained her doctorate from the Universidad de Zaragoza. Her research interests include music teaching and learning, the history of music education, and Baroque music in Spain and Latin America. Dr Sarfson has presented papers at conferences in Argentina, Bolivia, Chile, Italy, México, Perú, Poland and Spain.

Jane Southcott is a Senior Lecturer in the Faculty of Education, Monash University, Victoria, Australia. Her main research focus is the history of the music curriculum in Australia, America and Europe. She is a narrative historian and much of her research is biographical. Dr Southcott also researches multiculturalism, and music and positive ageing. She is Director of Postgraduate Education Programmes, teaches in postgraduate and pre-service teacher education programmes, and supervises postgraduate research students. Dr Southcott is a past President of the Australian and New Zealand Association for Research in Music Education and is a member of the editorial boards of several international and national refereed journals.

Robin Stevens was formerly Associate Professor of Music Education at Deakin University, Melbourne, Australia and is now a Principal Fellow in the Melbourne Conservatorium of Music at The University of Melbourne. He has a long-standing interest in historical research in music education –

particularly the development and propagation of the tonic sol-fa method and notation. He has published articles in several national and international journals and has contributed historical entries to *The Oxford Companion to Australian Music* (1997). Dr Stevens is a member of the History Standing Committee of the International Society for Music Education.

Nancy F. Vogan is the Pickard-Bell Professor of Music at Mount Allison University in Sackville, New Brunswick, Canada where she has taught for over thirty-five years. Her major fields of research have been the history of music instruction and the history of music in Canada. She is co-author (with J. Paul Green) of *Music Education in Canada: A Historical Account* (1991). Her other publications include articles in numerous books, journals, and encyclopaedias. She is currently preparing a book on the history of singing schools and tunebooks in the Maritime Provinces of Canada.

Foreword

We know of no human culture without music and wherever music is present, music learning will take place as part of socialization processes, as will the transmission of cultural values and practices from one generation to the next. Taking my own home country – Sweden – as an example, compulsory schooling has existed there since the 1840s and the first school songbook was published during the same decade. This meant the introduction of a style of music that differed from the local traditions at that time – at least outside the major cities and the higher social strata of the society. Folk songs were rearranged into school songs and adapted to the new musical language. New children's songs were also composed and became a part of the class singing repertoire within the school curriculum. All this is now the basis for everybody's musical frame of reference even though there is, of course, still music and music learning taking place outside formal education.

Read the chapter on music education in Japan – or almost any other country represented in this book – and you will find a number of striking parallels with your own country. Compulsory music education has reached many corners of the world. Nevertheless, as is normally the case in the process of globalization, compulsory music education may at first glance seem rather similar in each country, but a closer examination will reveal a number of local adaptations. We often think of globalization as the 'West' versus the 'East' or the 'North' versus the 'South'. However, such broad categories are not sufficiently well nuanced for us to fully understand how compulsory music education has spread and been adapted to the national environment.

These are some of the perspectives opened up by this volume as a result of its focus on how compulsory music education was received and developed in a number of countries. It fills a gap in our knowledge about music education and provides a basis for increased understanding of the present situation in different parts of the world.

Many of the ideas that led to this publication were developed and modified within the context of the conferences and symposia of the International

Society for Music Education (ISME). On behalf of ISME, I convey my thanks to the editors of the collection and the authors of the individual chapters in this book for their engaged work. *The Origins and Foundations of Music Education* contributes significantly to the Society's aims of fostering global intercultural understanding and cooperation among the world's music educators and of promoting music education throughout the world.

Håkan Lundström, ISME Past-President,
Malmo Faculty of Fine and Performing Arts,
Lund University, Sweden

The International Society for Music Education (ISME) was founded in 1953 under the auspices of UNESCO. The mission of the Society is to build a worldwide community of music educators, foster intercultural understanding and cooperation, and nurture and promote music education worldwide. Its seven Commissions embrace a comprehensive view of music education. Website address: www.isme.org

Acknowledgements

It is a pleasure to thank our contributors for their great enthusiasm and for their engagement in debate with us in order to untangle as clearly as possible the often complex roots of music education and their continuing influence or otherwise today. The editorial process has been one of a stimulating and fruitful international dialogue for which we are indebted to our authors. Particular thanks must also be extended to Marie McCarthy, Chair of the ISME History Standing Committee, for her constant support and encouragement of the project since its inception, and to Håkan Lundström, then President of the International Society for Music Education, for so readily agreeing to contribute a foreword.

1

Introduction

Gordon Cox and Robin Stevens

Our purpose in this book is to assemble accounts of the origins and foundations of music education in compulsory schooling from a selection of representative countries. The idea arose from a concern that for too long we, as music educators, have been constrained by the national boundaries in which we work. Yet increasingly in music classrooms, we observe musical practices and musical tastes that draw on a wide variety of cultures across the world. We need to confront this reality and learn from those operating in different cultural settings. One way of doing this is to discover the roots of our present practice and to compare and contrast them with those of music educators working within different cultures around the world. Such a study should enrich our understanding of the ways in which music can act as a powerful educational force and also question our taken-for-granted pedagogies and our assumptions about the place of music in compulsory schooling. However, our shared knowledge of this historical phenomenon is currently fragmentary and there is a consequent need for a series of studies to provide more comprehensive documentation and analysis of this foundational aspect of school music from a variety of international perspectives.

But first, in order to orientate ourselves, we need to consider something of the wider context of the introduction of compulsory schooling (see Cummings 1997). The social origins of formal education go back many centuries, and in most settings derive from the initiatives of religious groups. Towards the end of the eighteenth century in Europe and later in other parts of the world, revolutionary convulsions created a new ideal – to educate large numbers of the body public – and to arrange this education in a series of levels. Cummings (*ibid.*) has proposed six core patterns of 'modern' education including the French, Prussian, English, American, Japanese and Russian patterns. In each instance, the nation-state responsible for building the modern educational system also decided to create an empire, including an educational dimension. Consequently, each system had a profound impact on global mass education. Williams (1997) provides us with a helpful chronology of compulsory schooling:

> Compulsory schooling began in the early 1700s in Europe ... [It] was initiated in the more peripheral European states, beginning in the various German states and in Austria, then in Denmark, Greece, and Spain. By the mid-1800s, states outside Europe began to institute compulsory schooling – Haiti, Argentina, Massachusetts in the United States, then Japan. European nations continued to enact compulsory schooling statutes – Norway and Sweden, then finally in the late 1800s, the industrial leaders – France, The Netherlands, and Britain (p. 120).

Today (2009) considerable progress has been made internationally in the provision of universal primary education, a development enshrined as Goal 2 of the United Nations Millennium Development Goals whose target is to 'ensure that, by 2015, children everywhere, boys and girls alike, will be able to complete a full course of primary schooling' (UN 2008: section 2: 10). However the UN report reminds us that in 2006 there were still some 75 million children not receiving a school education.

The potential for utilizing compulsory schooling as a research focus is considerable, both for its contemporary relevance and for its historical underpinning. In particular, compulsory schooling 'lends itself to a composite analytical approach' (Mangan 1994: viii). This is especially the case when considering what should be taught in schools, which brings with it the age-old question of 'what knowledge is of most worth?'. As Holmes and McLean (1989) argue in their comparative study of the curriculum, 'common educational problems find unique expression in national systems' (p. vii).

As far as international and comparative music education research is concerned, Kemp and Lepherd (1992) traced the beginnings of serious work in the field to the 1953 UNESCO Conference in Brussels by considering the Role and Place of Music in the Education of Youth and Adults. One of the principal outcomes was the formation of the International Society for Music Education (ISME) in that year (see McCarthy 2004). Since then Lepherd has undertaken pioneering work with his comparative studies of the systematic provision of music education from a variety of international perspectives (Lepherd 1988, 1994, 1995). However, while amply describing systemic aspects such as the current state of and provision for music in schools, there is little about the underlying historical processes involved in establishing music as a curriculum subject.

We believe that such a focus on the historical context is essential in order to provide a basis for an informed debate about present and future trends as far as music education internationally is concerned. In her paper 'Music education in the twenty-first century', Kertz-Welzel (2008) argues that comparative music education is a necessity, dealing as it should with issues of internationalization and globalization. But at the same time as comprising a distinctive field of research, international and comparative music education can, nevertheless, be part of other fields such as music education history. An emphasis on such a historical perspective is supported at a more general level by Crossley and Watson (2003) who maintain that, 'there are many different histories of comparative and international education that are still to be written. This is, in itself, an exciting prospect for the future' (p. 138).

Two further aspects of our approach in this book need to be considered. First, we have adopted a cross-cultural perspective, which Kertz-Welzel (2008) maintains can transcend the boundaries of the traditional comparative method by focusing on specific aspects such as learning music in and out of schools. Such an approach underpins two significant contributions to the field of music education: Campbell's *Lessons from the World: A Cross-Cultural Guide to Music Teaching and Learning* (1991) and Hargreaves and North's *Musical Development and Learning: The International Perspective* (2001). Second, our emphasis on music in compulsory schooling immediately links past and present. In this respect, Keith Watson (2001) affirms that 'there is a real need for comparative education to re-establish its unique role in providing comparative historical insights for future policy action' (p. 24).

As a first step in developing these ideas, the two editors put a proposal to the meeting of the History Standing Committee of the International Society for Music Education in Kuala Lumpur in 2006 for a project that would assemble accounts of the origins and foundations of music in compulsory schooling from a variety of countries. For the subsequent ISME World Conference in Bologna in 2008, we contacted prominent authors from eight different countries to contribute to a symposium. Since then the project has expanded to include some 14 countries and 19 authors. This book is the result. While it makes no attempt to be comprehensive in its scope, it does illustrate the potential richness of cross-cultural historical research in music education.

We asked contributors to explore some core issues concerning the introduction of music as a mandated part of the curriculum in compulsory schooling. These comprised the following:

- historical and political contexts
- aims and content of music as a compulsory subject
- teaching methods
- training of teachers
- experiences of pupils
- reflections on the present state of music education in the light of past developments.

However, we became strongly aware that too tight a focus would unnecessarily force the great diversity of historical factors into a straitjacket. Such issues as federal versus centralized nation-states, the unequal treatment of minorities, and the influences of colonialism, revolution and war have all meant that there were as many differences as similarities and as many discontinuities as continuities in the progress of music as a curriculum subject. Accordingly, readers will notice that different writers have placed different emphases on these core issues according to the historical contexts they have been researching.

In order to give coherence to the structure of the book, we have organized it based on three main areas – Africa and the Asia-Pacific region, the Americas and Europe. We decided to start the book with Europe simply because, first, that was the region where compulsory schooling began (Williams 1997) and, second, it became apparent that, through colonialism and missionary and military influences, it was European ideas that were the most influential in the pioneering days of mass compulsory schooling across the countries we have selected.

The six core issues we invited our contributors to focus on were intended to provide a thematic underpinning of the book and we now provide a brief overview, drawn from the succeeding chapters.

From the very beginnings of studies into comparative and international education, it was recognized that the contexts in which schools developed (historical, cultural, religious, economic, political and social etc.) were crucial to explaining the subtle but distinctive differences between each system (see Crossley and Watson 2003). The point is emphasized by Michael Sadler (in Bereday 1964: 310):

> In studying foreign systems of education we should not forget that the things outside the schools matter even more than the things inside ... A national system of education is a living thing, the outcome of forgotten struggles and difficulties and of 'battles long ago' ... It has in it some of the secret workings of national life.

In particular, the influence of the political ideologies of colonialism and nationalism on the aims and content of the music curriculum is apparent in the accounts that follow. For example, Britain was at the height of its imperial power in the nineteenth century, which coincided with the rise of compulsory mass schooling. Accordingly, various forms of 'imperial nationalism' were manifested in the celebrations of Empire Day in Australian schools and in the more politically motivated imposition of British cultural norms on the Irish. As Gordon Cox points out in his chapter, patriotism in Britain was all pervasive, there being hardly a school in the country that did not use *The National Song Book*. In Australia with contingents of colonial soldiers being sent to the Sudan and South Africa, songs with patriotic and nationalist sentiments were popular as a means of promoting 'imperial citizenship'. In Canada, European immigrants were taught singing in order to develop their English language skills and to instil a sense of patriotism.

Inextricably linked with colonialism was missionary endeavour that saw mission schools established in South Africa, often with strong musical traditions being developed, as well as in China where congregational singing was promoted most commonly through John Curwen's tonic sol-fa system. In their account of developments in South Africa, Robin Stevens and Eric Akrofi remind us that an unfortunate consequence of missionary activity was a disregard for and dismissal of indigenous musical and educational traditions, such as the initiation schools of the Xhosa-speaking people.

In the context of Spanish imperial expansion in Latin America, there were Jesuit missionaries who promoted music making in Argentina, while, in Cuba, it was Spanish musicians and educators who sought to strengthen the musical skills of the local population, encouraging a school of Cuban composers of Western European art music to emerge. At the same time, as Lisa Lorenzino explains, Afro-Cuban institutions (as distinct from those of Spanish origins) were developed in order to control and inhibit. The *cabildos* or *cofradías*, set up by slave owners, served as centres for drumming, singing and dancing and, rather than focusing on note reading and literacy skills, were aurally based, using imitation and rote learning. Ironically, Afro-Cubans found themselves being encouraged to become professional musicians – as a profession, however, this was a financially unstable option at the time.

It was the struggle for political independence and the defence of national interests that particularly shaped what went on in schools. In Argentina, for example, school singing was intended to revive patriotic feeling inspired by the revolutionary process of establishing a representative, republican and federal system of government. Similar patriotic fervour was promoted through music in the French school system as a result of the disastrous Franco-Prussian War right up until the 1920s. The situation was paralleled in Prussia, where a new national identity was being forged under Bismarck and supported by a school song repertoire, the greater part of which was of a strongly nationalist character. In Norway, with independence in 1905, there was a desire to express patriotic feelings through music and song in school settings. In Ireland, as Marie McCarthy shows, political independence after 1921 resulted in an enhanced profile for music as the result of the language revival movement, the musical culture of Catholicism and a national effort to improve musical culture and the 'national fibre'. Consequently, music in schools was able to promote the authentic Irish culture and language. During the Second Sino-Japanese War of 1937–1945, a large repertoire of national songs was promoted in Chinese schools to inspire resistance to the Japanese invasion and achieve national liberation. With Castro's Cuban revolution in 1959 there was a specific focus on education, literacy and national pride which, in turn, influenced musical education.

But revolutions and political movements could also have a negative effect. China's Cultural Revolution between 1966 and 1976 meant that music was severely restricted to the service of political ideology, so that the singing of one song was to achieve one 'political' lesson learnt. In Spain, the end of the civil war saw the imposition of a fundamentalist Catholic and gender-segregated educational system with fascist principles that dominated what went on in schools – resulting specifically in the selection of a school music repertoire that incorporated a mixture of folk, religious and fascist songs. In Germany, the rise of Nazism precluded many of the then current liberalizing influences in the music curriculum and, from an educational perspective, led to a period of stasis.

Alongside these patriotic and nationalist sentiments, there was no shortage of high-minded justifications for music in the curriculum that were related to music as a humanizing and civilizing force. During the 1830s in the USA, as in many other countries, it was religious motives that predominated in the justification of music as a curriculum subject. For the British schools inspector Arthur Somervell, music could help build up the 'ideal citizen'. This idea had a long historical lineage, including the European Platonic notions of balance in physical and aesthetic elements in character building and the Chinese Confucian belief that music could help enhance social harmony and promote morality. More specifically, it was held that music could refine individuals living in difficult social contexts, such as the Australian goldfields and in inner city schools in London. For Egerton Ryerson in Canada, music was believed to be a 'powerful agent of moral culture' as it was for Isawa Shūji, the father of music education in Japan, who maintained that the most important benefit of music was its effect on moral development. However, this high mindedness could become paternalistic: in South Australia, it was believed that singing could assist in combating slovenly speech and Australian 'twang and slang' and, in Argentina, that it could help modify the unpleasantness of the provincial accent.

A more fundamental problem with these justifications was that music was rarely incorporated into the curriculum for its own sake. Masafumi Ogawa demonstrates in his chapter on Japan that if music merely exists as a means to an end, its fate is decided not on its own merits, but on that associated with other areas of learning, more specifically moral education. This makes for vulnerability.

When it comes to considering the methods employed in teaching school music, it will become apparent that the main emphasis in the pioneering days of compulsory schooling was on the skill of singing at sight. Much of this teaching was based on solmization – the application of sol-fa syllables as a mnemonic or memory aid for reading pitch. This teaching technique goes back in Western culture at least to Guido d'Arezzo in the eleventh century. According to Stevens (2008), 'solmisation is not only the most ancient form of teaching the pitch dimension of vocal music, but is now also the most widely used form of music pedagogy' (p. 194). The debate over the relative merits of the fixed-doh system (where 'doh' is always 'C') and the movable-doh system (where 'doh' is always the keynote) has been well covered in the literature, particularly by Kenneth Simpson (1976).

In Europe, the bastion of the fixed-doh method was France as demonstrated in the work of G. L. Bocquillon Wilhem and his classes for working men in Paris where the method later become known as *solfège*. In his chapter, François Madurell argues that, although the fixed-doh system may be seen as important for specialized training, based on the belief that perfect pitch is a benchmark for musical acumen, its dominance in France at least appears to have been counterproductive for school music. The fixed-doh method has traditionally been firmly entrenched in Argentina, as shown in the account of Ana Lucía Frega, Alicia de Couve and Claudia Dal Pino, where the influence of Italian and French conservatoires was particularly strong.

In England, John Hullah was so inspired by Wilhem's method that he adapted it for use in British schools and the instructional manual on Hullah's method carried with it the imprimatur of the government of the day. As will become clear in later chapters, this was a deeply flawed method, whose reliance on the fixed-doh system for teaching children led to its collapse, but not before having been adopted, albeit unsuccessfully, in most of the countries within Britain's sphere of influence including Australia, Canada and Ireland.

The movable-doh method was originally developed by Sarah Glover as Norwich sol-fa and further developed by John Curwen as tonic sol-fa, and was soon adopted as the most effective way of introducing children to music reading. Tonic sol-fa spread throughout the British Empire – and beyond – by missionaries as well as by teachers who had been trained in its methods and had worked abroad.

Cipher or numeral notation was developed by Jean-Jacques Rousseau and Émile Chevé. Indeed, its use was originally proposed in France to overcome the difficulties pupils found in mastering the traditional staff notation system. It became embedded in the Prussian school system, where solmization was never a matter of pedagogical contention. Similarly in Norway, the *ziffer* (or numeral) method was widely used, often in conjunction, according to Bjørnstad and Espeland, with the one-string instrument, the *psalmodikon*. However, perhaps the most interesting example of the use of cipher notation was in China, where the *jianpu* system was adapted from the numeral system via Japan where it had been introduced by a French musician. But intriguingly, Wai-Chung Ho argues that the *jianpu* is a natural extension and unification of the much more ancient Chinese *gongche* notation.

In most countries, alongside singing 'by note', there was also considerable recourse to teaching songs 'by ear', due principally to the limited musical expertise of many teachers. But singing by ear was also associated with educational philosophies that stressed spontaneity and naturalness. For example, in Cuba, singing by imitation was a reflection of the rote learning style of the *zarzuela*.

While there was an emphasis on developing formal ways of teaching pupils to sing at sight, there are also scattered references to instrumental teaching including the drum and fife bands of Australia as well as the Manby violin teaching method, and to the percussion band movement in Britain. More specialized instrumental teaching developed within the school systems in the USA and Cuba and, in parallel, 'schools of music' and local conservatories outside school systems in Spain and Norway.

Although it was generally believed that music was a subject that all pupils should experience, there was a minority view that considered music to be a 'feminine' subject. In France during the 1830s, for example, while the practice of singing was mandatory for girls, it was optional for boys. Gabriel Rusinek and Susana Sarfson point out that over a century later in Spain following the victory of Franco in the Civil War in 1942, there was an emphasis in the newly reopened teachers' colleges on preparing female instructors to teach music specifically to girls as part of 'home skills'.

When we come to consider the issue of teacher training, it was expected in the majority of cases during the pioneering days that every teacher would teach music and it was therefore the role of teacher training courses to provide them with the necessary musical skills. This made considerable demands on both students and their teachers. In France, the programme of musical instruction was designed to enable students to sing in tune, to acquire an elementary knowledge of music, as well as the rudiments of *solfège*. In Argentina, the detailed requirements concerning musical knowledge demonstrate something of the didactic nature of the training – the approach was a long way from the 'sound before the symbol' principle. Much the same situation existed in Britain, which led to the damning comment that teacher training during the Victorian era had neither instilled a love of music nor imparted any understanding of it. In some countries, student teachers were required not only to be able to sing at sight, but also to develop elementary instrumental skills that would enable them to accompany classroom singing. In Germany, they were taught to play the violin, and in Norway, the *psalmodikon* and the harmonium.

Gradually systems of teaching specialization developed. In Japan, there was a brave attempt by the government to educate leaders among music educators with the establishment in 1880 of the Music Study Committee (*Ongaku torishirabe kakari*). As a part of its remit, 22 students enrolled to study singing, *koto*, reed organ, *kokyū*, violin, harmony, theory of music, history of music and teaching methods. Some were court musicians and others came from noble families. Despite the fact that they had no background in Western music, most of them showed considerable progress and later became faculty members of normal schools involved with training teachers. In both Cuba and Argentina, the role of music conservatoires was key to the development of a specialized musical training that, in turn, influenced teacher training, although, surprisingly, Cuba did not have a state-funded teacher training institute until 1961. In the USA, Jere Humphreys explains that it was textbook publishers who first of all sponsored summer institutes for music supervisors, while a specialist normal school for music teacher training was established in Potsdam, New York, in 1882. Prior to 1914 in the USA, 'public school music departments' began springing up in teachers' colleges and some universities. Between the wars, France instituted a 'teaching aptitude certificate', enabling the holders to teach in upper grades and in teachers' colleges. By 1952 in China, teacher education reforms, based on the Soviet Russian model, resulted in nine compulsory music courses being available for student teachers.

When it comes to uncovering the experiences of children in making music at school, it must be admitted that describing what actually happened in nineteenth century classrooms is a real challenge because of the absence of direct records – although Finkelstein (1989) has undertaken a particularly revealing historical study of US primary school teachers at this time. However, in their chapter on Australia, Robin Stevens and Jane Southcott present us with the kind of data that can demonstrate children's music making – school newspapers, reports of school concerts and photographs of children performing. Moreover, the utilization of contemporary prints in Wilfried Gruhn's discussion of school music in Germany provides some unique insights into music teachers and their classrooms.

Finally, we come to reflect on the present state of school music education in the light of past experiences. It appears that, in most of the accounts, the teaching of music in elementary schools is still largely in the hands of generalist teachers, although in the USA, elementary schools are largely served by credentialed music teachers. But what emerges in most of the chapters is the need for education systems to support the classroom teachers by providing them with a comprehensive training in music that ensures that they will possess the necessary skills, knowledge and confidence to implement an effective classroom music programme.

It will become apparent to readers that while there have been many developments in and strengthening of compulsory music in schools as well as a record of fine innovative work, there are concerns that increasingly music becomes just one of a number of learning areas – many of them optional – under the generic title of 'artistic education'. We see this as a concern in Argentina, Australia, France, Germany, South Africa and Spain. Similarly, there are a number of reports that the concentration on the basic or core subjects – literacy, numeracy, science, languages etc. – have begun to squeeze music out of the curriculum – such as in Britain, France, and Norway. In the USA and Britain, much of the tension in these situations results from a top-down control over national educational standards. We might contrast this with Canada, where, as Nancy Vogan points out, there is a general wariness about the very idea of a national music curriculum.

Of course, there are alternatives or supplements to the notion of 'general music for all', including the development of the American system of the elective instrumental ensembles and, from Cuba, a model for the effective provision of both music as a general subject and as a highly developed specialism for gifted students. The work of 'Musical Futures' in Britain is a hopeful sign of the renewal of general music, with its emphasis on informal learning and a greater connection with popular music in the classroom.

We have been very much aware during the course of working on this book that it is something of a pioneering venture. Much remains to be done. We suggest six priorities for future action:

- To extend the geographical and cultural scope of the study – for example, to consider Russia and its former satellite states, in which music education has often been a powerful force, as well as countries like Israel with its rich Jewish musical heritage, and Indonesia and Malaysia with their predominantly Muslim culture.
- To undertake analytical comparisons – such as the transfer of a concept from one context to another as Gruhn (2001) has demonstrated in his paper on the transfer of Pestalozzian principles in Europe to American singing instruction. Through such studies we may come to a clearer understanding that 'concepts and ideologies may change their meanings when moved to a different context' (*ibid.*: 3).
- To chart the historical impact – for good or ill – of compulsory music in schools on the musical lives of indigenous peoples. This has been touched on to a greater or lesser extent in the chapters concerned with Australia, Cuba, Japan and South Africa, but perhaps with the United Nations Millennium Goal of providing universal primary education, this may become a priority for researchers and for music educators in the future.
- To investigate the exponential growth historically of instrumental teaching of school-age children, as a counterbalance to the emphasis in this book on vocal teaching.
- To extend cross-cultural historical research to specialist music instruction for the musically gifted and to higher education – for example, music conservatoires have been particularly influential on some school music programmes. In this regard, Fend and Noiray's (2005) book entitled *Musical Education in Europe (1770–1914)* represents a brave attempt to

historically document such institutions – a study that they describe as entering a *terra incognita*. There are clearly rich possibilities for investigating such institutions outside of the European domain.

- To undertake cross-cultural historical accounts of the rise of national associations of music educators, many of which have influenced policy (for example, the Music Educators National Conference (MENC) in the USA, the National Association of Music Educators (NAME) in the UK and the Canadian Music Educators Association (CMEA) to name but a few).

It is indeed the task set before music education historians to adjust to such an ambitious agenda so that their research has a global, inclusive reach. Through such work we may prevent music education, in Keith Swanwick's words, 'drifting into the margins of education ... we must recognize that music is a big player in the market-place of ideas' (1997: 2). Of course music education history is just one of the research fields that are appropriate to such a study, alongside international and comparative education, the philosophy of education, ethnomusicology and folklore. We should remind ourselves, however, of the words of Émile Durkheim in relation to the unique goal of educational history (1977): '[I]t is only by carefully studying the past that we can come to anticipate the future and then to understand the present' (p. 9).

We hope that the book will help to serve one of the purposes of international exchange among music educators – that we may all learn from the histories of different pedagogical traditions and so help to empower us with greater insights into our own and other education systems, so that there is a greater sense of belonging to a global community of like-minded professionals who share a passion for the teaching and learning of music.

References

Bereday, G. Z. F. (1964), 'Sir Michael Sadler's "Studies of Foreign Systems of Education"', *Comparative Education Review*, 7, (3), 307–14.

Campbell, P. S. (1991), *Lessons from the World: A Cross-Cultural Guide to Music Teaching and Learning*. New York: Schirmer.

Crossley, H. and Watson, K. (2003), *Comparative and International Research in Education: Globalisation, Context and Difference*. London: Routledge Falmer.

Cummings, W. K. (1997), 'Patterns of modern education', in W. K. Cummings and N. F. McGinn (eds), *International Handbook of Education and Development: Preparing Schools, Students and Nations for the Twenty-First Century*. Oxford: Pergamon, pp. 63–86.

Durkheim, E. (1977), *The Evolution of Educational Thought: Lectures on the Formation and Development of Secondary Education in France*. London: Routledge & Kegan Paul.

Fend, M. and Noiray, M. (eds) (2005), *Musical Education in Europe (1770–1914): Compositional, Institutional, and Political Challenges*. Berlin: Berliner Wissenschafts-Verlag.

Finkelstein, B. (1989), *Governing the Young: Teacher Behavior in Popular Primary Schools in 19th Century United States*. New York: Falmer Press.

Gruhn, W. (2001), 'European "methods" for American nineteenth-century singing instruction: a cross-cultural perspective on historical research', *Journal of Historical Research in Music Education*, 23, (1), 3–18.

Hargreaves, D. J. and North, A. (eds) (2001), *Musical Development and Learning: The International Perspective*. London: Continuum.

Holmes, B. and McLean, M. (eds) (1989), *The Curriculum: A Comparative Perspective*. London: Routledge.

Kemp, A. E. and Lepherd, L. (1992), 'Research methods in international and comparative music education', in R. Colwell (ed.) *Handbook of Research on Music Teaching and Learning*. New York: Schirmer, pp. 773–88.

Kertz-Welzel, A. (2008), 'Music education in the twenty-first century: a cross-cultural comparison of German and American music education towards a new concept of international dialogue', *Music Education Research*, 10, (4), 439–49.

Lepherd, L. (1988), *Music Education in International Perspective: The People's Republic of China*. Darling Heights, Queensland: Music International.

Lepherd, L. (1994), *Music Education in International Perspective: Australia*. Toowoomba, Queensland: University of South Queensland.

Lepherd, L. (1995), *Music Education in International Perspective – National Systems: England, Namibia, Argentina, Russia, Hungary, Portugal, Singapore, Sweden, the United States of America*. Toowoomba, Queensland: University of Southern Queensland.

Mangan, J. A. (ed.) (1994), *A Significant Social Revolution: Cross-Cultural Aspects of the Evolution of Compulsory Education*. London: Woburn Press.

McCarthy, M. (2004), *Toward a Global Community: The International Society for Music Education 1953–2003*. Nedlands, Western Australia: ISME.

Simpson, K. (1976), 'Some controversies about sight singing', in K. Simpson (ed.), *Some Great Music Educators: A Collection of Essays*. Borough Green: Novello, pp. 107–122.

Stevens, R. (2008), 'Solmisation past and present: the legacy of Guido D'Arezzo', in M. Baroni and J. Tafuri (eds), *Abstracts: 28th ISME World Conference: Music at all Ages*. Bologna: ISME, pp. 193–4.

Swanwick, K. (1997), 'Editorial', *British Journal of Music Education*, 14, (1), 3–4.

United Nations (2008), *The Millennium Development Goals*. New York: United Nations.

Watson, K. (ed.) (2001), *Doing Comparative Educational Research: Issues and Problems*. Wallingford: Symposium.

Williams, J. H. (1997), 'The Diffusion of the Modern School', in W. K. Cummings and N. F. McGinn (eds) (1997), *International Handbook of Education and Development: Preparing Schools, Students and Nations for the Twenty-First Century*. Oxford: Pergamon, pp. 119–36.

Part 1

Europe

2

Britain: Towards 'a long overdue renaissance'?

Gordon Cox

In this chapter, I will focus principally on the period in British music education from 1870 until 1927, as these were the crucial years for the introduction of 'singing' into the school curriculum. The overriding emphasis was on the teaching of singing at sight. It was not until 1927, significantly soon after the introduction of gramophone recordings into schools and of school radio broadcasts, that the nomenclature was changed by the Board of Education (1927), when the subject became known as 'music'. At the end of the chapter, I shall briefly summarize recent developments. My main focus is on the English scene, bearing in mind that England, Wales, Scotland and Northern Ireland have shared in many aspects of a common educational history. However, their educational patterns have never been identical and differences are becoming sharper with the passage of time.

Historical context for the introduction of music into the school curriculum

From the 1840s Britain witnessed what Rainbow (1967) referred to as the 'phenomenal growth of school music' (p. 13). Previously there had been a distinguished tradition of song schools in the medieval period and until the Reformation such schools were necessities for monasteries and cathedrals (see Plummeridge 2001). One of the outcomes of the Reformation was that provision for music started to decline, largely as a result of the closure of the majority of song schools. Consequently, for the majority of young people to whom schooling was available, opportunities for the learning of music were severely curtailed. In the seventeenth and eighteenth centuries, educational thought was characterized by its utilitarian and materialistic tendencies. The arts were regarded as mere diversions, although singing and instrumental playing were looked on as worthy 'accomplishments', particularly for females. By the nineteenth century, working- and middle-class education had clear identities. They were separated by different curricula, length of school life, attendance rates and cultural and social objectives (see Lawson and Silver 1973).

The Industrial Revolution prompted concerns about the social tensions arising in districts with sizable populations that were without water supply, sanitation or policing – and, furthermore, without church or school. Consequently, in 1833 a grant of £20,000 was voted for public education, to be distributed through the British and National School Societies, representative of the mainstream religious institutions.

The *Elementary Education Act of 1870* was the 'most workable piece of compromise legislation in English nineteenth-century history' (*ibid.*: 314). Although it did not introduce free or compulsory education, it made both possible: it brought the state into action in education as never before. By 1880 education was made compulsory up to the age of 13. For Scotland, an education act passed in 1872 likewise made attendance compulsory.

Turning the focus to musical concerns, we find that the nineteenth century in England was known as the 'Sight Singing Century' (Scholes 1947: 1). In the 1840s a sight singing mania had gripped the country. Two men were to dominate this movement and came to influence profoundly the direction of compulsory musical instruction in schools after 1870: John Hullah (1812–1884) and John Curwen (1816–1880).

In his early days John Hullah was much influenced by his mother's musical gifts and his father's democratic tendencies (F. Hullah 1886). His education linked this connection between art and democracy. After studying at the Royal Academy of Music in London, the idea formed in him of developing schools for popular instruction in vocal music. He visited Paris to see for himself the work of the German musician Joseph Mainzer who had established singing classes for working men, but in the end Hullah allied himself with the French music educator, G. L. B. Wilhem, who had written a music manual for use in the monitorial system of schools. As well as holding classes in schools, Wilhem was committed to spreading musical skills to as wide a spectrum of adults as possible, particularly to working people (Rainbow 1967: 94–107).

By 1840 Hullah had been taken up by the educational reformer James Kay (Secretary to the Committee of Council on Education), who requested that Hullah translate Wilhem's method into English for school use. This became known as *Hullah's Manual* (1842) and was the basic text for his singing schools, which spread like wildfire throughout the country. When we consider Hullah's teaching we have to remember that his vehicle for such sight singing was the fixed-doh method. Unfortunately, the method encapsulated in *Hullah's Manual* was not a success, with one critic calling it 'diffuse, circumlocutory, confused and superficial' (Barnett 1842: 6): few pupils got further than the end of the first book as its later stages proved to be impenetrable.

John Curwen became the great promoter and evangelist of the tonic sol-fa method, whose foundation lay on the 'movable doh': the tonic of the new key was always 'doh'. His book *Singing for Schools and Congregations* (1843) heralded the start of a new era: Curwen's tonic sol-fa swept the country and the Empire under its banner 'Cheap, Easy and True' (see Rainbow 1980). Curwen's method was based on the work of Sarah Glover (1786–1867), which he synthesized and publicized. In 1867 he founded the Tonic Sol-fa College, which provided the home of his movement and was to provide generations of teachers opportunities to develop their sight singing skills through its part-time and vacation courses.

The introduction of music into schools: music inspectors

The *Elementary Education Act of 1870* as we have seen made both free and compulsory education possible (Lawson and Silver 1973). Schools at this time were subject to payment by results, introduced in the 1862 Revised Code. Briefly, annual financial grants to schools became conditional on the proficiency of the children as tested by the inspectors. Music education was at a low ebb; in fact in 1871 it was omitted from the government code. Pressure was placed on the government to reinstate it and, in 1872, it was announced that the grant to day schools would be reduced by one shilling per scholar, unless inspectors were satisfied that vocal music were part of the ordinary course of instruction. But in order to earn the grant, schools could simply teach a few songs by ear. This was a clearly unsatisfactory and negative state of affairs, so that as a result of further pressure the Code of 1874 provided that one shilling per scholar should be paid if singing were taught satisfactorily. In order to police this, a music inspector was appointed by the government – none other than John Hullah. It was his job, and that of his immediate successor, John Stainer, to monitor standards of musical teaching principally in the training colleges of England, Wales and Scotland as well as providing crucial advice on policy matters and documentation.

However, increasingly, school inspectors were complaining of a deterioration in public elementary schools. It appeared that most pupils were being taught to sing by ear rather than by note. Hullah was dispatched to the continent to investigate musical instruction in elementary schools between April and July 1879. Significantly, Rainbow (1985) has pointed out that Hullah omitted to visit France and this might have been a quite conscious decision as it would have exploded the fact that the Wilhem system had been abandoned in the 1840s and that cipher notation was gaining ground. One of the outcomes of his journey was that he recommended that, after 1882, no financial award would be made for singing unless it were taught by note (although this was never fully implemented). The problem was that his system obfuscated the process of sight singing, rather than clarifying it.

Hullah's successor as inspector, in 1882, was John Stainer (1840–1901) who was a musician of considerable stature (see Dibble 2007) – he was one of the finest organists and improvisers in the country, organist at St Paul's Cathedral and Professor of Music at Oxford. However, he had little (if any) experience of teaching in schools. He solved this by appointing as his assistant W. G. McNaught (1849–1918). McNaught had considerable experience as a teacher and was also a keen advocate of the ideas of John Curwen and the tonic sol-fa method.

The partnership between Stainer and McNaught flowered into a period of consolidation for music in schools. They had developed a theory into a practice, well researched and suited to 'payment by results'. The situation now was that schools that only taught singing 'by ear' would only receive six pence per pupil per annum while those teaching 'by note' received one shilling. The payment by results system was withdrawn in 1901.

There was a feeling of optimism in the air. McNaught pointed out that 1,504,675 children had gained the grant for singing by note in one previous year (Browne 1885–6). It led him to claim somewhat extravagantly that: 'So far as the elementary musical education of the children in our schools is concerned we are accomplishing more than any other nation in the world' (*ibid.*: 19).

Moreover, they had reached the children whom Hullah had failed to reach. It was expressed vividly by a London head teacher, quoted by McNaught:

> You have enabled us to tame wild spirits which we could not otherwise have tamed. It is the experience of those who know best that there is no power in the schools in the lowest neighbourhoods which can exercise a refining influence on the wildest and roughest spirits like this teaching of music. We use this teaching as a recreation, as a relief and as a change in our schools, nothing makes the schools so popular and attractive to the children as the music that goes on in the 300 or more schools in London. (McNaught 1884: 417–18)

On Stainer's death, it was expected that McNaught would be his successor as music inspector, but instead the appointment of Arthur Somervell (1863–1937) was announced in 1901. There was an outcry because although Somervell was establishing himself as a composer, he had little experience of schools. His 30 years in office coincided with a profound shift away from utilitarian traditions towards an artistic and educational liberalism (see Cox 2003). Somervell's contribution, as we shall see, lay in the introduction of national songs into schools and the development of an idealist justification for the teaching of music.

Justifications for music's place in the school curriculum

What values impelled this quest to spread musical instruction into the school curriculum? John Hullah was particularly influenced by the Victorian Christian Socialists who believed that social suffering might be alleviated by Christian works of charity and the elevating consequences of popular education. First, he believed music could refine and civilize, principally through the process of sight singing. Individuals could be fashioned into productive members of the community by reconciling 'cotton spinning and counterpoint, husbandry and harmony' (Hullah 1846: 20). Hullah became known as someone who could transform popular amusement into valuable instruction. He believed that music encouraged positive moral values: 'patience, temperance, power of attention, presence of mind, self-denial, obedience and punctuality' (Hullah 1854: 15). He admitted there might not be a direct connection, but performers could never manage without acquiring such qualities. Here we see stated the extrinsic values that music might serve. The results of such an education would be seen in a socially redemptive context, but we should note that the redemptive power of music was linked by Hullah to its activity, with no mention of its content.

Both Stainer and McNaught were practical men – we might describe them as conviction politicians who acted within a narrow sphere most effectively and became almost populist figures. As a result they tended to dismiss high-flown claims for the educative power of music. Nevertheless, Stainer had no doubt there was a connection with the beautiful and the good. He believed that listening became a creative process in which art, thought, action and the moral were energized. This led him to the practical conclusion that 'our real want in England at this moment is not professional performers or even composers, but intelligent hearers' (Stainer 1892: 57–8). McNaught concurred and declared he was wary of making exorbitant claims for the subject (*School Music Review*, October 1896, 96). His musical friends were no better ethically than his non-musical acquaintances. Of course, he conceded, there may be an indirect moral influence through the emotions and there certainly was intellectual value, but music did not get rid of Original Sin! Both men talked of music's extrinsic values cautiously. The danger was that music could suffer a narrowing of interests and a concentration on methods and techniques for their own sakes.

Arthur Somervell was an idealist – a key phrase in his writings is the 'Whole of Things' and he subscribed to the Platonic notion of 'the True, the Good and the Beautiful'. There was a need for balance between science, art and moral ideas and such a unity of experience could heal divisions in society. Care should be taken not to limit the aim of music education to the creation of greater numbers of singers and instrumentalists – music might build up the Ideal Citizen. It was simply Somervell's belief that 'your only really practical man is the one with a trained and cultivated imagination' (Somervell 1905: 151). The arts provided such a sure foundation. By seeking a theory based on Plato and Aristotle, Somervell was placing his formulation of music education within the tradition of Matthew Arnold who had revived the old humanist notion of the centrality of literature as an energizing moral force (*ibid.*). For Somervell, like Arnold, art took over many of the functions of religion.

Content and methods

It is hard to re-create what went on in an elementary school singing class. We have to rely on the writings of the inspectors. Hullah carried out an experiment in 1876 in which he taught 65 infants for 20 minutes daily for a fortnight and occasionally for 5 minutes in odd periods of recreation. By the end of this time he claimed the children could name notes correctly and give utterance to diatonic scale notes. They could beat time with their hands, distribute notes in measures, touching on their hands (using the hand as a manual stave) a tune that they sang accurately. Moreover, they could sing at sight from the blackboard, were intensely interested and had 'sympathy of ear and eye' (Hullah 1878: 6). He concluded that these children reached a better standard than two-thirds of teacher training college candidates.

Both Stainer and McNaught had to work under the payment by results scheme, with schools receiving a greater grant if singing 'by note' were taught, rather than singing 'by ear'. The tendency was that this encouraged mechanical teaching. However, McNaught believed fervently that true tonic sol-fa teaching could be invested with feeling. How was this to be achieved in practice? One of the chief means of disseminating ideas to music teachers was the monthly periodical, the *School Music Review*. McNaught wrote three series of articles that considered three crucial questions:

1 What were the necessary steps to enable effective note singing to take place?
2 What was the relationship of tonic sol-fa to staff notation?
3 How could tonic sol-fa cultivate the power of observing sounds and mentally hold them for analysis?

He believed that teaching had to illuminate the relationship between tones and he vividly outlined how the theory of mental effect could be approached through the 'doh' chord:

Demonstrate (not merely assert) the firm repose of 'doh', the bold cheerfulness of 'soh', the plaintiveness of 'me', the exultation ('hurrah' would be a better word for children) of the high 'doh' ... Make a great deal of each note, so that the impression is vivid. Suppose the keen, bright, eager expectancy of 'te' and the meeker expectancy of 'ray' have been amply demonstrated, and that 'fah' is to be introduced. You have got somehow to build up in your pupils' minds an impression of gravity, sternness, dignity and expectancy. You must make them feel it by a variety of well-chosen illustrations. (McNaught 1894–5: 23–4)

As with everything else he touched, McNaught produced a simple practical scheme. As a start he concentrated on the teaching of a timeless tune, next he dealt with the teaching of time and rhythm. It was only when regular pulse, variety of accent and the distribution of sounds over or in a pulse were mastered that notation should be introduced. But this skill was crucial, because McNaught believed the only rational test of such teaching lay in the ability of pupils to perform rhythms from signs and to write down signs on hearing musical patterns.

The *Report on Singing in the London Elementary Schools* (Board of Education 1913) provides a useful guide to progress. Four items of concern were noted. First, voice production: there was a pleasing insistence on the use of the head voice, but there was a mismatch between the decent sound of the vocal exercises and the inferior quality of the voices in song singing; special classes might be formed to deal with the issues of boys' breaking voices. Second, organization proved difficult, with too little care that there was a graduated course of instruction. Third, notation gave rise to the greatest concern: in too many cases tonic sol-fa was worshipped for its own sake; children should have a greater acquaintance with staff notation. Finally, although the music chosen for competitive festivals was frequently sentimental or worthless, praise was given to the improved quality of song repertoire, particularly national and folksongs.

The relation between music and national feeling permeated popular music education during the latter half of the nineteenth century. The culmination of this relationship was reached with the publication of *The National Song Book* (Stanford 1906), produced very much under the auspices of Arthur Somervell, Stainer's controversial successor as Music Inspector in 1901 (see Cox 2003) – its influence was so widespread that by 1917 it could be boasted that there was hardly a school in the country that did not possess a copy. National songs were supposed to express the emotions of a people; they were long established and were individually composed, frequently by esteemed musicians. The national song was 'popular by destination' (Greene 1935: xcviii). As far back as 1842 the relationship between music and national feeling had been reckoned to be important from an educational perspective: as many legends were expressed in songs, the teaching of singing could fix the words in children's minds (Hullah 1842: iv).

National songs were at the peak of their popularity around the turn of the century. But how do we know what songs were actually sung in school? For the purposes of this chapter, I shall note the number of times a song was reprinted in six major collections of songs published between 1884 and 1906 (see Farmer 1895; Hadow 1903; Nicholson 1903; Sharp 1902; Stanford 1884, 1906). We find eight songs common to all: 'The British Grenadiers', 'Early One Morning', 'The Roast Beef of Old England', 'Come Lasses and Lads', 'The Mermaid', 'Here's a Health unto His Majesty', 'Hearts of Oak' and 'Rule, Britannia!'. The values these songs encapsulate are clear – the need to respect authority, contempt for one's enemies, superiority over others and a looking back to rural life and the values of the past. As for the musical qualities, the songs are all in the major key and all but two are in simple duple or quadruple time. The vocal range, however, varies considerably.

The principal resistance to the hegemony of the national song in schools was the folksong. This was generally reckoned to have been communally composed expressing the feelings of the collective soul, springing from the oral tradition: 'popular by origin' (Greene 1935: xcviii).

The oral tradition that promulgated folksong without the aid of notation understandably threatened music educators whose main aim was to encourage the ability to sing at sight from notation. The two traditions collided in the controversy of 1905, when the Board of Education (1905) published a list of 'national or folksongs'. Cecil Sharp (1859–1924), the great folksong collector, was furious about the bracketing together of the two categories (see Cox 2003). He maintained that the list contained 'scarcely a single genuine peasant-made folk song' (*School Music Review*, June 1906: 1). He was to wage the battle for a genuine folksong repertoire in schools for the next 20 years. It is ironic that folksongs eventually became part of a rigid orthodoxy that linked them inseparably with the values of national songs.

But whatever the pros and contras of folksongs compared with national songs, everyone agreed that music education had to fight the pernicious effects of popular culture – in particular, this meant music-hall songs. Somervell's position was that national songs were morally superior and that popular music vulgarized and exerted a harmful influence on character. Bad music was popular because it was attractive.

Music in teacher training

From their earliest days training colleges instructed all their students to teach singing and, by the end of the nineteenth century, many were also providing facilities for practising instrumental music. But none trained specialists. The annual inspection of individual students included a note test, a time test, an ear test and the performance of a solo song. In addition, the students presented a choral performance and were required to sit a theory examination. Stainer and McNaught had to submit detailed reports (Committee of Council on Education Reports 1883–1899, hereinafter referred to simply by date) and these provide us with detail concerning musical training.

In his first report, Stainer (1883) drew attention to the lack of musical training of most students. No great change would come, he believed, until elementary schools were able to produce teacher candidates with a musical ear. He estimated that this might take 10 or 15 years to achieve. He praised the college teachers for working against the odds, when students arrived with untried voices, untrained ears and ignorant of any musical notation. In spite of this, he witnessed that much valuable work was being carried out; in fact, he declared that wonders were performed. Indeed, throughout his inspectorship, Stainer found 'proof of the upward tendency of musical taste among students in training colleges' (1897: 354). One of the actions Stainer took was to remove the study of harmony from the requirements in 1885. He felt too much time was devoted to it and the majority of candidates took it to be a technical puzzle. This was all part of a general strategy on his part, to discourage the thinking that theory was more important than practice.

Ideally, Stainer wished he could observe students giving music lessons in a practising school, but this was not practically feasible (1886). In McNaught's opinion, students should leave college with the code requirements: a dozen or so songs and fruitful lessons of time, tune and expression. Stainer, however, cautioned against expecting too much from training colleges. It was unrealistic to expect them to turn out cultivated and practical musicians.

A critique (Board of Education 1928) of the teaching of music in training colleges during the Victorian era, however, pointed to some of the drawbacks of the system for which Stainer and McNaught had been responsible. It concluded that what had been provided had been essentially non-cultural, cramped by its close dependence on the requirements of the elementary school and by its adherence to a syllabus framed in an *ad hoc* fashion: 'it inspired no love of music and failed to impart any understanding of it' (*ibid.*: 6).

From 'singing' to 'music'

The change in nomenclature from 'singing' to 'music' was officially confirmed in the Board of Education's publication, *Handbook of Suggestions for Teachers* (1927). It signalled an enlargement of scope of the subject and included two new sections – melody training (in which children were encouraged to make tunes of their own) and appreciation (regarded as the climax of 'ear training'). By 1933 it was reported that the class teacher of music was suffering an 'embarrass de richesses', including appreciation of music, community singing, the gramophone, the school orchestra, the percussion band, rhythmic work and wireless (radio) lessons (Board of Education 1933). The report finished on a triumphant note: 'The whole history of musical England from 1850 onwards is one of emergence from darkness to light, and undoubtedly the treatment of music in the schools has played a great part in the gradual transformation' (*ibid.*: 7).

After 1945 there was a considerable expansion in secondary school music making, with choirs, orchestras, madrigal groups, brass bands and operatic ventures. Instrumental teaching in schools was encouraged and the methods of Kodály and Orff gained some prominence. The 1960s witnessed a growing interest in the use of contemporary music in the classroom, with children as both performers and composers. By the 1970s a division could be discerned between, on the one hand, those music educators who advocated a subject-centred curriculum model focusing on skills, literacy and the Western music tradition and, on the other hand, those who subscribed to a child-centred curriculum model encompassing experiment, creativity and contemporary musical styles (see Cox 2002). Much of this debate came to be resolved in the 1980s and 1990s with the introduction of the National Curriculum.

Towards the present and future

The most significant event of recent history regarding music as a school subject has been the development, for the first time in England, Wales and Northern Ireland, of a National Curriculum. As a result of the publication of the Great Education Reform Bill in November 1987, all pupils aged 5 to 14 were to be taught the new National Curriculum core subjects (English, mathematics, science (and Welsh in Welsh-speaking schools in Wales)) by September 1989 and the foundation subjects, including music, by September 1992. The inclusion of music should not be regarded as having been automatic. There had been talk about not making it compulsory (see Barber 1996). Integral to the reforms was the creation of the Office for Standards in Education (Ofsted), which was to carry out regular detailed inspections of schools and their teaching in order to maintain and improve overall standards.

As far as the music curriculum was concerned, there was a focus on composing and performing, listening and appraising. This practical, hands-on approach has remained, albeit in revised form, in subsequent revisions of the National Curriculum and owes much to the pioneering work of John Paynter and Keith Swanwick. The latest version of the Curriculum was unveiled in 2008 and according to a newspaper headline at the time, promises to promote 'a classroom revolution as curriculum embraces modern life' (*The Independent* 13 July 2007). More specifically, a distinctive feature lies in the encouragement of cross-curricular themes in secondary schools (see www.curriculum.qca.org.uk).

An influential justification for music as a curriculum subject that came to particular attention in the late 1990s was the notion of the transfer of learning. Scientific research, according to Everitt (1998), demonstrated that music played a key role in the functioning of the brain. Behavioural psychologists had demonstrated how music could aid the learning process. Consequently, it was argued that giving more time to 'the 3 Rs' was counterproductive if it led to fewer music classes. This notion that music could help children improve their learning in a number of areas such as mathematics and literacy appealed to politicians such as David Blunkett, then Minister of Education, who declared that his priority lay in the raising of standards in 'the 3 Rs', but also that if music could contribute to this, it was all the better (*The Times Educational Supplement* 22 May 1998).

Teacher training today is very much shaped by a national curriculum and tests and targets. One significant development, however, is that nearly a quarter of new teachers now train in schools rather than universities (*The Economist* 11 April 2009). However, training in both schools and universities is based on the same set of national standards for teachers.

There have undoubtedly been a number of encouraging developments taking place in recent years. The *Music Manifesto* (DfES 2004) promised a new 'joined-up' policy for music education. The School Standards Minister, David Miliband, reiterated the government's commitment that over time any primary school pupil who wanted to would be able to learn a musical instrument. The government's commitment to music was based on five key resources: the vital foundation of the Music National Curriculum; professional collaboration; new flexibilities so that schools and professional musicians could work together; creativity and innovation in music charting new directions; and financial resources. In 2007 the government announced a £332 million settlement for music education.

Current initiatives (2009) receiving government funding include: the Wider Opportunities Scheme, enabling all children within specific age groups (key stages) in primary education to receive tuition in a musical instrument; the Sing Up campaign, which aims to have every child in primary education involved in singing before 2012; and projects in England and Scotland working to replicate Venezuela's *El Sistema*, a 30-year-old scheme that 'has changed the lives of thousands of children from the barrios by immersing them, every day of their lives, in classical music' (Higgins 2009). This is not to mention the highly influential Musical Futures initiative, funded by the Paul Hamlyn Foundation, which aims to devise new and imaginative ways of engaging young people in music activities as an entitlement for all 11 to 19 year olds (see www.musicalfutures.org.uk). More specifically, it attempts to bring together formal education and informal learning (see Green 2008).

As an aside, we should note some historical resonances in at least two of these schemes. First, the notion of music as a socially regenerative force in *El*

Sistema relates to much of the thinking of the early inspectors of music regarding the justification for music's place in the curriculum. Second, related to the national song controversy of the early twentieth century, was an intriguing report from the *The Daily Telegraph* on 14 May 2008, headlined, 'National song-book project falls flat'. It had been hoped by government ministers that the Sing Up campaign might be based on 30 songs that every 11 year old should know. It was not to be. Gareth Malone, a leading figure in Sing Up explained: 'It's simply a hot potato culturally' (*ibid.*). In the place of a national songbook is now a national song bank, which contains over 100 songs. A consideration of the similarities and differences of views then and now regarding the national song issue could illuminate some of the continuities and discontinuities that underpin curriculum thinking.

Alongside the signs of real progress that have been outlined are counterbalancing concerns, which were reported in a recent Ofsted (2009) report, *Making More of Music: An Evaluation of Music in Schools 2005–08*. While the report welcomed the considerable amounts of much needed extra funding, it was felt this needed to be better targeted to have even more impact. The conclusion was that while this should be a very positive time for music in schools, too much was being developed in isolation and initiatives were not always reaching the schools and teachers that needed them most.

Summary

Music's status as a curriculum subject in Britain has almost always been ambivalent. On the one hand, it has an ancient and distinguished educational pedigree, forming part of the medieval and Renaissance *quadrivium* based on its intellectual rigour; on the other hand, it is frequently regarded as a piece of educational frippery, associated with leisure and mass media manipulation. In this historical study, there are correspondences between the past and the present – the place awarded to music in the school curriculum, always there, but somehow conditional; the diversity of justifications for the subject ranging from the severely practical, to the high flown; the fierce debates about pedagogy and about the musical content of the curriculum; arguments about whether the training of music teachers should follow the practice in schools or seek to change it.

More recently there has been talk of 'a long overdue renaissance' in British music education (see Rainbow with Cox 2006: 361). However, at the time of writing (February 2011), music education is in a state of flux in the light of financial constraints and a thorough-going curriculum review by the new coalition government. The provision of music education as a statutory requirement as part of the National Curriculum is under consideration, and will be resolved later in the year.

References

Barber, M. (1996), *The National Curriculum: A Study in Policy.* London: Keele University Press.

Barnett, J. (1842), *Systems and Singing Masters: An Analytical Comment Upon the Wilhem System as Taught in England with Letters, Authenticated Anecdotes and Critical Remarks Upon Mr John Hullah's Manual and Prefatory Minutes of the Council in Education.* London: W. S. Orr.

Board of Education (1905), *Suggestions for the Consideration of Teachers and Others Concerned in the work of Public Elementary Schools.* London: HMSO.

Board of Education (1913), *Report on the Teaching of Singing in the London Elementary Schools.* London: HMSO.

Board of Education (1927), *Handbook of Suggestions for Teachers.* London: HMSO.

Board of Education (1928), *Report on Music, Arts and Crafts and Drama in Training Colleges.* London: HMSO.

Board of Education (1933), *Recent Developments in School Music.* Educational Pamphlets No. 95. London: HMSO.

Browne, M. E. (1885–6), 'Music in elementary schools', *Proceedings of the Musical Association,* 12, 1–22.

Committee of Council on Education (1873–1899), *Reports of the Committee of Council on Education.* London: HMSO.

Cox, G. (2002), *Living Music in Schools 1923–1999: Studies in the History of Music Education in England.* Aldershot: Ashgate.

Cox, G. (ed.) (2003), *Sir Arthur Somervell on Music Education: His Writings, Speeches and Letters.* Woodbridge: Boydell Press.

Curwen, J. (1843), *Singing for Schools and Congregations.* London: Curwen.

Daily Telegraph, The, 'National song-book project falls flat', 14 May 2008.

Department for Education and Employment (DfEE) (1999), *The National Curriculum for England: Music.* London: DfEE.

Department for Education and Skills (DfES) (2004), *The Music Manifesto.* London: DfES.

Dibble, J. (2007), *John Stainer.* Woodbridge: Boydell & Brewer.

Economist, The, 'Not so loony', 11 April 2009.

Everitt, A. (1998), 'Cerebral software', *Times Educational Supplement,* 24 April.

Farmer, J. (1895), *Gaudeamus: A Selection of Songs for Schools and Colleges.* London: Cassell.

Green, L. (2008), *Music, Informal Learning and the School: A New Classroom Pedagogy.* Aldershot: Ashgate.

Greene, R. L. (1935), *The Early English Carols.* Oxford: Clarendon Press.

Hadow, W. H. (1903), *Songs of the British Islands: One Hundred National Melodies selected and edited for the Use of Schools.* London: Curwen.

Higgins, C. (2009), 'Now for a samba', *The Guardian,* Wednesday 14 January, www.guardian.co.uk/uk/2009/jan/14/scotland-venezuela/print.

Hullah, F. (1886), *Life of John Hullah LLD.* London: Longmans Green.

Hullah, J. (1842), *Wilhem's Method of Teaching Singing Adapted to the English Use under the Superintendance of the Committee of Council on Education.* London: John W. Parker.

Hullah, J. (1846), *The Duty and Advantages of Being Able to Sing. A Lecture Delivered at the Leeds Church Institution.* London: John W. Parker.

Hullah, J. (1854), *Music as an Element of Education: Being One of a Series of Lectures Delivered at St Martin's Hall, in Connexion with the Educational Exhibition of the Society of Arts, July 24, 1854*. London: John W. Parker.

Hullah, J. (1878), *How Can a Sound Knowledge of Music be Best and Most Generally Disseminated? A Paper read...at the Twenty-Second Congress of the National Association for the Promotion of Social Science*. London: Longmans Green.

Independent, The, 'A classroom revolution as curriculum embraces modern life', 13 July 2007.

Lawson, J. and Silver, H. (1973), *A Social History of Education in England*. London: Methuen.

McNaught, W. G. (1884), 'Music in primary schools', in *The Health Exhibition Literature XIII. Conference on Education*. London: William Clowes, pp. 417–30.

McNaught, W. G. (1894–5), 'How to teach note singing pleasantly and expeditiously', *School Music Review*, 3, 15–16, 23–4, 61–62.

Musical Futures initiative, www.musicalfutures.org.uk.

Nicholson, S. H. (1903), *British Songs for British Boys: A Collection of One Hundred National Songs: Designed for the Use of Boys in Schools and Choirs*. London: Macmillan.

Ofsted (2009), *Making More of Music: An Evaluation of Music in Schools 2005–08*. London: Ofsted.

Plummeridge, C. (2001), 'Music in schools', in S. Sadie and J. Tyrrell (eds), *The New Grove Dictionary of Music and Musicians* (2nd edn). London: Macmillan, pp. 614–29.

Qualifications and Curriculum Authority (2008), www.Curriculum.gov.qca.org.uk.

Rainbow, B. (1967), *The Land without Music: Musical Education in England 1800–1860 and its Continental Antecedents*. Borough Green: Novello.

Rainbow, B. (1980), *John Curwen: A Short Critical Biography*. Borough Green: Novello.

Rainbow, B. (1985), 'The land with music: reality and myth in music education', in A. E. Kemp (ed.), *Research in Music Education: A Festschrift for Arnold Bentley*. Reading: ISME Research Commission, pp. 19–32.

Rainbow, B. with Cox, G. (2006), *Music in Educational Thought and Practice* (2nd edn). Woodbridge: Boydell Press.

Scholes, P. (1947), *The Mirror of Music 1844–1944: A Century of Musical Life in Britain as reflected in the Pages of the Musical Times*. London: Novello and Oxford University Press.

School Music Review, October 1896, June 1906.

Sharp, C. (1902), *A Book of British Song for Home and School*. London: John Murray.

Somervell, A. (1905), 'The basis of the claims of music in education', *Proceedings of the Musical Association*, 31, 149–66.

Stainer, J. (1892), *Music in its Relation to the Intellect and the Emotions*. London: Novello, Ewer.

Stanford, C. V. (ed.) (1884), *Song-Book for Schools (being a Graduated Collection of Sixty-four songs in One, Two and Three Parts adapted for the use of Children)*. London: National Society's Depository.

Stanford, C. V. (ed.) (1906), *The National Song Book*. London: Boosey.

Times Educational Supplement, The, 22 May 1998.

Woodford, P. (2005), *Democracy and Music Education: Liberalism, Ethics, and the Politics of Practice*. Bloomington: Indiana University Press.

3

France: An uncertain and unequal combat

François Madurell

In his landmark article devoted to 'L'enseignement musical à l'école' (the teaching of music in the school), Maurice Chevais (1880–1943) offered an in-depth analysis of the situation in France, and gave voice to the following hope:

> May we one day show esteem in France both for popular musical education and for those who assume the task of propagating it, and at last become aware of everything that can be asked of music and of choral singing in the aim of furthering [the] harmonious development of the child. (Chevais 1931: 3683)

His wish has never been fully realized. This observation points to a structural difficulty with incorporating music education into schools and reveals deep-seated, longstanding disagreement about methods, goals and curricula. The causes of this situation include: the historical circumstances, the power of patriotic sentiment, the virulence of pedagogical disputes and the problem of teacher training. They are inextricably bound up with different perspectives on the functions of music education in school. To offer musical instruction to all children was to go against the ideology of 'the gift', strongly rooted in French musical culture. Possessing a gift for music was most often seen to be an advantage received from God or from nature, not as a matter of education or training.

The focus of this chapter will be on the years between 1870 and 1940, more specifically tracing the origins of music as a school subject in France, the relationship of music education to patriotism, two pedagogical issues relating to cipher notation and to pitch, and the training of music teachers. Finally, after a consideration of the significant influence that Maurice Chevais had on French school music education, there will be some observations about the present situation.

The introduction of music as a subject in the school curriculum

Music was introduced to primary schools in Paris as early as 1819. As a subject it enjoyed a high degree of prominence due to Guillaume Louis Bocquillon, known as Wilhem (1781–1842), a staunch advocate of choral singing, who became director of this branch of instruction in the schools of Paris in 1835. Wilhem had compiled a singing manual (1836) for use in the monitorial system of teaching (large classes split into small groups, each under a monitor). In his textbook, Wilhem broke down the rudiments of music into a series of easy steps following a carefully planned sequence. His preparatory vocal exercises were based on the 'vocal staircase', which visually represented the diatonic scale as a set of stairs, with the semitones as appropriately smaller steps. At a later stage he used *phonomimie*, in which the hand was used as a stave. Exercises could be pointed out one note at a time on the hand. Wilhem's method aimed at overall musical instruction stretching into adulthood with his adult classes bringing together mechanics and labourers and their employers. The method nevertheless clearly established the fundamental principles for musical progression at the first level in schools. Wilhem insisted on a systematic course of ear training for children as well as a reliance on *solfège* (he employed the traditional French 'fixed-doh' sol-fa). Around 1841 it was estimated that some 12,000 children were receiving singing lessons using his method in the schools of Paris and that his adult classes included 1,500 students (see Rainbow 1967).

However, what has been called the 'Parisian exception' (Fijalkow 2003) cannot conceal the difficulty that music education had in becoming an integral part of French education and acquiring full status as a school subject. Although the Guizot Law (1833) required each town to open a school for boys and stipulated a place for music, by 1836 girls schools were also required by law, but although the 'practice of singing' became mandatory for girls, it was to be merely optional for boys. This discrimination reflects the power of social roles and their influence on the school. Far from being a sanctuary, the school – which claimed to be a source of values – remained subject to prevailing traditions. In 1850, the Falloux Law – at once regressive and inconclusive – saw music return to being optional in status for all pupils. The law, furthermore, saw the status of music in schools to be subjected to the whims of the governing authority.

The matter came up again in 1881. Following a series of seven reports by educational experts (Alten 1995), the official syllabus issued as 'Programme du 27 juillet 1882' did away with any and all sex discrimination and set out a clear political intention that singing (*chant*) would be mandatory for all children within compulsory primary instruction. It had therefore taken until 27 July 1882 for singing to claim its rightful place in primary education within the framework of non-parochial schooling. Nevertheless, *chant* remained at the end of the subject list. Because musical instruction was based on singing, the teaching gradually came to incorporate the fundamental principles of the *solfège* method. The 1882 syllabus remained in force until 1923, when a mandatory test in singing was prescribed for the granting of the Primary Studies Certificate (*Programmes et instructions* 1923). This measure was put into effect from 1924. But many primary school teachers did not have sufficient training in music to implement the syllabus leading to the mandatory test. Aside from the crucial issue of adequate training for school teachers in music, introduction of the mandatory test epitomized the complex nature of the problem presented by music education in the schools of the Republic.

On the one hand, there was the problem of the comparatively unambitious requirements for music together with limited scheduling of class time (most often 1 hour weekly) and, on the other hand, the significant socio-cultural and political expectation that music should be provided for in the education of all citizens and that music should serve as a means of promoting patriotism. There was also the ongoing debate about the subject matter to be taught and the goals to be achieved, which were aggravated by conflicting opinions within the music profession – for some teachers, recommendations given by conservatories tended to emerge as a point of reference (Gédalge 1926) whereas other teachers who considered these recommendations unrealistic, supported a music education approach best suited to the school context, thus taking into account school teachers' sometimes limited musical skills. Vançon (2004) has further elaborated on this ongoing issue.

Music education and patriotism

The disastrous Franco-Prussian War resulted in the fall of Napoleon III and the proclamation of the Republic. Bismarck demanded Alsace-Lorraine (under the Treaty of Frankfurt of 1871), which would only be returned to France at the Treaty of Versailles in 1919. Thus, according to the *Tribune des Instituteurs*, the attempt in schools at 'making sincere patriots' (Ferro 2003: 10) was seen as a benchmark for success in achieving a sense of national pride.

It comes as no surprise, therefore, that patriotic songs have had a significant place in the repertoire of school songs, especially in the context of an increasingly threatening international climate. Michèle Alten (1995) has analyzed the rise of patriotic fervour in school music and has revealed remnants of it up to the beginning of the 1920s. In the two decades preceding the First World War, the return of Alsace-Lorraine to France and the surge for revenge permeated a 'pro-Republican' focus in the teaching of morals and citizenship. Children were imbued with a growing patriotic spirit in which military heroism was glorified. Thus an entire generation was unobtrusively prepared for immense sacrifices to follow.

After the First World War – although the cult of the *patrie* or fatherland was maintained through ceremonies commemorating the Great War in which school teachers and students took a major role – the songs taught in classrooms focused more on the folklore of the regions of France, for example: *Chansons populaires du val-de-Loire* (Traditional songs from the Loire Valley) (Chevais 1925), *Chansons populaires des provinces de France* (Traditional songs from French provinces) (Société française l'art a l'école 1925) and the first part of *Anthologie du chant scolaire et post-scolaire (*Anthology of school and after-school songs) (Société française l'art a l'école 1925). Gradually school teachers forsook nationalist ideals as pacifism gained ground, (particularly with the emergence of the trade union movement) and a new social perspective emerged.

This patriotic focus was not the only social imperative at the time. The incorporation of music education into the school curriculum came about in a period in which France – then still essentially a rural society – was undergoing massive industrialization. Many children from rural areas were to swell the ranks of workers tethered to exhaustingly repetitive tasks in the new factories. There was a growing realization that singing could also be beneficial for adult workers in such circumstances (Alten 1995: 38).

Music education in schools had survived major political and social changes but despite recognition of these extra-musical benefits, its status in the curriculum remained tenuous and its methods and practices lacked universal acceptance.

Pedagogical issues: Cipher notation and the debate over absolute and relative pitch

It was a member of an influential educational committee, Amand Chevé, who, in 1882, pointed out the hurdle represented by the learning of music reading within the limited time allotted for musical instruction in schools (see Alten 1995; Vançon 2004: 42). Accordingly, he made a case for the use of the Galin-Paris-Chevé method (see Chevé 1852, 1862; Lee-Forbes 1977), which was based on Galin's (1818) cipher notation (*méthode chiffrée*), which, in turn, built on the principles set out by Rousseau in his *Projet concernant de nouveaux signes pour la musique* (1742). Put simply, in cipher notation, the degrees of the major scale are represented by the numerals 1 to 7, where the numeral 1 refers to the keynote of a major key. It was intended to be used as the initial stage in learning to sing at sight, making it possible to forgo the learning of conventional staff notation, although it was intended to facilitate this at a later stage. Although the official 1882 texts recommended no particular method, the ministerial decree of 23 July 1883 did authorize the use of cipher notation in schools (see Chevais 1931: 3648). Following the later ministerial decree of 4 August 1905 (Article 119), cipher notation was included in the curriculum of teachers' colleges and finally appeared in the *Manuel Général* in 1905.

bias?

Although 'Galinism' (the Galin-Paris-Chevé method) represents only one of many possibilities tried up to and including the 1920s, it fed one of those paralyzing polemical bouts of which France is so fond. Galinism certainly made the learning of simple melodies much faster than other approaches and offered certain advantages within a curriculum that had singing as its focus. With this in mind, the official texts based on this approach were introduced to teachers' colleges (*écoles normales*). Even Chevais, who was hardly well disposed toward this method, admitted that it had certain pedagogical merits, in particular the simplification of pitch and duration signs and the reduction of all major and minor keys to two scales: C for the major mode and A for the minor mode. Chevais (1931) considered that simplified methods were useful 'as temporary means of musical instruction' (p. 3648), but that staff notation became necessary whenever more complex types of music were likely to be encountered.

The use of cipher notation gave rise to an extended debate over a period of some 30 years. Cipher notation was not suited to instrumental learning and therefore opposed by specialist music teachers. Accordingly, from 1923, it was no longer included in official syllabi.

Another key pedagogical issue was the French preference for the fixed-doh as opposed to the movable-doh method. France, like other Latin countries, saw considerable discussion about the merits of relative solmization and 'absolute' *solfège*. These methodological disputes poisoned the debate over music in the schools. Eventually, the 1859 ministerial decree determining standard pitch (435 Hertz at a temperature of 18C), followed by the international congress of 1885, had unexpected consequences in France – something that, at the outset, was no more than the adoption of a mere convention. However, this gradually led to a music instructional approach based exclusively on actual (fixed as opposed to relative) pitch and misgivings about whatever methods employed a relative pitch approach, such as those devised by Curwen, Ward, Kodály and Gédalge. This unfortunate orientation to fixed pitch has prevailed to this day. The focus on an absolute pitch approach was opposed by the musicologist Jacques Chailley who, after a period of hesitation, finally acknowledged the need for a large-scale reform of music teaching methods and pointed out the negative effect of this methodological standoff (Chailley 1980, 1983). Other more concrete attempts, such as the French adaptation of the Kodály method put forward by Jacquotte Ribière-Raverlat (1975, 1978) did not meet with sufficient support to enable this innovation to flourish.

The excessive prominence given to perfect pitch as a benchmark of musical

unfortunate? *it isn't...*

acumen, the excessive importance accorded to *solfège*-orientated skills and the dichotomy in focus presented by specialized musical instruction and more general classroom music education in schools were counterproductive to the development of music in schools. Furthermore, many generalist teachers felt that their training did not provide them with sufficient confidence to hold their own in music.

The training of music teachers

The relationship of generalist teachers to musical knowledge depends essentially on two factors: prior experiences in practical music making at a personal level and the amount of specific musical training included in a course of teacher education. Some among the schoolteachers trained during the period of the Third Republic (1870–1940) had prior experience as singers or instrumentalists. This at least gave them a degree of self-confidence to take on musical activities in the classroom. A few even played their instruments in class, which was not the norm in the then highly rationalist educational context. Music, as the 'last subject of instruction' in the curriculum, was deemed to be associated with emotional and bodily engagement, which frequently aroused misgivings among teachers. The exception to this view was that of those certain favourably disposed inspectors who were themselves musicians. In most cases, however, schoolteachers were ill at ease with music.

Despite official directives, the quality of teacher training in music varied considerably. Singing in tune, possessing an elementary knowledge of music and – in the best of cases – the rudiments of *solfège* placed considerable demands on teachers who were expected to devote most of their time and energy to teaching French children to read, write and count. It was not until the period between the two world wars that a 'teaching aptitude certificate' for voice, at two levels, was instituted and gave recognition to the competencies of musician-teachers, enabling them to teach in the higher grade (*école primaire supérieure*) and in teachers' colleges. Alten (1995) has noted that the situation in many regions remained so difficult that in 1933 André Ferré, Inspector for Primary Instruction, was seriously considering establishing ongoing professional training for teachers, with classes being organized at the various levels of France's administrative system (national, department-level and even inter-canton sessions). However, teacher training programmes are still inconsistently applied across France and only Paris, with its intense cultural life and more highly specialized teachers, provides a high degree of consistency in its training of teachers in music.

Maurice Chevais

As a centralized state equipped with an educational system long considered to be exemplary, France has never satisfactorily resolved the problem of music education in the primary schools, whereas specialized musical training in music conservatoires and music schools has made spectacular progress.[1] The lack of a hard-headed approach, the absence of strong political will, fruitless conflicts hardly conducive to dispassionate reflection, have all overshadowed the basic pragmatism that a handful of more insightful pedagogues were able to implement at an early stage. The pioneering efforts of Wilhem have already been discussed, but the work of another highly influential musical pedagogue, all too readily forgotten today, is Maurice Chevais.

Between the two world wars Maurice Chevais was the dominant figure in the development of a suitable musical pedagogy for schools (see Fijalkow 2004). His thinking, in its epistemological breadth, overlooked none of the many aspects associated with music education. Based on actual knowledge about the child, it embraced the kinds of knowledge to be taught, teaching curricula, goals, pedagogical strategies, the training of schoolteachers and, more generally, the purposes of school music instruction. By focusing on the contribution of Chevais, we can discover more about the prevailing thought concerning musical pedagogy in the interwar period.

From the start Chevais was keen to move towards a subject that had greater breadth and scope, so he preferred to talk about *enseignement musical* or *education musicale* rather than the more restricted *chant* (see Chevais 1925). He asserted the primacy of a sensory approach over any theoretical endeavour. At the first level, from 6 to 9 years of age, abstraction was avoided: the instruction was oral and relied primarily on singing. The aim was to educate the voice, the ear and musical taste. Singing thus was no longer the mere illustrative phase of a previously propounded theoretical approach but the main vehicle for music *education*. Chevais envisaged activities in terms of play, rhythm and physical exercise, being pleasurable and being able to instil lasting motivation for learning in children.

At the second level, from 9 to 12 years, music education continued with the gradual introduction of musical signs and recourse to its visual representation. This was the beginning of musical instruction that should not impede the process of education in vocal, listening or aesthetic skills commenced in the previous level, a pitfall which many teachers did not know how to avoid. The rudiments of *solfège* were incorporated into the active and empathic environment of the classroom in which the teacher was constantly relating to the children. Chevais grounded his instructional system in a broad repertory of folksongs and mimed songs, intended for school festivals, which Chevais had collected. In 1909 Chevais had published a collection entitled *Chansons avec gestes* (Songs with gestures) that later was to become *Chants scolaires avec gestes* (School songs with gestures) (n.d.) in which the link between text, music and body movement came to the fore. Chevais did not reject previous methods such as *phonomimie* – an ingenious system of representing the C major scale and highlighting the notes of the common chord to the left of the vertical axis, with the remaining notes being located to the right.

The instruction carried out at the third level, from 12 years onwards, was essentially based on choral singing in both harmonic and polyphonic styles. Chevais was convinced of the effectiveness of choral activity outside the school to supplement classroom music and as a social activity of considerable civic and artistic value in adult life.

The models and progression advocated by Chevais may be debated, particularly the choices resulting from his belief in the innate nature of tonal feeling. But the humanitarian underpinning of his work should also be acknowledged, as should his concern for making the child, under the guidance of the teacher, a fully fledged participant in the co-construction of his/her musical skills. Within the context of French education, Chevais's method is indisputably the first of those identified as 'action based'. Moreover, it is now well established that his approach influenced music learning outside the school setting, particularly within the movement advocating popular education (see Andrieux, in Pistone 1983).

In hindsight, the contribution of Chevais to music education is considerable (see Mialaret, in Fijalkow 2004), particularly in changing the focus from a theoretical to a sensory approach. By bringing the sensory approach to the fore and identifying the impediments to learning, Chevais became part of a major pedagogical innovation that, together with the work of Montessori and Dalcroze, informed research into child psychology. Chevais became interested in the work of Alfred Binet (1857–1911), who at the turn of the century had directed the *Société pour l'étude psychologique de l'enfant* (see Avanzini 1974; Binet and Simon 1908). Binet's influence on Chevais can be seen in his application of Binet's work on the psychological functioning of the child and his incorporation of a developmental perspective in his pedagogical procedures.

Without undertaking an in-depth exposé of the 'progressive' method advocated by Chevais (see Mialaret 1978), it is quite possible to grasp the significant psychological principles using present-day research tools. As opposed to most of his predecessors, for whom learning to read notes remained a prime issue, Chevais's psycho-pedagogical approach did not rely initially on the visual mode of learning but on the combining of listening and singing (see Drake and Rochez 2003). This enlightened decision bypassed the prevailing practices in instrumental training in France, where visual-semantic and visual-motor combinations occupied a pre-eminent position. The priority granted to practice and the refusal to include abstract prerequisites brought

Chevais considerably closer to the later methodologies of Jaques-Dalcroze, Kodály and Orff. Again, due recognition should be given to Chevais's intuition in making singing the most important part of music education. Today it is well established that singing contributes greatly to the transfer of knowledge and skills from one area of music to another (see Drake, McAdams and Berthoz 1999; Drake, Rochez, McAdams, McAdams and Berthoz 2002).

The introduction of music into the school and its somewhat difficult integration into a centralized education system have provided the opportunity for an ongoing and fruitful discussion about musical pedagogy. Faced with a milieu that was anything but hospitable, music pedagogues attempted in successive stages to adapt to the structures of the school as an institution. The evolution of practices and manuals (see Augé 1889; Bouchor 1895; Marmontel 1886) demonstrates that classroom music education has broken loose, albeit slowly, from the prevailing model of musical instruction intended primarily for instrumentalists and singers. Hence recognition of a specific status for music education in the school and the hard-won acknowledgement of music as a specialism within the school system forms a common thread throughout the first two periods in the history of musical education in France (1833–1882 and 1882–1923).

But what meaning should be attributed to school music education? Successively and at times simultaneously, the benefits of music – such as its promotion of social harmony, the encouragement of patriotic pride and the enhancement of aesthetic sensitivity – were recognized for this latecomer to the mandated school curriculum. This was achieved largely through Chevais, who saw music as a necessary means of personal expression for the development of the child and a pathway towards the increasing of human sensitivity. Herein lies the 'great lesson' offered by the last in a line of music education pioneers.

aesthetic value of music ed – Similar to Reimer

The present

In 1984 Annie Labussière, in a short study of music in general education, presented a damning critique of the situation in schools (emphases by Labussière):

> Musical education in the contemporary school, despite its apparent renewal and flourishing, is tainted and shackled by a certain number of external problems (economical, political, social), but more still by internal ones (methods, repertory, pedagogical orientation) which may not be solved empirically but by a constant give-and-take between *scientific procedure* (musicology, experimental psychology, psycho-pedagogy) and *curricula* and *teaching modes*. Furthermore, since the beginning of the century

it has been possible to observe a succession of reforms, projects, amendments and sub-amendments whose practical application (often short-lived or insufficient, and sometimes open to criticism) fails or else founders on the shoals of indifference, essentially in a country in which music has never been fully integrated into the overall school curriculum. (Labussière 1984: 440-41)

Today, while the psychological underpinnings of music education are generally acknowledged, the same does not apply in the case of discipline-based content within the school system – that has recently been promoted under the guise of 'artistic education' (*Bulletin Officiel*, 3 February 2005) and placed in competition with other artistic practices. Thus music education has lost its former clarity of definition. Its survival as a readily identifiable school discipline is no longer assured. It is striking to note the contemporary significance of the major questions raised by the pioneers of school music. A comparison of past and present – a painful one indeed – shows a persistence of problems for which no convincing solution has been offered. The lack of confidence often felt by generalist teachers in teaching music has not subsided (see Jahier 2006). It is recurring at a time when very severe restrictions are weakening the musical training of future generalist teachers, within institutes where teachers are supposed to receive adequate training to carry out their mission. The credibility of the generalist teacher in the area of music – a difficulty brought to light early on by the pioneers of music education – remains as an unresolved problem. Music, having entered the relative sanctuary of the schools of Third Republic through the back door, eventually became more firmly entrenched in specialized structures determined by locally controlled governmental entities (*collectivités territoriales*) such as music schools and conservatories. The gap between these two types of instruction has widened considerably, although the 'action-based' methods used in general education have ultimately contributed to the evolution of more innovative practices in the initial phases of specialized music teaching. The larger historical perspective is that the effort required today in order to set up a partnership between the primary school and specialist musicians, while laudable in itself, will only achieve positive results if the teacher in charge of the class is capable of following up the work of these artists. The effective training of teachers is an indispensable prerequisite to maintaining the status quo in music education and remains a very sensitive issue.

Pressed into service at the beginning of the twentieth century on behalf of extra-musical aims (most often social or political), school music education – today as in the past – is forced to justify its existence through arguments beyond the purely musical. In this respect, it is emphasized that music represents an indisputable contribution to the socialization of children and the transfer of more or less closely related competences or, at the very least, an enhancement in other spheres of learning from a study of music. Research in this area (see Drake and Rochez 2003) has been carried out on populations for whom the amount of time spent in music practice is considerably more than that of French children in primary schools. This is the reason why this argument – potentially a double-edged sword – may only be used in the context of French school instruction with caution.

The first defenders of what today we call 'music education' were committed musicians who were fully aware that music had no need to hide behind an external justification, however laudable, in order to justify its presence in the school curriculum. The obligation to place their discipline at the service of other competencies or other educational aims has only been in response to the stubbornness of education authorities to fully recognize the intrinsic values of music. The place of music in the hierarchy of knowledge and skills that is represented in the curriculum remains fragile.

Ultimately the difficulties of music education in schools mirror the ambiguities of the status of music in French society, which sometimes has been distorted to the point of caricature. Although highly valued by the social elite whenever it is associated with prestigious music training institutions, music is restricted to its function as entertainment for the lower and upper middle classes – in education, the practice of music is well regarded as long it is not to the detriment of basic subjects that are considered to be more important. As for the musical activities of the majority of students, these fail to connect with life outside the school. In other words, there is a disjunction between didactic action and social knowledge so that musical activities in school rarely attain the status of 'referent social practices' (see Martinand 1981). The introduction of music education to the school curriculum has brought with it the legitimacy accorded to other disciplines. As set out in the official regulations – for example, *Bulletin Officiel*, 9 March 1995 – governments will still adhere to the rhetoric of supporting school music, but this is not the case in reality. A plan for the inclusion of music in teacher training, at once ambitious and systematic, is indispensable if a major change is to be effected. Moreover, recognition of music education as an active ingredient in forming the child will necessarily entail a major curriculum reform that can be applied to all schools. This change has only been partial and hesitant attitudes have never fully disappeared.

Thus, pedagogues who devote their efforts to music education and expend considerable energy to convince a rather sceptical public opinion also struggle within the school system to have their ideas accepted. The efforts expended by these music educators, often in very restrictive environments, cannot but result in only modest results that are barely perceptible to political decision makers and to their hierarchy. Yet it is this basic work, made up of unceasing efforts and small victories, that should have deserved the overwhelming support of government agencies. Failure to perceive the benefits of school music education has remained a major obstacle to the development of a discipline that is prisoner to a reticent educational hierarchy and a hard-to-convince public opinion.

In hindsight, the interaction between society and the school system seems to have made music education a 'hot spot' around which a consensus has never been truly established. School music education turns out to be something of a litmus test of significant trends in French society with regard to perceptions about the art of music. This is manifest in a fascination with high-level musical practice that provides reassurance about the primacy of the cultural power of France as a breeding ground for great performers and composers, as opposed to music education for the masses that is crucial to any education of the wider population, which is treated condescendingly. High-profile manifestations of excellence have led to a neglect in building solid foundations within the school milieu. The continuum that spans the entire range from school music practice to the most sublime performances of great musicians has never succeeded in firmly establishing itself, despite the best intentions and efforts of numerous music teachers, composers and other enlightened minds.

These particular socio-historical conditions set France apart from other European countries such as Germany or Hungary. French musical life is affected by a division between elitists, and those who favour a musical education for the majority of children. One cannot delve into the introduction of music education in the French school system without thorny socio-cultural questions being asked, or at least puzzling over the attitudes of government, one prone to legislating but which, when it comes to matters of musical education, has shown itself to be rather weak willed than assertive. It is with self-sacrificing devotion that the most motivated teachers have striven to provide their students with a music education adapted as best they might to the unfavourable conditions in which teachers and students alike find themselves. This has brought about great diversity in pedagogical approaches and with it perhaps a lack of a clear focus.

Conclusion

The inroads made by music education into school curricula represent a succession of advances and retreats, of enthusiasms and abandonments. At the end of this brief overview, the overriding impression may well be one of an uncertain and unequal combat – the history of music education in schools seems to be marking time. Yet, within the course of a century, music has gradually managed to clarify its goals and content, adjusting them to the rather paltry means that were allotted to it within schools. Music has also shown itself to be capable of incorporating contributions from child psychology and has been receptive to the great psychological debates. The official regulations and successive programmes reveal the drawn-out changes that have caused music to proceed from being an entertainment to a decoration and more recently to being recognized as a discipline essential for the development of personality. However, it still remains for the true worth of music education to be felt by all those within the education community and for its significance to be clearly formulated to those authorities entrusted with oversight of the school curriculum. Today, as in the era of the pioneers, these conditions have not been met.

The situation to the present day remains very inconsistent, juxtaposing admirable successes – often inadequately acknowledged by schools and given little or no media exposure – with serious shortcomings. The current orientation of French school curricula as set out in the *Bulletin Officiel* 29 (20 July 2006) is to emphasize the 'basics' and to relegate music to the larger framework of artistic education. These measures are part of a conception of teaching in which utilitarian preoccupations merge with criteria of scientific and technological efficiency. In this context, the convictions and commitments of the pioneers of music education need to be recalled and forcefully reasserted, so that music educators may find a path to renewal and may become aware of how to adapt to the demands of a world that is now constantly on the move.[2]

Notes

[1] As far as secondary schools were concerned, music was taught to girls at the end of the nineteenth century, but it was only in 1937 that it was also taught to boys. The situation was not really improved until the 'plan Landowski' in 1969 (see Landowski 1979).

[2] The following additional references should prove helpful for researchers wishing to explore further the historical development of music education in France: Chailley (1965, 1966); Chevais (1937, 1939, 1941); Dauphin (2004); Genet-Delacroix (1992); Kleinman (1974); Lescat (2001); Prost (1968); Roy (2002).

References

Alten, M. (1995), *La musique dans l'école de Jules Ferry à nos jours*. Issy-les-Moulineaux: EAP.

Augé, C. (1889), *Le Livre de musique*. Paris: Vve P. Larousse.

Avanzini, G. (ed.) (1974), *Binet: Écrits psychologiques et pédagogiques. Choisis et présentés par Guy Avanzini*. Toulouse: Privat.

Binet, A. and Simon, T. (1908/2004), *Le développement de l'intelligence chez les enfants*. [Reprod. en fac-sim. de l'édition de 1908, Paris: Masson]. Paris: l'Harmattan.

Bouchor, M. (1895), *Chants populaires pour les écoles. Poésies de Maurice Bouchor*. Paris: Hachette.

Buisson, F. (1887), *Dictionnaire de pédagogie*. Tome 2. Paris: Hachette.

Bulletin Officiel n 5, 9 March 1995, 'Nouveaux programmes de l'école primaire'.

Bulletin Officiel n 5, 3 February 2005, 'Circulaire d'orientations sur la politique d'éducation artistique et culturelle (...)'.

Bulletin Officiel n 29, 20 July 2006, 'Socle commun de connaissances et de compétences'.

Chailley, J. (1965), 'Solmisation relative ou solfège absolu', *L'éducation musicale*, 21, (123), 26–7.

Chailley, J. (1966), 'Solmisation relative ou solfège absolu', *L'éducation musicale*, 21, (125), 18.

Chailley, J. (1980), 'Hauteur absolue, hauteur relative', in H. P. M. Lithens and Gabriel M. Steinschulte (eds), *Divini cultu splendori, studia musicae sacrae necnon et musico-paedagogiae. Liber festivus in honorem Joseph Lennards*. Rome, pp. 125–30.

Chailley, J. (1983), 'La solmisation Kodály, révélateur des problèmes de hauteur absolue et de hauteur relative dans les pays latins', *L'Éducation musicale*, 40, (295), 7–10.

Chevais, M. (1909), *Chanson avec gestes*. Paris: A. Leduc.

Chevais, M. (1925), *Chansons populaires du Val-de-Loire. Orléans-Blois-Tours et des pays avoisinants*. Paris: Heugel.

Chevais, M. (1931), 'L'enseignement musical à l'école', in A. Lavignac and L. de Laurencie (eds), *Encyclopédie de la musique et Dictionnaire du Conservatoire* (Part II, vol. 6). Paris: Delagrave, pp. 3631–83.

Chevais, M. (1937), *L'éducation musicale de l'enfance*. Vol. 1: *L'enfant et la musique*. Paris: A. Leduc.

Chevais, M. (1939), *L'éducation musicale de l'enfance*. Vol. 2: *L'art d'enseigner*. Paris: A. Leduc.

Chevais, M. (1941), *L'éducation musicale de l'enfance*. Vol. 3: *Méthode active et directe*. Paris: A. Leduc.

Chevais, M. (n.d.), *Chants scolaires avec gestes sur des mélodies recueillies ou composées par Maurice Chevais [...] 1er recueil*. Paris: A. Leduc.

Chevé, E. (1852), *La routine et le bon sens ou les conservatoires et la méthode Galin-Paris-Chevé*. Paris: Chez l'auteur.

Chevé, E. (ed.) (1862), *Galin, P., Exposition d'une nouvelle méthode pour l'enseignement de la musique*. Paris: E. Chevé.

Dauphin, C. (2004), 'Les grandes méthodes pédagogiques du XXe siècle', in J-J. Nattiez (ed.), *Musiques. Une encyclopédie pour le XXIe siècle*. Vol. 2: *Les savoirs musicaux*. Arles: Actes Sud, pp. 833–53.

Drake, C. and Rochez, C. (2003), 'Développement et apprentissage des activités et perceptions musicales', in M. Kail and M. Fayol (eds), *Les sciences cognitives et l'école*. Paris: PUF, pp. 443–79.

Drake, C., McAdams, S. and Berthoz, A. (1999), 'Learning to sing a novel piece of music facilitates playing it on the violin but not the other way round: evidence from performances segmentations', *Journal of the Acoustical Society of America*, 106, (4), 2285.

Drake, C., Rochez, C., McAdams, S. and Berthoz, A. (2002), 'Sing first, play later: singing a novel piece of music facilitates playing it on an instrument but not the other way round', *7th International Conference for Music Perception and Cognition (ICMPC) Proceedings*, Sydney: ICMPC. CD-ROM.

Ferro, M. (2003), *Histoire de France*. Paris: Odile Jacob.

Fijalkow, C. (2003), *Deux siècles de musique à l'école: chroniques de l'exception parisienne, 1819–2002*. Paris: L'Harmattan.

Fijalkow, C. (ed.) (2004), *Maurice Chevais (1880–1943). Un grand pédagogue de la musique*. Paris: L'Harmattan.

Galin, P. (1818), *Exposition d'une nouvelle méthode pour l'enseignement de la musique*. Paris: Rey et Gravier.

Gédalge, A. (1926), *L'enseignement de la musique par l'éducation méthodique de l'oreille*. [The teaching of music by the methodical education of the ear. English trans. by Anna Mary Mealand.] Paris: Libr. Gédalge.

Genet-Delacroix, M-C. (1992), *Art et état sous la IIIe république: le système des beaux-arts, 1870–1940*. Paris: Publications de la Sorbonne.

Jahier, S. (2006), 'L'éducation musicale à l'école: les pratiques pédagogiques et le rapport au savoir musical des enseignants du primaire' (doctoral thesis, University of Paris X-Nanterre).

Kleinman, S. (1974), *La solmisation mobile: de Jean-Jacques Rousseau à John Curwen*. Paris: Heugel.

Labussière, A. (1984), 'Pédagogie et éducation musicale ', in J. Chailley (ed.), *Précis de musicologie*. Paris: PUF, pp. 431–42.

Landowski, M. (1979), *Batailles pour la musique*. Paris: Le Seuil.

Lee-Forbes, W. (1977), 'The Galin-Paris-Chevé method of rhythmic instruction: a history'. London: University Microfilms International.

Lescat, P. (2001), *L'enseignement musical en France de 529 à 1972: 71 plans, chronologie, lieux, élèves, maîtres, études, emploi du temps, classes, manuels*. Courlay: J. M. Fuzeau.

Manuel général de l'instruction primaire (1905). Paris: Hachette.

Marmontel, A. (1886), *La première année de musique. Solfège et chants à l'usage de l'enseignement élémentaire*. Paris: A. Colin.

Martinand, J-L. (1981), 'Pratiques sociales de référence et compétences techniques. À propos d'un projet d'initiation aux techniques de fabrication mécanique en classe de quatrième', in A. Giordan (ed.), *Diffusion et appropriation du savoir scientifique: enseignement et vulgarisation. Actes des Troisièmes Journées Internationales sur l'Education Scientifique*. Paris: University of Paris (Paris 7), pp. 149–54.

Mialaret, J-P. (1978), *Pédagogie de la musique et enseignement programmé*. Paris: EAP.

Pistone, D. (ed.) (1983), *L'éducation musicale en France. Histoire et méthodes*. Actes du colloque de l'Institut de recherches sur les civilisations de l'Occident moderne, 13 March 1982. Paris: Presses de l'Université de Paris-Sorbonne (Paris IV), p. 8.

Programmes du 27 juillet 1882, *Bulletin administratif du ministère de l'Instruction publique*. Paris: Imprimerie Nationale.

Programmes et instructions de l'enseignement élémentaire (1923). Chambéry: Éditions Scolaires.

Prost, A. (1968), *Histoire de l'enseignement en France*. Paris: A. Colin.

Rainbow, B. (1967), *The Land without Music: Musical Education in England 1800–1860 and its Continental Antecedents*. London: Novello.

Ribière-Raverlat, J. (1975), *Chant-Musique. Adaptation française de la méthode Kodály: Livre du maître. Classes élémentaires, 1re Année*. Book 1. Paris: A. Leduc.

Ribière-Raverlat, J. (1978), *Chant-Musique. Adaptation française de la méthode Kodály: Livre du maître.* Book 2. Paris: A. Leduc.

Rousseau J. J. (1781), *Projet concernant de nouveaux signes pour la musique, lu par l'auteur à l'Académie des sciences le 22 août 1742.* Geneva.

Roy, J. (ed.) (2002), *La formation des professeurs des écoles en éducation musicale.* Paris: University of Paris-Sorbonne, Documents de Recherche OMF, Série Didactique de la Musique 31.

Société Française L'art à l'école (ed.) (1925), *Anthologie du chant scolaire et post-scolaire.* (Anthology of school and after-school songs), 1ère série, *Chansons populaires des provinces de France.* (Traditional songs from French provinces). Paris: Heugel.

Vançon, J. C. (2004), 'De la polémique galiniste (1882–1883) au conflit Chevais/ Gédalge (1917–1923): l'histoire de la musique à l'école à la lumiére de ses querelles pédagogiques', in C. Fijalkow (ed.) *Maurice Chevais (1880–1943).* Paris: L'Harmattan, pp. 39–56.

Wilhem, G. B. (1836), *Manuel de lecture musicale et de chant élémentaire à l'usage des collèges, des institutions, des écoles et des cours de chant (. . .).* Paris: Perrotin.

4

Germany: Educational goals, curricular structure, political principles

Wilfried Gruhn

Introduction

Music instruction in public schools in Germany has a rather long history (for review see Braun 1957; Ehrenforth 1995; 1997; Gruhn 2003; Günther 1967; Nolte 1982; 1991; Schmidt 1986; Sowa 1973). However, when considering the development of music education, it is necessary to bear in mind that as a political unit Germany has changed many times and has existed in its present form only since 1990. The long history of the *Heilige Römische Reich Deutscher Nation* united various smaller states and local tribes (for example, Saxons, Prussians, Bavarians, Franks, Kelts etc.) and lasted from the Middle Ages until 1806. During the seventeenth and eighteenth centuries, Germany was scattered into innumerable kingdoms, duchies, archduchies, counties and principalities, so that Germany could not be thought of as a homogeneous political entity; rather it was a culturally and linguistically related assemblage of member states.

During the nineteenth century the House of Hohenzollern in Prussia became the most influential and powerful counterpart to the House of Habsburg in Austria. Therefore, Prussia will be taken as a model for music education in Germany because the other states followed in adopting its educational policies. After the Second World War, Germany became a Federal Republic of ten states; since reunification in 1990, it now consists of sixteen states that are culturally autonomous – the so-called *Kulturhoheit der Länder*. This caused and still causes many differences in school organization, curricula and educational policies in particular states that correspond to the ruling parties and their political agendas. The history of these divergent developments will not be addressed in this chapter; rather some general principles that initially determined and then emerged from compulsory schooling and mandatory music learning will be discussed.

FIGURE 4.1 Latin school (*Lateinschule*) in the sixteenth century. The board with notation on the wall indicates that choral singing was part of schooling. (Woodcut from 1592; © H. Schiffler & R. Winkler, 1991, *Tausend Jahre Schule*. Stuttgart: Belser Verlag, p. 67)

Historical premises

Singing of Gregorian chant 'by ear' and later from notation had always been part of the education in monastic schools since the Middle Ages (see Figure 4.1).

But this form of education cannot be thought of as schooling in the modern sense. Only the very few students who were seen as having the potential to take over clerical or governmental positions were introduced to reading and writing. Formal education as such did not exist. The Augustinian monk Martin Luther (1483–1546), who was the first to codify a common German language (as distinct from the many dialects of the different Germanic tribes), recognized the importance of congregational singing in building and unifying a community. Accordingly, singing came to be widely taught in monastic and Latin schools and was no longer confined to its original liturgical function.

Through an edict of King Friedrich the Great (*Generallandschulreglement*), Prussia became the first state to introduce compulsory schooling in 1763. However, it took a long time before this law could be applied to the whole

FIGURE 4.2 Cartoon by J. Nussbiegel (1825) reflecting the situation of teaching during the seventeenth and eighteenth centuries. (Reproduced with permission of Germanisches Nationalmuseum Nürnberg)

country. It has only been since the end of the eighteenth century that compulsory schooling in the German states and in the German kingdoms (e.g. Saxonia and Bavaria) came into being, albeit with limited effect. Teachers were not recognized in society as professionals, many of them being disabled soldiers who had adequate literacy and numeracy skills and a knowledge of bible stories. They were poorly paid by parents so that they needed additional income to maintain their daily lives. Therefore, it was not uncommon that pupils came to the teachers' homes and were taught all together by the teacher and his wife who also had to perform household duties in between their teaching (see Figure 4.2).

Although great differences occurred between city and country schools, singing (or 'singing instruction') was always included in compulsory schooling. However, there was neither methodical teaching of singing and other subjects nor formal teacher training in place. Contemporary illustrations of singing masters depict teachers as lacking enthusiasm and being lethargic and indicate a feeling of depression and resignation to a poor lot in life (see Figure 4.3). Moreover, music journals of the time include complaints and reports about desperate conditions in schools, poor discipline and numerous calls for pupils to be excused from singing. By the same token, musical life flourished at the aristocratic courts – for example, at Köthen, Dresden, Mannheim, Munich etc. – and in cities such as Berlin and Leipzig. All this set a standard of musical excellence in performance and composition

FIGURE 4.3: A typical music teacher of the nineteenth century. The violin was the standard instrument for the accompaniment of singing, the bow served as a pointer and often for punishment as well. (Print by Kauffmann 'Der Herr Cantor'; © H. Schiffler & R. Winkler, 1991, *Tausend Jahre Schule*. Stuttgart: Belser Verlag; reproduced with permission of Horst Schiffler)

that spread to the rest of Europe. The dichotomy presented by the gap between educational and artistic standards is very characteristic of this period.

At the turn of the nineteenth century the educational reforms of the Swiss philanthropist Johann Heinrich Pestalozzi (1746–1827) profoundly influenced education on the continent. Teachers travelled to Switzerland to meet with and learn from him and the German poet Johann Wolfgang von Goethe reflected and transfigured Pestalozzi's educational philosophy in his novel *Wilhelm Meisters Wanderjahre* (1821–29/1981), referring to this as *Pädagogische Provinz*. The interest aroused by Pestalozzi's ideas and their profound influence on early nineteenth-century education in Europe and the USA (see Gruhn 1993; Pemberton 1985)[1] were probably due to a desire for a clearly defined, formalized general teaching method. Pestalozzi's friends Michael Traugott Pfeiffer (1771–1849) and Hans Georg Nägeli (1773–1836) applied his ideas to singing in schools and edited the first instructional method book for singing according to Pestalozzi's principles (*Gesangbildungslehre* 1810).

However, their strict and highly systematized method was a misinterpretation of Pestalozzi's new understanding of the psychology of learning and the educational philosophy that aimed to follow children's natural development by supporting sensual experiences before introducing formal (verbal) knowledge. Unfortunately, Pestalozzi had never enunciated a psychologically grounded learning theory, but in essence this was reflected in his published works. Nevertheless, Pfeiffer and Nägeli's formalized instructional approach became more successful and influential than any other contemporary method book and made Pestalozzi famous all over Europe.

Singing during the nineteenth century was always part of the school curriculum in elementary education but was dominated by the debate about the optimal teaching method to employ. Formal aspects of a methodical approach to teaching – as reflected in *Formalstufen* (formal stages of teaching) by Johann Friedrich Herbart (1776–1841) – became the principal educational idea of that century and overshadowed all other aspects.

Philosophical and socio-cultural contexts: four paradigms

In reflecting on compulsory music in school education and on how and why it was set up, four overarching paradigms can be identified: singing under the supervision and for the benefit of *the church*; singing as serving and promoting the values of *the state*; music (not specifically singing) as a component of *general public education* (*Volksbildung*);[2] and music learning based on, and as a component of, the developmental growth of *the child/pupil*. Each of these paradigms will now be discussed in turn.

Singing as liturgical support

From the early Middle Ages, singing had been an integral part of the religious education of the German people. Even after the Royal Edict of 1763 singing remained under the control of the church. The main purpose of singing as a mandatory subject for all children in schools was to learn and commit to memory the melodies and words of hymns and chorales, with the aim of enhancing church services with the tuneful singing of children that would elevate the spirit of the community and enlighten the mind. Indeed, this idea of elevation and enlightenment gained through singing and listening to liturgical songs was fundamental to the teaching of singing in schools. This liturgical context also determined the song repertoire and curriculum content of music as a school subject – namely, congregational songs and music notation. Accordingly, the issue that dominated the music curriculum during the course of the nineteenth century was that of teaching methodology. This is reflected in the countless singing instructions that were published in each

FIGURE 4.4 Notation with numbers according to Bernhard Christoph Ludwig Natorp's *Anleitung zur Unterweisung im Singen* (Introduction to singing instruction), Essen, 1813 (p. 52).

region by numerous singing teachers and supervisors (Abs 1811; Hientzsch 1829/18930; Hohmann 1838; Kübler 1826; Natorp 1813, 1820; Pfeiffer and Nägeli 1810; Schulz 1816; Zeller 1810; also see Gruhn 2003: 66–88).

Interestingly, solmization – whether using the movable- or fixed-doh approach – was never a matter of contention, as cipher notation, where numerals indicate the position of tones in a scale, was introduced through Pfeiffer's and Nägeli's *Gesangbildungslehre* (1810) and then more systematically through Natorp's *Anleitung* (1813) (see Figure 4.4).

Singing in the service of the state and its values

In 1809 Wilhelm von Humboldt (1767–1835) became the Prussian Minister of Culture with control over the school system for the entire kingdom. He developed a new way of thinking about school education. The basis of his educational reforms (known as *Preußische Schulreformen*) was set out in his proposals for the schools in Königsberg (Prussia) and in Lithuania (*Königsberger und Litauischer Schulplan*) (Humboldt 1964, *Werke*, Vol. IV: 168–95). He maintained that each student should have the opportunity to develop individually according to his/her potential (*Kraft*). Humboldt deliberately chose to use the term *Bildung* (formation), which stems from the reflexive verb *sich bilden* (to grow, form) in the sense that the goal of schooling and teaching is to support the *growth of the potential* of every individual. The function of the state, he maintained, should be to guarantee academic freedom for the learning and growth of the individual. Accordingly, the main purpose of the state was to establish boundaries for school education within which teaching and learning could develop without state control or prescription (see Humboldt 1964, *Werke*, Vol. I: 56–233). The idea of academic freedom and general education (*Allgemeinbildung*), as opposed to occupational training (*Berufsbildung*), was at the core of Humboldt's conception of a university where learning was based on the apprenticeship model and students formed a research group and learnt by assisting their professor in his research. During his short period as Prussian Minister, Humboldt framed a broad set of philosophical ideals for education and outlined more general structures for schools. For the practical applications of teaching and learning, Humboldt specifically referred to Pestalozzi's principles and sent Prussian teacher trainees to Switzerland for instruction in methods of teaching.

Humboldt's conception of education was obviously not aligned to the official view and appeared somewhat subversive to state officials with the result that Humboldt resigned after 10 months in office. Some decades later another educational model came to the fore. During the time of *Kulturkampf* (cultural conflict) from 1866, Reichskanzler Otto von Bismarck (1815–1898) broke the nexus between church and state, and the school system became controlled by government (see Figure 4.5). This was part of the development

FIGURE 4.5 A school prior to the transfer of educational authority from church to state. In his (1858) print, Adolf Menzel depicts King Friedrich Wilhelm I of Prussia (1688–1740) visiting a typical village school. (© H. Schiffler & R. Winkler, 1991, *Tausend Jahre Schule*. Stuttgart: Belser Verlag, reproduced with permission of Horst Schiffler)

of a new national identity in Germany (Prussia) during the nineteenth century. Given the emergence of a new nationalism, the singing of patriotic songs was employed to establish a sense of national identity among students and to imbue them with feelings of patriotism and loyalty and, as such, was made an obligatory part of what was by then a system of compulsory schooling for young people (Lemmermann 1984). Accordingly, the music curriculum for each administrative district consisted of a mandated repertoire of songs that had to be memorized as well as a prescribed syllabus involving voice training (*Stimmbildung*), sight reading and music theory (scales and intervals) (Nolte 1975). However, singing was recognized as neither an artistic nor an academic subject, but rather as belonging to technical subjects such as calligraphy (*Schönschreiben*) and drawing.

The change in the function of music in schools from serving the church to serving the state effectively saw only a change in repertoire – namely from liturgical to patriotic and folksongs – and a change in purpose – singing at church services and on church holidays was replaced by singing at celebrations of national commemoration days. Otherwise, there were no significant changes in teaching and learning, which were mainly based on the materials of the particular subject matter (*materiale Bildung*) and the memorization of verbal knowledge such as music theory and song texts. Although the structural change in school policy affected the function and the content of music in schools, it did not impinge on the methods of teaching singing.

Music as part of general education

In 1924 the subject called *singing* was redesignated as *music* by the Prussian school reforms of Leo Kestenberg (1882–1962). Kestenberg was preoccupied by his belief in the power of a general public education (*Volksbildung*). As a Jewish musician who had studied with the pianist and composer Ferruccio Busoni (1866–1924), Kestenberg began his career as a brilliant pianist, but soon became deeply involved in educational and political issues associated with the Social-Democratic Party. He organized working-class concerts, designed cultural programmes in Berlin and was appointed in 1918 after the First World War as an Official Adviser for Music (*Musikreferent*) in the Prussian Ministry of Culture. From this position, he initiated a significant reform of music education that was outlined in a new policy for schooling in general and for music in particular when the subject was mandated as part of the curriculum.[3] When 'singing' was replaced by 'music' in the school curriculum, the intrinsic aesthetic aspects of music as an art form came to the fore. Consequently, the various musical genres available at that time (which, for the want of other forms of media, could only be performed on a piano) were incorporated into the curriculum and singing as such was no longer seen as the most appropriate form of musical expression to promote creative experience and intellectual understanding within the new educational order.

The new subject of 'music' continued to be mandated as part of the state-supported school system, although its function, content and methods were continually revised. In general, however, the fundamentals of school music in Germany were still based on Kestenberg's principles: (i) music was an artistic (as opposed to technical) subject; (ii) music was taught by an academically trained professional school music teacher who was also trained in a second academic subject (as opposed to a singing master only able to provide singing lessons); (iii) music teachers undertook training in artistic, scientific and pedagogic aspects of a comprehensive course of music teacher education. Kestenberg can therefore be accorded the status of founder of modern school music development in Germany[4] (see Gruhn 2004; Kestenberg 1921).

From an international perspective, it is surprising that neither the pedagogical methods of Carl Orff (1895–1982) nor that of Zoltán Kodály (1882–1967) had any direct influence on German music education. Although school music teachers make use of the Orff-type classroom instruments, the pedagogical *Orff Schulwerk* approach has never been formally introduced into German schools probably because the basic ideas underpinning Orff's conception of musicianship were seen as being at odds with the innovative reform initiatives of the progressive education.

The implementation of the Kestenberg reforms in German schools slowed and finally ceased during the years of the Third Reich – the 12 years of Nazism did not witness any new educational paradigm. Because of a demarcation of responsibility for school education between the Ministry of Culture and the Nazi Party (NSDAP), the old syllabi continued to remain in place for some time under the authority of the Ministry of Culture. However, there were comparatively few teachers who were trained during the period of educational reforms who were able to implement classroom teaching according to Kestenberg's ideas (see Gruhn 2003: 259 ff.) Although new curricula were issued between 1937 and 1942 (Gruhn 2003; Nolte 1975), it was only after the Second World War that the reform process could be renewed. This process was aided by the philosopher and sociologist Theodor W. Adorno (1903–1969) who, from his exiled home in America, addressed the main representatives of the old 'musische' ideology in his *Thesen gegen die musikpädagogische Musik* (Theses against pedagogical music) (Adorno 1954/ 1973), in which he strongly criticized the aesthetic foundations of their educational philosophy and, by this, opened a general debate about music education and initiated an educational change in the 1960s.

Music and child-centred learning

Based on the ideas of *Das Jarhundert des Kindes* (The century of the child*)* (Key 1902) and motivated by the challenge of the launch of Sputnik 1 by the Russians in 1957, a new model of child- and student-centred learning and teaching emerged as a result of innovative theories to emerge from cognitive developmental psychology. With regard to curriculum reform, the selection of the musical content and its relation to appropriate teaching methods had to be organized into a systematic teaching progression – a sequential and developmental curriculum as opposed to a canon of mandatory objects or contents. The development of new curricula – different in each of the German states – caused a radical change in the way that teaching was perceived as a legitimate professional discipline. The focus on the development of the child's potential as an individual represented a totally new perspective and resulted in new materials, new textbooks, and new pedagogical approaches (Gruhn 2003: 327 ff.). As a consequence, new trends of youth culture, pop, rock and jazz, contemporary music, film music, music for use in commercials etc. as well as many possibilities of music production and perception were included into the curriculum. This changed the way music was recognized in schools. It was now predicated on enabling all students to participate in the broad variety of musical forms and practices within a democratic society. This has strongly influenced the principle of general music as an educational right offered to everybody as a compulsory subject in school.

Teacher training

It seems both reasonable and obvious that the various phases of music as part of a compulsory school education should be reflected in different models of teacher training. When the function of school music (then singing) was to serve church liturgical purposes, the teacher in elementary schools and the church organist (*Kantor*) were often one and the same person especially in smaller villages. The 'teacher-Kantor' who taught pupils in the school and at the same was organist and choir director in the church was a common occurrence especially in Saxonia.[5]

When the state took control of schools and the development of education became the responsibility of the Ministry of Culture, new training institutions were established, so-called teacher seminars (*Lehrerseminare*), where graduates from the so-called *Volksschule* (comprehensive elementary school) continued their education and were trained to teach all subjects including singing. All teacher trainees were required to play an instrument (the organ for church services and the violin as a portable instrument for classroom teaching). They also received tuition in vocal music within teacher training programmes. The convention of a generalist elementary (primary) teacher who teaches all school subjects originates from this early model of teacher training.

With the broadening of curriculum content associated with the move from 'singing' to 'music', together with a further expansion to include the new challenge of 'arts education', additional demands were put on teacher training programmes. Today, music teachers – specifically those in secondary schools (so-called *Gymnasien*) – need to be trained as musicians first and then to specialize in music pedagogy. The requirement that secondary teachers should be highly trained musicians resulted from the introduction to the school curriculum of music from across a broad span of historical periods and incorporating a wide variety of genres. This approach also called for 'symphony concerts for children'[6] through which students were introduced to symphonic music. In order to prepare their students for these concerts teachers were required to demonstrate the pieces by playing them from a piano score. Accordingly, secondary music teacher education programmes were established at music academies, which then became academic institutions (*Musikhochschulen*), equivalent to universities in status. Teachers in elementary schools were trained in new academies for teacher training (*Pädagogische Akademien*) where music was included as an elective study within the generalist training course. Later, these institutions became pedagogical universities (*Pädagogische Hochschulen*), which were then integrated into universities during the 1970s in most German states.

It is not surprising, therefore, that a change of paradigm relating to the purpose, function and structure of music education in schools caused changes in teacher training courses. Music education as part of the general educational system has a strong social dimension and is therefore reflective of the prevailing social, political, and socio-cultural context in Germany.

However, underlying the development of music in schools and in the social life of Germany, there is a common belief in the emotional power of music. This can be traced back to the late eighteenth century when, with the prevailing aesthetic of *Empfindsamkeit* (sensitive style), music was evaluated in terms of its emotional and affective power. Music was understood as a *language du coeur* (Rousseau 1782) or in Hegel's (1967) terms as *tönende Innerlichkeit* (sounding intimacy), which is still deeply engraved on the popular understanding of music and has resulted in the widely held belief that music in schools has an effect on *Charakterbildung* (formation of mind and personality). This has its origins in eighteenth-century aesthetics and perpetuates a belief in the earlier doctrine of embellishment and elevation as the main power of music that marks it as an indispensable part of a human being's physical and psychic endowment.

New directions in compulsory music education

Music as a compulsory school subject for all children became the new imperative and this brought with it new challenges and difficulties for educators. Several compelling questions arise:

- How can we understand the culture of the new generation?
- How can this youth culture be integrated into a school curriculum?
- How can music educators deal with questions of the divergent musical cultures in a globalized world which are reflected in contemporary classrooms?

It is not only a question of being able to motivate students, but also of connecting music in school with their individual life worlds (*Lebenswelt*) – a term introduced by the philosopher Edmund Husserl (1859–1938). The dichotomy between the musical experience of everyday life and the demands of music as an art form collide in the classroom and result in a clash of contradictory cultures, a challenge that has to be met by the teacher. There are many inspiring and persuasive new ideas as to how students might be involved in music making, but there are nevertheless significant problems in dealing with the demands of different cultures and the experiences of students in a methodically cogent manner.

Therefore, it must be noted that each model or paradigm creates its own problems, difficulties and challenges that must be solved within the environment of particular social, cultural and educational contexts. Mandatory classroom music as part of compulsory schooling produces a multitude of educational questions and demands because obligatory class music teaching is different from individual and presumably optional instrumental lessons. The two different but equivalent demands call for didactic solutions based on clearer insights into teaching and learning procedures that is nowadays being informed by the findings from ongoing brain research (see Gruhn and Rauscher 2008).

Conclusions and prospects

This review of music in compulsory education from a German perspective shows that curricular decisions and educational concepts are always embedded in a socio-cultural and historical context.

The four dominant paradigms discussed provide a broad perspective for music in compulsory schooling, but they do not offer a single convincing model of how music should be introduced into schools. In Germany, the situation demonstrates a rather broad variety of educational policies with regard to music. In relation to music in elementary education, the situation is that in all states music is compulsory and is taught by the generalist classroom teacher although teacher training programmes offer music as an elective for special focus. However, in elementary schools, about 80 per cent of music lessons are given by non-specialist teachers.

In secondary education (*Gymnasium*), the situation is quite different. Here, well-educated and highly specialized music teachers implement general music education as a compulsory subject and aim to provide a set of rich musical experiences for students both within and outside formal schooling. Generally speaking, music belongs with the core curriculum which is mandatory at least until grade (year) 10 in all types of secondary school in the various German states although there are differences between states; afterwards music becomes an elective.[7] Accordingly, music is present in all schools and every student receives a music education for at least several years in general music classes. School choirs, bands, orchestras are supplementary and may be chosen by the students according to their interests and abilities. String and wind classes have become very popular in recent times. This marks a new trend of practical music making as the core of the curriculum.

By way of contrast, there has been a slight tendency in a few states to eliminate music as a discrete subject and integrate it into the larger context of *aesthetic education* or alternatively to build a new subject area that relates to life sciences (biology, nature, culture). It is obvious that this development weakens the function of music as a compulsory subject. Where implemented, this political decision has resulted in a reduction in the number of specialist music teachers in elementary schools which follows an all-too-common belief that one art form may be replaced by any other because all of them deal with aesthetic objects. However, this argument completely fails to fulfil the demand of genuine music learning as an essential goal of compulsory music in schools.

With regard to compulsory education, another possibility is beginning to come to the fore – after centuries when the church or the state regulated and organized comprehensive education by funding personnel and physical infrastructure, it has now become apparent that the state may withdraw from its responsibility by handing over the implementation of education to private providers. First steps in this direction saw the introduction of tuition fees for higher education which replaces the time-honoured principle of free education guaranteed by the state. Whether this trend will continue and how it might affect music as a compulsory subject in schools in the future has yet to be seen.

Notes

[1] As a matter of interest, it was a more or less literal translation of a local German singing instruction book by J. G. Kübler (1826) that laid the foundation for Lowell

Mason's famous *Manual of the Boston Academy of Music* (1834). For further details see Gruhn (1993); Pemberton (1985).

[2] The term *Volksbildung* is difficult to translate. It refers to the social aim of providing everybody, including those of the lower social classes, with the opportunity to participate in the values of education. The principle of *Volksbildung* is embedded in the ideals and mission of education within the labour movement during the late nineteenth and early twentieth centuries.

[3] Because of the importance of Kestenberg as a leading figure in Prussian/German music education, his complete literary works are to be published in a four-volume edition in 2009 (see Gruhn 2009).

[4] Kestenberg expended the same effort in developing music education in Israel when he immigrated to Tel Aviv in 1938 and became an Israeli citizen immediately after the proclamation of the state of Israel in 1948.

[5] One of the most prominent examples was Johann Sebastian Bach, who taught at the *Thomas Schule* and was music director at the four main churches in Leipzig.

[6] Similar to the initiatives of Robert Mayer in England and Walter Damrosch in the USA, Richard Barth started his first *Volksschülerkonzerte* (concerts for pupils of elementary schools) in Hamburg 1899/1900 (see Gruhn 2003: 211).

[7] As mentioned earlier, it is extremely difficult to present a general overview of the German school system and of music education as part of it because of the many differences resulting from the cultural sovereignty (*Kulturhoheit*) of the federal states. In general, there is the policy of a three-tiered school system consisting of the elementary school (*Grundschule*), which then divides into main (*Hauptschule*), middle (*Realschule*) and high school (*Gymnasium*), all of which offer different qualifications. However, there are other models in some states where main and middle schools are merged into a regional school (*Regionalschule*) or where a four-tiered system is established in which an integrative comprehensive school (*integrierte Gesamtschule*) parallels the *Gymnasium*.

References

Abs, T. (1811), *Darstellung meiner Anwendung der Pestalozzischen Bildungsmethode*. Halberstadt: Bureau für Literatur und Kunst.

Adorno, T. W. (1973), 'Thesen gegen die musikpädagogische Musik [1954]', in R. Tiedemann (ed.), *Gesammelte Schriften*, vol. 14. Frankfurt am Main: Suhrkamp, pp. 437–40. [First unauthorized publication *Junge Musik*, 1953/54, 111–13.]

Braun, G. (1957), *Die Schulmusikerziehung in Preußen*. Kassel: Bärenreiter.

Ehrenforth, K. H. (1995), *Geschichte der musikalischen Bildung. Eine Kultur-, Sozial- und Ideengeschichte in 40 Stationen von den antiken Hochkulturen bis zur Gegenwart*. Mainz: Schott.

Ehrenforth, K. H. (1997), 'Geschichte der Musikerziehung', in L. Finscher (ed.), *Die Musik in Geschichte und Gegenwart. Allgemeine Enzyklopädie der Musik*, vol. 6. Kassel and Stuttgart: Bärenreiter & Metzler, columns 1473–99.

Goethe, J. W. von (1821–29/1981), *Wilhelm Meisters Wanderjahre*, in *Werke Hamburger*, vol. 8. Munich: Beck.

Gruhn, W. (1993), 'Is Lowell Mason's "manual" based on Pestalozzian principles?', *Bulletin of Historical Research in Music Education*, 14, (2), 92–101.

Gruhn, W. (2003), *Geschichte der Musikerziehung. Eine Kultur- und Sozialgeschichte vom Gesangunterricht der Aufklärungspädagogik zu ästhetisch-kultureller Bildung*. Hofheim: Wolke.

Gruhn, W. (2004), 'Leo Kestenberg', *International Journal of Music Education*, 22, (2), 103–129.

Gruhn, W. (ed.) (2009), *Leo Kestenberg. Gesammelte Schriften vol. 1, Die Hauptschriften*. Freiburg: Rombach.

Gruhn, W. and Rauscher, F. (eds) (2008), *Neurosciences in Music Pedagogy*. New York: Nova Sciences.

Günther, U. (1967), *Die Schulmusikerziehung von der Kestenberg-Reform bis zum Ende des Dritten Reiches*. Neuwied: Luchterhand.

Hegel, G. F. W. (1967), *Einleitung in die Ästhetik*. Munich: Fink.

Hientzsch, J. G. (1829/30), 'Der Gesang-Unterricht in Schulen' *Eutonia*, (1) 1829, vol. I, 42–9, 205–222; vol. II, 210–231; *Eutonia*, (2) 1830, vol. III, 229–43.

Hohmann, C. H. (1838), *Praktischer Lehrgang für den Gesang-Unterricht in Volksschulen*. Nördlingen: Becksche Buchhandlung.

Humboldt, W. von (1960–1964), *Werke in 5 Bänden*. Darmstadt: Wissenschaftliche Buchgesellschaft.

Kestenberg, L. (1921), *Musikerziehung und Musikpflege*. Leipzig: Quelle & Meyer.

Key, E. (1902), *Das Jahrhundert des Kindes*. Berlin: Fischer.

Kübler, G. F. (1826), *Anleitung zum Gesang-Unterrichte in Schulen nebst einem Anhange von 55 zwei- und dreistimmigen Gesängen*. Stuttgart: Metzlersche Buchhandlung.

Lemmermann, H. (1984), *Kriegserziehung im Kaiserreich*, 2 vols. Bremen: Eres.

Mason, L. (1834), *Manual of the Boston Academy of Music for Instruction in the Elements of Vocal Music on the System of Pestalozzi*. Boston, MA: Wilkins & Carter.

Natorp, B. C. L. (1813, 1820), *Anleitung zur Unterweisung im Singen für Lehrer in Volksschulen*. Essen: Bädeker.

Nolte, E. (1975), *Lehrpläne und Richtlinien für den schulischen Musikunterricht in Deutschland vom Beginn des 19. Jahrhunderts bis in die Gegenwart* (Musikpädagogik. Forschung und Lehre, vol. 3). Mainz: Schott.

Nolte, E. (1982), *Die neuen Curricula, Lehrpläne und Richtlinien für den Musikunterricht an den allgemeinbildenden Schulen in der Bundesrepublik Deutschland und West-Berlin. Einführung und Dokumentation: Teil I: Primarstufe* (Musikpädagogik. Forschung und Lehre, vol. 16). Mainz: Schott.

Nolte, E. (1991), *Die neuen Curricula, Lehrpläne und Richtlinien für den Musikunterricht an den allgemeinbildenden Schulen in der Bundesrepublik Deutschland und West-Berlin, Teil II: Sekundarstufe I*, 3 Bde. (Musikpädagogik. Forschung und Lehre, vol. 17). Mainz: Schott.

Pemberton, C. A. (1985), *Lowell Mason: His Life and Work*. Ann Arbor, MI: UMI Research Press.

Pfeiffer, M. T. and Nägeli, H. G. (1810), *Gesangbildungslehre nach Pestalozzischen Grundsätzen*. Zurich: Nägeli.

Rousseau, J. J. (1782), 'Essai sur l'origine des langues', *Œuvres complètes*, vol. 16. Deux-Ponts, pp. 153–231.

Schiffler, H. and Winkler, R. (1991), *Tausend Jahre Schule*. Stuttgart: Belser Verlag.

Schmidt, H.-C. (ed.) (1986), *Geschichte der Musikpädagogik* (Handbuch der Musikpädagogik, Bd.1). Kassel: Bärenreiter.

Schulz, K. (1816), *Leitfaden bei der Gesanglehre nach der Elementarmethode mit besonderer Rücksicht auf Landschulen*. Leipzig: Darnmannsche Buchhandlung.

Sowa, G. (1973), *Anfänge institutioneller Musikerziehung in Deutschland (1800–1843)* (Studien zur Musikgeschichte des 19. Jahrhunderts, Bd. 33). Regensburg: Bosse.

Zeller, C. A. (1810), 'Elemente der Musik', in *Beiträge zur Beförderung der Preußischen Nationalerziehung*, 4. Heft, Königsberg.

Ireland: Curriculum development in troubled times

Marie McCarthy

The first state education system, the National School System, was established in Ireland in 1831, although it was not until 1926 that compulsory schooling for children aged 6 to 14 years was first legislated, shortly after political independence was gained from Britain and the Irish Free State was founded. This chapter traces the development of music in primary education from colonial times in the nineteenth century through the decades of cultural nationalism in late nineteenth- and early twentieth-century Ireland to political independence in 1921, which was followed by a wave of educational reform. Emphasis is placed on the influence of political and cultural circumstances on music in schooling at each stage of development. Although compulsory schooling was not mandatory until 1926, music was introduced into primary education as an extra subject beginning in the 1840s, and vocal music became an obligatory school subject in 1900.

Introducing music into the National School System, 1831–1871

Valuing music in the National School System

Ireland had been a colony of Britain for centuries before a national education system was put in place and any consideration of the role and nature of music in the community and in education must be made within this socio-political context. Through the agency of Lord Stanley, Chief Secretary for Ireland, the National School System was established in 1831 and a board of seven commissioners of national education was to represent various religious denominations in the country (Coolahan 1981: 12–13). Earlier efforts to provide schooling for the Irish were seen by the native people as a strategy to proselytize them and make them loyal subjects of the British Crown, so when the National School System was founded on non-denominational principles, with the goal of keeping religious instruction separate from literary and moral instruction, the native Irish remained suspicious, even though the members of the board were drawn from various religious denominations to represent the total population.

As the National School System began to develop in the 1830s, there was considerable discussion about the value of including music in the curriculum and the most efficient method for teaching it. Values assigned to music were its strong humanistic base and its power to inculcate moral, religious and social values in the young. These values were central to discussions that guided the development of music in the National School System. In the *Report from the Select Committee on Foundation Schools and Education in Ireland* (National Commissioners of Education 1837), there are many references to the social influence of music on the lower classes of an increasingly industrialized society – how music would serve to humanize and civilize the people, provide them with a source of innocent recreation, elevate their lifestyle and social manners and, particularly in the Irish context, provide a pastime for those who spent too much time in the alehouses.

The importance of music as an adjunct to religious practice was also central to the report, but given the sensitivity to religious matters in Ireland, this value was presented with great care. While the report of the select committee focused mostly on social, religious and moral values of music, Catholic MP Sir Thomas Wyse looked to the aesthetic and cultural aspects of a musical education. In his speech to the House of Commons in 1835, and in his book *Education Reform* in 1836, he presented his view of the state of Irish music and culture. As he looked around the country, he saw a gloomy picture of native musical culture, was critical of the standard of music in religious worship and asked why music making was so rare, why people were discordant and why their musical taste was inferior. Based on the impoverished musical culture he saw, Wyse advocated an aesthetic approach to music education, one that would educate the 'whole spiritual man' and nurture 'all the finer perceptions and higher sensibilities' of human nature (Wyse 1836: 195, 197). Like most educated people at the time, he viewed folk traditions as unworthy of inclusion in popular education and omitted reference to the rich instrumental, song and dance folk traditions of the country. His emphasis on developing a love of the arts through education was a noble one, but perhaps premature for people who were struggling to make a living and as yet not literate or socially mobile as they later would become. As one school inspector later commented in this regard: 'So long as the children can read, write, calculate the price of a load of hay, or a bag of flour, they [parents] are perfectly satisfied' (Commissioners of National Education 1863: 189; hereinafter referred to as 'Annual Reports').

The introduction of music to the curriculum was surrounded by political, religious, economic and cultural tensions. In the official rhetoric, music was seen to elevate cultural taste, build moral fibre, provide an innocent pastime and improve church singing. However, not one of these arguments was relevant or acceptable to the majority of communities in which national schools were established. The one context in which they were accepted was the model schools, a class of school originally set up in Dublin for teacher training purposes but which later spread to towns throughout the country, *de facto* to serve the children of Ango-Irish, middle-class families. It was in these model schools that music was first developed as a curricular subject beginning in the 1840s.

Finding a method for teaching music in the National School System

In the early nineteenth century, Britain depended heavily for its cultural and musical models on the continent, regarding its own music as inferior (Rainbow 1967). This was the case when the British Committee of Council on Education set out to find a method for teaching music. Having observed and reviewed many continental schemes, the Council sanctioned the use of the French Wilhem method – published in *Manuel Musical* – in 1840. In this method modelled on teaching language, Wilhem (1836) approached music as a science and focused on breaking down music theory into a carefully planned sequence. A British version was prepared by John Hullah and published in 1842 as *Wilhem's Method of Teaching Singing*. It was granted government approval for use in British schools. Without further investigation or modification, it was adopted by the Commissioners of National Education in Ireland. Two Irish music teachers were sent to the Battersea Training College in Britain in 1840 to learn the method and bring it back into the model schools.

In addition to the pedantic, overly scientific nature of the method, an even greater problem with the Hullah approach was the content of the songs – for these were songs that were created for use in British schools and were designed to illustrate theoretical aspects of music. After Head Inspector James Keenan listened to children singing these songs, he wrote that they 'do not pretend to any national character ... are foreign to all sympathy ... belong to no country, ... [and] are sung in no home' (*Twenty-Second Annual Report* [Appendix] 1855: 74). The weakening of identity with native Irish culture was one of the aims of the National School System and the teaching of Hullah's tunes was in accord with that aim. The method never took root in Irish education. An alternative song repertoire, Thomas Moore's *Irish Melodies* (1834), released in ten volumes between 1808 and 1834, became popular in schools, as they were seen as being inoffensive, mildly nationalist in sentiment and classical in genre.

Barriers to the development of music in the curriculum

When examining the entry of music into national schools in Ireland beginning in the 1840s from an official vantage point, it seems to have been founded on a sound, comprehensive philosophy that was carefully constructed and supported and on a foreign teaching method that was well established. In reality, however, the introduction of music into the National School System was surrounded by barriers that worked against its widespread development – barriers caused by political mistrust, social and economic inequities, diverse cultural values, religious beliefs and educational aspirations.

The use of religious music in the school song repertoire was viewed with utmost sensitivity due to the socio-political implications of such repertoire and the goal of keeping religious instruction separate from literary and moral instruction. The use of music to elevate musical taste resonated with certain middle-class communities but not with the majority of the native, lower class Irish. Promoting the national songs of the people brought up the question of whose nation. Whereas in Britain, such songs were seen as an important means for engendering the national spirit and forming an industrious, loyal working class, the use of British national songs in Irish schools would have caused protest among the native Irish. At the same time, Irish national songs would be in direct opposition to the British policy of cultural assimilation, songs that may incite nationalism among the young Irish and contribute to advancing a rebellious spirit. Songs in the Irish language were of the peasant, suppressed class and not appropriate for a colonial educational system. In any case, the majority of parents were eager to have their children learn English in order to be economically mobile and prepared for emigration.

Music developed first in model schools where the middle-class values of Victorian society complemented those developed in the Hullah music curriculum. In the majority of ordinary national schools, however, the Hullah songs and method were culturally and socially foreign compared with the values of the majority of people and, in the end, the method failed. As denominational education developed during the nineteenth century and the Catholic clergy had more say in the running of national schools, Moore's melodies and songs of Irish origin were taught, using methods such as rote singing and John Curwen's tonic sol-fa system of sight singing.

Music and schooling in an era of accountability and political upheaval, 1872–1921

Music in the payment-by-results system

In the period leading up to compulsory schooling – the decades of the late nineteenth and early twentieth century – music in primary or national schools came under the influence of economic climate, changing educational philosophy and political nationalism. In 1872 a payment-by-results system was introduced into the National School System and continued until 1899 when it was abolished. Highly structured syllabi were laid down for each subject, student progress was evaluated regularly by board inspectors and teachers were paid according to pupils' results. As teachers' salaries were dependent on the results of their pupils, they were forced to comply with the system and to succumb to its regulations even if they were opposed to them.

The curricular status of music improved in 1883 when it was changed from being an 'extra' and therefore non-compulsory subject to being an 'ordinary and optional subject' – a subject that was accepted for examination along with the basic subjects. Commenting on the change of status for music, School Inspector Connellan considered it as 'the first recognition of what all educationalists and all men of reflection regard as one of the most potent and subtle elements of culture' (*Fiftieth Annual Report* [Appendix] 1883: 211). Yet, there were many obstacles impeding its development in the curriculum. Due to the focus on students' results, those aspects of music that could be standardized, quantified and measured were emphasized. When teachers put forward students for examination in music, there were additional risks when compared to other subjects. Fees paid for pupils in the lower primary classes were dependent on the musical proficiency of pupils in the upper class levels and the annual gratuity for teaching music first made available in 1859 was now granted only to teachers employed in model schools, or teachers in ordinary national schools who taught music outside normal school hours (*Thirty-Ninth Annual Report* 1872: 25).

The 'rote-note' controversy – singing by ear, as opposed to singing from staff notation – was widely debated during this period of payment by results. Singing by ear was not recognized as legitimate for examination purposes and this policy was criticized by many teachers and inspectors, on the basis that in Britain, from 1882 onward, singing by rote gained half the fees out of the possible grant for singing by note (Sneyd-Kynnersley 1908: 287). Many inspectors believed that singing by note was inappropriate for primary-age children and they supported the tonic sol-fa method because it was more accessible to children (*Fiftieth Annual Report* [Appendix] 1883: 144). An inspector's report from Limerick in 1893 illustrated how singing taught through tonic sol-fa before school hours improved school attendance and punctuality: 'The pupils are enthusiastic about Tonic Sol-fa; they beam with delight when asked to sing by it. This ardour has been utilized to insure punctuality in several schools' (*Sixtieth Annual Report* 1893: 234). Whether this practice was regional or national, it does provide evidence of the success of the tonic sol-fa system, a method of sight singing that by the end of the nineteenth century had received strong official support. In 1884 it was granted official recognition and a programme was designed for teachers using this method

(*Fifty-First Annual Report* [Appendix] 1884: 82-83). It became an institution of Irish primary education until the introduction of *An Curaclam Nua* (The new curriculum) in 1971.

During the payment-by-results era, teachers became discouraged and irate due to new conditions (*The Irish Teachers' Journal* 12 April 1873; *Thirty-Ninth Annual Report* [Appendix] 1872: 295). The number of pupils presented for music examinations decreased in the 1870s and 1880s; at the same time the percentage pass rate increased, making the subject exclusive and serving a minority of students. By 1896 only 14 per cent of national schools presented students for music examination, compared to 99.8 per cent of schools in Britain and 96.6 per cent of schools in Scotland in the same year (Commissioners of National Education 1898: 54). It is clear that music did not thrive in national schools during the payment-by-results era. In 1899, music inspector Peter Goodman advocated change in the approach to music in national schools, heralding the new educational philosophy of the twentieth century after the abolition of payment-by-results in the same year:

> Payment by results of individual examinations has not succeeded in making our teachers cultivate art for art's sake. Would it not be well, therefore, to seek to make Music loved and cherished in the school for its own sake, and so to deal with it that each teacher will come to regard it, not merely as a source of money making for himself, but rather as a means of bringing pleasure and happiness into the lives of the little ones entrusted to his care? (*Sixty-Sixth Annual Report* 1899: 193)

Music, schooling and changing educational philosophy

The early twentieth century brought reform within education and much thought was given to making the system democratic and more in touch with the realities of the surrounding culture (Selleck 1968: 102–238). Music in national schools came under the influence of this new thinking – it began to be valued as a medium for establishing self and group discipline, for confronting moral issues and for linking home, school and community. Attention was focused on the needs and characteristics of the child and the provision of age-appropriate instruction. At the same time, national schooling became increasingly associated with the process of nation building and the promotion of patriotism, civic responsibility and common national ideals. When taken as a whole, the new education movement addressed the total development of the child – physical, social, intellectual, aesthetic and emotional – and set it in the larger socio-cultural context.

Reflecting this new educational philosophy, vocal music became an obligatory subject of the new *Revised Programme of Instruction in National Schools*

(Commissioners of National Education 1900) and the beginning years of the century were marked by waves of reform in school music.

The elitist attitude towards music that dominated previous decades gave way to a more democratic one. An effort to disseminate music to the remotest regions of the island was evident in the increasing percentage of schools that offered music instruction, from 17 per cent in 1899 to 78 per cent in 1907 (*Annual Reports* 1899, 1907).

To assist teachers with the goal of universal music education, an intensive programme of teacher in-service training was provided by the commissioners. Between 1900 and 1904 168 teachers' classes were held, attended by about 6,400 teachers, nearly equally distributed over all parts of Ireland. Care was taken to reach teachers in remote, rural districts, based on the assumption that 'outside the towns, Music in Ireland is practically an unknown art' (*Seventy-First Annual Report* 1904: 4). Tonic sol-fa was the recommended method of sight singing and Curwen's music education charts and modulators were supplied to schools.

In addition to vocal music, this period saw development in instrumental music in the National School System. While it had been granted status as an 'extra' subject in 1859, a new regulation of 1885 elevated it to a subject that could be taught to fifth and sixth classes within school hours. The curriculum described a 2-year programme for piano similar to the syllabus of the Royal Irish Academy of Music and other colleges of music of the day (*Fifty-Fourth Annual Report* 1887: 69). Instrumental music was primarily available in the schools of affluent communities and in convent schools where 'daughters of respectable well-off parents had many opportunities for practising at home' (*Fifty-Eighth Annual Report* 1891: 322). The number of schools presenting pupils for examinations in instrumental music increased from 47 schools in 1884, 168 in 1891, to 180 in 1899 (*Annual Reports* 1884, 1891, 1899).

School music attuned to the ideals of cultural nationalism

The nationalist movement of late nineteenth- and early twentieth-century Ireland impacted the course and direction of music in schooling. Literature on Irish education in the early years of the century reflected the country-wide preoccupation with nationalism (Ní Niocaill 1909: 258). The Gaelic League, founded in 1893, sought to revive Irish culture and build national identity. Primary schooling was seen as an important site for achieving such goals. Music in the schools was seen by nationalists as a primary source for stimulating nationalist ideals and the inheritance of native music traditions was considered central to the formation of Irish cultural identity. One critic questioned the absence of native music in the system's schools: 'why are the children not taught, first and foremost, to sing all the better-known national melodies before they touch melody of any other kind? This learning of the

"Songs of Our Land" should be a *sine qua non,* and go hand in hand with the study of the Gaelic tongue' (*Journal of the Ivernian Society,* October 1909: 124).

A circular issued by the London Board of Education to teacher training colleges in Great Britain in 1902 suggested that students in teacher training should be impressed with the importance of passing on the national songs of England and Wales, Scotland and Ireland to the next generation, thus setting 'a wholesome standard in musical taste' (*Irish School Weekly,* 6 December 1902, 10). The 'wholesome standard' envisioned here through use of national music was not the standard embraced by Irish cultural nationalists. The political agenda of the London statement represented Ireland's continued union with Britain; the nationalist agenda was diametrically opposed to this, as its goal was independence from Britain.

The teaching of Irish music in the schools received support from the teaching profession, but certain challenges needed to be overcome before implementation could be affected. First, no general consensus existed as to what constituted Irish music and opinions on the future of Irish traditional music varied. Second, it was only in 1904 that the Irish language was introduced into the schools as part of a bilingual programme and much native song material had Irish lyrics. Third, a repertoire of Irish music appropriate for primary school pupils was needed. From the early years of the century, those who published song materials began to balance their collections between Irish language songs and Anglo-Irish music. Examples of such collections were Peter Goodman's *The Irish Minstrel* (1907) and Father Walsh's *Fuinn Na Smól* (1913) and *Songs of the Gael* (1915).

The Irish Minstrel served as a symbol of official recognition of native Irish music in the curriculum of national schools. Its exclusive focus on Irish songs and airs may be interpreted as a response to the demands of cultural nationalists. Viewed from another perspective, it may be seen as part of the wider British discourse on the use and value of folksong in education that was maintained during the early years of the century. A second song collector, Father J. T. (Jack) Walsh, visited the Gaeltacht (Irish-speaking) regions of the island – 'those favoured glens and mountains where anglicisation has not yet triumphed' (Ó Casaide 1915: 33). There he transcribed songs that were still part of the living tradition and published them with tonic sol-fa notation in a series of seven booklets, *Fuinn na Smól* (1913). Recognizing that a great number of teachers and students did not understand the Irish language sufficiently well to be able to sing songs in Irish, he compiled another collection of 200 Anglo-Irish songs and ballads and wedded them to traditional Irish airs in *Songs of the Gael* (1915). Goodman and Walsh's efforts to provide Irish music for the national schools represent but a fraction of the rising tide of native Irish song materials in both languages in the early decades of the twentieth century.

Collections of hymns in the Irish language were also published – *Dia Linn Lá 'Gus Oídhche* (1917) and *Raint Amhrán* (1917). The provision of hymns in the Irish language in these decades was aimed at wedding Catholicism and nationalism and presenting them to the next generation as essential elements of Irishness. Irish-language songs and Catholic hymns, the staple diet of singing later in independent Ireland, were already established as the canon of Irish school music when the Irish Free State was established in 1921–22. Nationalist songs were also part of the canon, evident in the autobiographical writing of Patrick Shea (1908–1986). Shea described his Irish childhood in Deerpark in the midlands and recalled a singing class at Deerpark National School around 1916: 'We fairly belted out "The Minstrel Boy", "Let Erin Remember", "A Nation Once Again", and, out of respect for the Principal's native county, "The Bells of Shandon" ' (Shea 1987: 24).

A climate of war dominated the years between 1914 and 1921 – the First World War and the Irish War of Independence – and effected how music was perceived in the school curriculum. It brought a utilitarian mentality back into the education system. The 1916 Congress of the Irish National Teachers Organization was critical of the overloaded curriculum of the revised programme issued in 1900 and demanded a return to the basic subjects (*The Irish School Weekly*, 6 and 13 May 1916: 453). Music was once again relegated to the periphery as an additional subject, its availability dependent upon the staffing of the school and local needs and resources (*The Irish School Weekly*, 3 March 1917: 122).

On the positive side, the climate of war highlighted the power of school music to unite people for a common cause and to instil patriotic sentiments for the homeland. During the First World War, for example, many school concerts were organized 'on behalf of local distress caused through the war' (*The Irish School Weekly*, 3 October 1914: 714). In the early twentieth century, there is ample evidence to show the rise in popularity of the school concert so that by 1907 Goodman wrote that it had become 'a fixed institution' in many places (*Seventy-Third Annual Report* 1906–07: 165). The school concert provided opportunities for the performance of instrumental music. Although class instruction in instrumental music was not organized officially in primary schools, it did occur haphazardly, its development dependent on individual teachers, school traditions, or local musical traditions. While the first two decades of the twentieth century witnessed major developments in group instrumental teaching both in Europe and in the United States, political and economic conditions in Ireland did not support the development of instrumental music in formal education and this absence marks a major difference between music education in Ireland and other Western countries to this day.

Educational reform in a new nation, 1922–1926

After the Irish gained independence from Britain and a provisional government was set up in the Irish Free State in late 1921 and early 1922, one of the first tasks was to reform the educational system and align it to nationalist goals. In January 1922 Pádraig Ó Brolcháin, Chief Executive Officer of National Education, spoke to the agenda of education in the newly established state: 'It is the intention of the new Government to work with all its might for the strengthening of the national fibre, by giving the language, history, music and tradition of Ireland their natural place in the life of Irish schools' (Commissioners of National Education 1922: 2–3). Three aspects of this agenda influenced the course of music in primary education: the Irish language revival movement, the promotion of Catholic Church music and a national effort to improve musical culture and 'the national fibre'.

The language revival movement exerted the single most dominant influence in the early years of compulsory schooling in independent Ireland. Father Thomas Corcoran of University College, Dublin, a zealot for language revival and an active educational policymaker (Corcoran 1923, 1933), acted as a consultant in the preparation of a new curriculum issued in 1922, the *National Programme of Primary Instruction*. He advocated that 'the union of simple Irish with Irish music, in our Irish schools to-day, would certainly be the royal high road to the restoration of the spoken language and to the development of new literature, really Irish, for the people of Ireland' (Corcoran 1923: 340). The curriculum recommended that all songs taught should be in the Irish language and taught through the medium of Irish (National Programme Conference 1922: 14). This report was adopted by the government of the Irish Free State and came into operation in national schools on 1 April 1922. The tonic sol-fa system was already linked to the publication and teaching of Irish language songs and this practice of teaching song continued.

Catholicism, a second marker of Irish identity, also affected the direction of music in Irish culture and education in the Free State, in particular through the singing of hymns and the Plain Chant movement (Rooney 1952: 19-21). In his autobiography, Paddy Crosbie (1913–1982) described his early convent school music education in the 1920s, speaking to the centrality of hymns in the curriculum of national schools. He wrote:

> We were taught plenty of hymns e.g. 'I'll sing a hymn to Mary', the Lourdes hymn, and a hymn which we all thought was 'Oh Mother I could sweep the earth', but which in reality was 'Oh, Mother I could weep for mirth'. We learned also 'Sweet heart of Jesus', 'To Jesus Heart All Burning', 'Hail Glorious, Saint Patrick', and so on. We knew all of these songs and sang them lustily on the many occasions offered, particularly at the May Processions. (Crosbie 1981: 31)

Gregorian plain chant was another form of Catholic repertoire that found a home in Irish schools. Beginning in 1926 a summer school of plain song was founded by Father John Burke, Dean of University College, Dublin. Liturgical festivals were developed in many provincial centres such as Tuam, Ennis, Limerick, and Kilkenny – festivals that were characterized by the 'massed singing of the Ordinary of the Mass by thousands of children' (Rooney 1952: 219).

A third influential factor in national education was the effort to change the musical image of Ireland. At the 1926 Annual Congress of the Irish National Teachers Organization, Cork school teacher Denis Breen (Donnchadh Ó Braoin) focused on the 'national indifference to and contempt for music' and argued that the state of music in education was a reflection of its state in national life, each institution being 'a little microcosm of the people with all their faults and virtues displayed' (Breen 1926a: 558). From the beginning of the National School System, blame had been placed on music in education for this state of affairs. Now the blame was shifted to the lack of national policy. School music, Breen said, would remain mere school work 'unless it is vitalized by contact with some more significant activity from outside – some trend of the national will, some settled desire of the people, some movement sufficiently powerful to keep itself from decay or destruction in the hurly-burly of life' (1926a: 558). What was needed, in his opinion, was a comprehensive national policy for music in order to defeat the 'universal indifference' toward music so obvious in Irish life – 'a result of causes historical and otherwise with which all are familiar' (Breen 1926b: 620).

In a sense, national or primary schools had indeed contributed to the development of national life in their traditions of school concerts and participation in festivals and competitions from the 1880s onwards. These traditions received a further impetus with the coming of the Irish Free State. In 1925 the Cork School Music Committee, chaired by Breen himself, organized a school choir concert in Cork and 200 pupils were drawn from various schools in the city. In addition to the massed schools' choir, other items were featured in the programme – two convent choirs, instrumental selections, a play in Irish, and Irish step-dancing. This model, one observer remarked, was 'probably the first attempt of its kind in Ireland', with implications 'whose limits are not easily defined' (*The Irish School Weekly*, 11 July 1925: 852). Such events became popular in independent Ireland.

When compulsory school attendance legislation was introduced by the Department of Education in 1926, music held a firm footing in the curriculum, less as a subject in its own right and more as a servant to the advancement of nationalist ideals of language revival, the development of a Catholic ethos in school and society and the improvement of Ireland's musical image and culture.

The gift and burden of the past, legacy for the present

From the beginning of a national state-sponsored education system in 1831, music had a place in the curriculum, albeit not as a compulsory subject. Its development was impeded by a number of political, religious and cultural factors. Among them were the use of song repertoire that reproduced colonial values not accepted by the native Irish, the use of an inappropriate method to teach music and the negative effects of the payment-by-results system on music as a school subject. As schooling became de facto denominational in the mid-nineteenth century and Catholic orders played a more significant role in primary education, repertoire associated with Irish native culture and heritage began to be transmitted in national schools and the use of the Curwen tonic sol-fa system proved to be accessible to teachers and students alike.

In 1900 vocal music was introduced as a compulsory subject and subsequently gained a greater presence in the curriculum. This reflected a change in educational philosophy and coincided favourably with the rise of cultural and political nationalism. The climate of world war caused educators to turn again to a basic curriculum and the climate of the local war of independence focused the music curriculum on songs that advanced nationalist ideology. When compulsory education for 6 to 14 year olds was introduced in 1926, music lost its compulsory status and was not regarded as a basic subject. However, its role in the curriculum was regarded as vital to the core agenda of reviving the Irish language and promoting a Catholic ethos.

Contemporary music education in every nation is shaped by its past – the gifts transmitted as well as the burdens inherited. In the Irish context, music was considered as part of the curriculum from the beginning. Several leaders emerged to critique what was in place and to advance thinking about the repertoire and pedagogy. Singing was the primary activity promoted and over time this focus led to the development of a strong choral culture. Although no music specialists were employed to teach music, and classroom teachers received minimal specialist education in music, many national school teachers served important roles as teachers of singing in both the school and the parish church to which the school was attached. The colonial context and subsequently the period of nationalism that developed around the war of independence represented some of the most powerful factors in determining the direction of music in the national schools. Political ideologies dominated the rationale for and content of the music curriculum, a factor that does not feature in today's schools. Support for music education for its own sake was lacking and the poor economic state of the country in the twentieth century did not allow for the development of instrumental music education similar to other countries. Perhaps the single burden that was inherited from the past, the stigma surrounding Irish traditional music, has been resolved in recent decades. Just as the music itself has come from the backwaters of society into centre stage, so also has it entered the curriculum and is transmitted for its own sake, not for the political values it once represented. Some patterns from the past continue into the present – generalist teachers teaching primary school music, inconsistent governmental support for music in education and an underdeveloped system of instrumental music instruction.

Reflections on one nation's story

This case study of music and compulsory schooling in Ireland illustrates that music is a curricular subject that is deeply implicated with political ideologies, economic realities and socio-cultural values. When it enters the public space of schooling, its use continues to be grounded in those values. In the troubled times of nineteenth-century Ireland, any attempt on the part of Britain to advance an educational agenda perceived as increasing colonial control was met with opposition by the native Irish. The development of music was impeded on many fronts and not until the hidden curriculum rooted in colonial political ideology was past and Ireland gained political independence from Britain did compulsory education become legislated. And in that new brave world, the music curriculum was dominated by a new political agenda of a new independent nation state.

Evidence from this narrative also points to the complicated and vulnerable nature of music as a school subject and the contradictions that inhere in its status as a school subject. Music rides the waves with the values that dominate schooling and society. When a colonial agenda was associated with it, teachers focused only on 'safe' aspects of the subject matter; when an era of accountability set in and teachers were paid based on student examination results, music was treated as an examination subject but with several conditions not applied to other subjects. As the curriculum broadened to be more child centred, vocal music became obligatory but after an exploratory phase the reins were pulled in and music again lost its core status. When a nationalist agenda dictated educational values in independent Ireland and compulsory schooling was introduced, music regained its status quickly as it served a new political agenda. In the post-nationalist Ireland of today, the political burdens of the past no longer determine curriculum content.

The troubled times of nineteenth- and early twentieth-century Ireland complicated the introduction of compulsory schooling; yet music found its way into various types of national schools. The narrative of music in Irish primary schooling reflects a far more complicated set of values than those that were inherent in one legislative act to make school attendance compulsory.

References

Breen, D. (1926a), 'School-music: its place in the national life', *The Irish School Weekly*, 77, (1 May), 558.

Breen, D. (1926b), 'School-music: its place in the national life', *The Irish School Weekly*, 77, (15 May), 620.

Commissioners of National Education (1834–1921), *Annual Reports*. Dublin: Office of National Education.

Commissioners of National Education (1898), *Final Report of Royal Commission on Manual and Practical Instruction in Primary Schools*. Dublin: Office of National Education.

Commissioners of National Education (1900), 'Revised programme of instruction in national schools', in *Annual Reports 1900–1901* (Appendix). Dublin: Office of National Education.

Commissioners of National Education (1922), *Minutes of the Proceedings of the Annual Reports Commissioners of National Education at their Special Meeting on Tuesday, the 31st January, 1922*. Dublin: Office of National Education.

Coolahan, J. (1981), *Irish Education: History and Structure*. Dublin: Institute of Public Administration.

Corcoran, T. (1923), 'Music and language in Irish schools', *Irish Monthly*, 51, (July), 338–340.

Corcoran, T. (1933), 'National literature through national music', *Irish Monthly*, 61, (July), 410–12.

Crosbie, P. (1981), *Your Dinner's Poured Out*. Dublin: O'Brien Press.

Dia Linn Lá 'Gus Oídhche's Pádraig Aspal Éireann (1917). Baile Átha Cliath: Brún agus Ó Nualláin Teor.

Goodman, P. (1907), *The Irish Minstrel: A Collection of Songs for Use in Irish Schools*. Sel. and arr. by P. Goodman. Dublin: M. H. Gill.

Hullah, J. (1842/1983), *Wilhem's Method of Teaching Singing*, intro. B. Rainbow. Kilkenny: Boethius Press.

Irish School Weekly, The (1902), 'Circular to training colleges – music', 6 December, 10.

Irish School Weekly, The (1914), 'A new song', 3 October, 714.

Irish School Weekly, The (1916), 'Irish National Teachers Organization Congress: an influential gathering', 6 and 13 May, 453.

Irish School Weekly, The (1917), 'Memorandum on suggested changes in present school programmes', 3 March, 122.

Irish School Weekly, The (1925), 'Cuirm ceoil: successful schools' concert in Cork', 11 July, 852.

Irish Teachers' Journal, The (1873), 'Drawing and singing of national schools', 12 April, 101.

Journal of the Ivernian Society (1909), 'Notes', 2, (October), 124.

Moore, T. (1834), *Irish Melodies*. London: Power & Longman, Rees, Orme, Brown & Green.

National Commissioners of Education (1837), *Report from the Select Committee (of the House of Commons) on Foundation Schools and Education in Ireland*. House of Commons (H.C. 701).

National Programme Conference (1922), *National Programme of Primary Instruction*. Dublin: Browne & Nolan.

Ní Niocaill, E. (1909), 'Nationality in Irish education', *Irisleabhar na Gaedhilge*, 19, (19 Meitheamh), 258.

Ó Casaide, S. (1915), 'Father Walsh's Irish song books', *Irish Book Lover*, 7, (September), 33.

Rainbow, B. (1967), *The Land without Music: Musical Education in England 1800–1860 and its Continental Antecedents.* London: Novello.

Rooney, H. (1952), 'The plainchant movement', in A. Fleischmann (ed.), *Music in Ireland.* Cork: Cork University Press, pp. 218–21.

Selleck, R. J. W. (1968), *The New Education 1870–1914.* London and Melbourne: Pitman & Sons Ltd.

Shea, P. (1987), 'Sounds of thunder, from voices and the sound of drums', in A. N. Jeffares and A. Kamm (eds), *An Irish Childhood.* London: Collins Sons & Co. Ltd, pp. 272–6.

Sneyd-Kynnersley, E. M. (1908), *H. M. I.: Some Passages in the Life of One of H. M. Inspectors of Schools.* London: Macmillan & Co. Ltd.

Walsh, P. (1913), *Fuinn na Smól.* Dublin: Browne & Nolan.

Walsh, P. (1915), *Songs of the Gael.* Dublin: Browne and Nolan.

Wilhem, G. B. (1836), *Manuel de Lecture Musicale et de Chant Élémentaire à 'Usage des Collèges, des Institutions, des Écoles et des Cours de Chant (. . .).* Paris: Perrotin.

Wyse, T. (1836), *Education Reform.* London: Longman.

6

Norway: Educational progress or stasis on the outskirts of Europe?

Fred Ola Bjørnstad and Magne Espeland

When looking back at ideas and developments in music education, one sometimes wonders about the *quality* of ideas appearing at a moment so different from our own time. Sometimes our reflection might seem to be of a different kind, focusing on *why* events and ideas taking place in neighbouring countries never seemed to surface in one's own country. When writing this chapter the authors have frequently found themselves asking one another questions such as: How could this particular person write so powerfully about singing at this early stage? Why did Norwegian music education in schools seem to be so minimally influenced by ideas from other countries in Europe at certain times in history? As we dig deeper for possible explanations into our primary and secondary sources, we realize how the balance between the contextual and the personal also makes itself felt in our particular sector: how the general Norwegian political and historical situation may explain what happens in a particular singing lesson in a Norwegian classroom and how the engagement and enthusiasm of individual music educators may account for systemic changes in the teaching of music far beyond the particular singing or music lesson.

In this chapter, a short overview of Norwegian music education history will be given bearing in mind such questions. The emphasis will be on the development of song and music as a curriculum subject from its introduction to school programmes until 1960 when 'music' became a fully mandated subject within the curriculum of Norwegian public primary and secondary schools.

This narrative does not claim to represent the absolute truth as there is reliance on both our own and others' scrutiny of original documents, research studies and published books and bearing in mind that not all data are in documentary form; accordingly any examination of the past is inevitably speculative.[1]

After a short introduction to the political history of Norway, we will focus on the following four periods in Norwegian music education history: from medieval times until the eighteenth century; from the nineteenth century until 1939; from the outbreak of war until 1960; from 1960 up to the present. In our narrative, we will be more analytic than descriptive as there will be an attempt to provide answers to questions about the relationship between 'music' as a mandatory curriculum subject in Norway and similar developments in other countries. In an attempt to describe the evolutionary nature of this process, events will be treated holistically with a view to contextualizing information as well as analyzing and commenting on developments both in school education and in teacher education.

General historical and political context

A single chapter on the history of school singing and music in Norway does not allow for a comprehensive account of Norwegian political history. However, a short synopsis should provide sufficient background to enable a better understanding of the development of music education.

Norwegian political history is closely linked to that of Sweden and Denmark. After periods as independent Viking and monarchist entities during the early centuries of the first millennium, the three countries were united through the Kalmar Union – under a single monarch – from 1397. In 1523 this union was replaced by a provincial arrangement where Sweden and Denmark became independent and separate kingdoms whereas Norway became a province of Denmark. This arrangement, referred to as the '400 years' night', came to an end in 1814 when an awakening nationalism inspired by the French Revolution resulted in a limited, although separate Norwegian constitution, representative assembly and government. Even though the political situation resulted in Norway being conceded to Sweden as a result of Denmark's role in the Napoleonic Wars, the declaration of the Eidsvoll Constitution on 17 May 1814 became the basis for a growing Norwegian nationalism and political awareness. This led to the establishment of a parliament-based Norwegian government in 1884 and Norway's separation from Sweden, heralding the rebirth of Norway as an independent state in 1905. In the first decades of the twentieth century Norway became increasingly more industrialized. This development, although interrupted by German occupation during the Second World War, has been maintained through a thriving oil industry established during the early 1970s to the present focus on 'high-tech' industries today.

Music education from medieval times until the eighteenth century

The early history of music, or rather singing *and* music, in Norwegian schools is closely related to the history of the church. From the twelfth century, monasteries and cathedrals established schools where pupils (boys) were taught music as one of the 'artes liberales'. The main aim of education was to ensure the supply of clergy to perform the ecclesiastical offices that were supported in the service by the singing of the choir.

The curriculum consisted of song repertoire and music theory. This was maintained until just after the Reformation when the first school regulations under the union of Denmark and Norway appeared in 1539. According to extant documents and manuals from the period, the major focus of the music curriculum was on theoretical aspects. It was expected that the standard of singing by pupils at services should be at such a level that the congregation was not required to musically participate, except for joining in some responses and in the 'amen'. Curriculum requirements at this time dictated that one hour should be allocated to singing each day. Pupils in the lower classes were required to practise Gregorian chant, whereas those in the upper classes focused on 'figure song or descant' (Bergheim 1974: 8).

However, it was not until 1739 that a new decree established singing as a mandatory subject in the school curriculum. The 1739 decree of King Christian VI – 'by God's mercy, king of Denmark and Norway' – included not only a directive that schooling should be compulsory for all children, but also detailed descriptions, instructions and overall executive responsibility for the *klokker*,[2] a church official responsible for the singing as part of the liturgy. The *klokkerne* were called on not only to become schoolmasters but also teacher trainers in that they had to appoint 'substitutes' who could, after passing examinations, become schoolteachers in their own right.[3] In addition, the 1739 decree set out a specific rationale for including singing in the school curriculum:

In the same way as the morning starts with Reading, so too should there be Singing, Prayer, and the reading of the Holy Scripture. The evening should end in this way: there needs to be sung a Spiritual Psalm, after which all children must kneel while reading the Evening Prayer; afterwards a chapter of the Holy Scripture is read, and finally the day ends with the singing of an Evening Psalm. However, be aware that in case of bad and foul weather during the winter, only a couple of verses need to be sung, so that the children can arrive home before darkness, and not be hurt or lost in snowstorms and darkness. (Tønnessen 1966: 36 [authors' translation])

It is interesting to note that, in the detailed instructions given to school teachers, there were directives regarding the welfare of their pupils and the need to take account of the harsh climatic context in which schooling took place. Not surprisingly, however, the detailed directives included in the 1739 decree became very unpopular in the rural areas and some of the regulations were consequently not carried through. Even when laws enacted in 1809 saw the separation of education from the church, the singing of psalms was retained as the main focus of musical content in the school curriculum. For this reason, schools and the church appear to have been more or less inseparable during this first period in the history of Norwegian music education.

From the nineteenth century to 1939

It was not until 1834 that what might be called 'music education methods' revealing influences from central Europe are mentioned in the national decrees (or ordinances) affecting education. The decree that appeared in 1834 was described as a 'Plan, in accordance with which the Teaching and Disciplines in the Public Schools in the Country should be adapted, and Instruction for teachers in the Public Schools'. It continued the link between singing and the psalms, but there is also reference to an instrument called the *psalmodikon* and a system of numeral notation. Section 8 of the decree says: 'In the teaching of singing, for the moment, Bohr's psalm melodies with numeral signs should be used with [the] psalmodikon' (Norsk Skolemuseums Venner 1960: 679 [authors' translation]). The system obviously drew on the ideas of the French philosopher Jean-Jacques Rousseau who numbered the notes of the major scale from 1 to 7.[4]

The *psalmodikon* was a bowed monochord with frets that was developed by the Swedish priest J. Dillner in the 1820s (Stålmarck 1962: 225, in Hole 1999). It is a one-stringed wooden instrument designed to be played from *ziffer* (numeral) notation with the use of a bow. Different fret boards could be used for different types of scale. The best known pioneer of this instrument in Norway was Lars Roverud, a music teacher who, having been commissioned by the Ministry of Education, travelled extensively in Norway between 1835 and 1847 to promote its use (Berghcim 1974: 12). Roverud used the *psalmodikon* to teach congregations as well as school teachers and their pupils to sing psalm melodies in tune and accurately according to notation.

But Roverud was highly critical of organists and musical life in Norway in general, suggesting that little musical knowledge was apparent. 'Organists', he complained, 'have in general little education, some play wildly, i.e. not knowing notes, or accompanying psalms in their own peculiar ways; the more hocus-pocus, ornaments and scales introduced at every beginning of a musical phrase, the better' (quoted in Bjørnstad 2001: 33 [authors' translation]).

Roverud also criticized the teaching of singing by church officials (the *klokkeren*) as being incompetent and of doing great damage to the overall standard of singing in churches. He argued:

> In most churches there is no organ. The singing is led by so-called *klokkere*, among whom one out of fifty hardly knows a single note, or has any music education whatsoever; and from where should they have got such a thing? Most of them sing the psalms according to their own rules, i.e. including all kinds of ornaments, and the higher and stronger they are able to scream, the better ... Also, in almost every community there is one amongst the public, who competes with the *klokkeren* in screaming and shouting and such a stentor[5] has a high standing for his ability to take the tune away, i.e. overcome the *klokkeren*. (*ibid*.: 33)

However the reform of the singing practices long entrenched in Norwegian churches did not happen without conflict. A local report from the time describes this discord in the following way:

> But now there was a conflict in most congregations in that most of them wanted the old traditional tunes, whereas the teachers and their pupils tried to lead the singing in accordance with the new authorized melodies. There was conflict over the melodies, and this conflict escalated to such an extent that, in the end, churches were emptied of the congregation during singing. The congregation came in when the priest entered the pulpit, and left when he descended. This situation lasted nearly half a century until the congregations little by little became used to the authorized melodies. (*ibid*.: 34 [authors' translation])

There is little doubt that, as a dedicated and enlightened pioneer, Lars Roverud affected more general reforms to music education well beyond the particular singing or music lesson. Roverud strongly believed that the improvement of music education, in particular singing, was dependent on well-established teaching methods and on a curriculum designed to promote knowledge of musical notation and theory. In assessing his contribution, however, it is important to recognize that Roverud's zeal and endeavour may very well have resulted in the loss of some traditional singing practices and repertoire of the so-called 'common people', traditions that are highly valued in modern Norwegian society.

Teacher training and resource books for schools

The new practices introduced to congregational singing soon found their way into the new teacher training 'seminaries' as they were called. Several of these 'seminaries' were established in the late 1830s across Norway in rural districts as well as in cities, one of them being Stord Seminarium, south of Bergen, to which the authors of this chapter are attached.

The 1837 national curriculum for teacher training colleges largely adopted the approach promoted by Roverud and recommended, among other things, the use of the *ziffer* notational method. The requirements were set out as follows:

> The students should, when we talk about psalmody, be introduced to the theory of this popular music and by the use and help of *ziffers* in singing as well as in playing the psalmodikon with skills, be able to play the most common psalm melodies, and, as far as possible, one of the associated descants or bass lines. Also they should learn how to play the harmonium, and as far as possible, learn specific folk songs. In order for the students to be prepared as church singers, they should regularly attend services in the nearest church and, in cooperation with the singing master, lead the singing. (quoted in Bergheim 1974: 11 [authors' translation])

This excerpt from the requirements for teacher education also points to two other major elements of music education at this time – namely, a focus on the harmonium as an accompanying instrument and a growing awareness of singing as a vehicle for rebuilding a national identity. One of the ideas behind the introduction of the harmonium was its capacity to lead group singing in a way that could cope with the then unwanted ornamentation of notes that was common in the folk style of singing (Storækre 1965: 925). The immediate context of the focus on folksongs was the nationalistic movement, increasing after 1814 when Norway freed herself from 400 years of Danish rule and re-established its own constitution and parliament.

The emphasis on singing as a compulsory subject in early teacher education seemed to have naturally complemented the role of singing in public schooling. However, in 1869, the official title of the subject in teacher education courses was changed to *musik* (music) and it might seem strange that this change did not take place in public primary and secondary education until 1960 when music became fully mandated in Norwegian schools.

The promotion of teaching music through staff notation in addition to *ziffer* notation was not apparent in the official Ministry of Education documents until 1877 when the reading of the C major and C minor scales from staff notation was specified as one of the aims for singing lessons. This change seems to have been influenced by teacher courses taught by the composer J. D. Behrens in the years 1866–73. In the foreword to one of his books on singing methodology, he wrote:

If singing in schools is to be useful in building a life of good quality, the methods for teaching normally accompanying this skill, and which consist of plain and mechanical rote learning, must be changed ... In addition to this comes the fact that the teacher proceeds without a plan ... [Therefore] it is very understandable that the majority of the pupils at the end of schooling stop singing completely. A good result of song teaching can only be gained through the use of methods, where the theoretical and the practical walk hand in hand from the very start of teaching. (Behrens 1868: preface [authors' translation])

Behrens' ideas appear to have dominated the methods of teaching singing in schools towards the end of the nineteenth century and at the beginning of the twentieth century. There seems to have been very little influence from corresponding debates in other European countries reflecting a focus on other important issues in music education – for example, the opposing methodologies of fixed doh and tonic sol-fa, which, by this time, were well established respectively in France and in England. There was also nothing to indicate a mirroring of the debate over music appreciation that was beginning to surface in America and England or so-called 'rhythmic movement practice' ('eurythmics') pioneered by Émile Jaques-Dalcroze in Switzerland in the 1890s.

In 1917 the curriculum for singing in primary schools still emphasized the ability of pupils to sing simple melodies and to understand music theory in the tradition of Behrens. Additionally, the curriculum required that pupils from the third grade should learn to use *solfège*. In the secondary school curriculum, it was prescribed that the pupils should be trained according to the so-called 'formula method', a melody-reading approach with strong links to similar movements in England and France. Based on the use of *solfège*, the pupils were taught small melodic formulas that were supposed to help them in their sight reading from staff notation and also to perform simple musical phrasing. In the same period a music teacher named Ole Koppang developed an alternative to this methodology called the 'sound method' (*klangmethod*), which had its basis in *harmonic* formulas. Other early music educators advocated new methods for enhancing the vocal style of *skjönn sang* (beautiful singing) that emulated the Italian classic 'bel canto' song tradition and was proposed by Hans Georg Nägeli as early as 1810 in his comprehensive 300-page *Gesangbildungslehre nach Pestalozzischen Grundsätzen*. Lars Søraas, another Norwegian pioneer and teacher educator of the first part of the twentieth century, supported this approach. He advocated the ideal of 'beautiful singing' not only for music education, but for reading and speech as well. This influence can be clearly identified as German in origin in this quotation from Søraas:

A good resonance – as well as a good pronunciation – is particularly well achieved by using Professor Edvard Engels' methodology for singing. Through the formation of the tone the resonance is developed, and by positioning the tongue towards the lower teeth and curling it, the tip of the tongue will be trained, the articulation becomes easy and clear, the tone carries more easily, and the back of the throat opens up. In Germany this methodology has spread widely in primary as well as secondary schools. It is widely used for class teaching in schools (in conjunction with the sound method in reading) and has gained praise from teachers as well as doctors for the advantages it brings in relation to hygiene as well as the excellent sound of language in reading, speech and singing ... Professor Engels' method is being used in the courses for singing teachers provided by the Ministry. (quoted in Espeland 1974: 17 [authors' translation])

In the curriculum plans of 1922 (KUD 1922), there are further indications of the wider aims for singing lessons than just learning songs and notation. A statement such as 'the children should [be] help[ed] to develop their voice and ear. They should learn to sing the most well known songs and psalms correctly, nicely and in pitch' is an early example of a focus on child development issues in and through music. However, there were still no real outward signs of music appreciation or other progressive educational approaches in compulsory schooling in Norway.

From the outbreak of war until 1960

It was not until a curriculum reform in 1939 (KUD 1939) that new and progressive pedagogical ideas developed at the beginning of the century by John Dewey and William H. Kilpatrick were adopted by the Norwegian school system. However, in contrast to other aesthetic subjects – for example, visual art – there was almost no sign of creative elements or even an orientation towards a broader view of the role of music in compulsory schooling in this document. In an article from 1966, Finn Benestad and Ingmar Fottland, two postwar reformers of Norwegian music education, summarized the development of music in schools until 1945 thus:

If we examine books, regulations and methodologies in Norway before 1945, very little new was added as compared to the latter part of the 19th century. This seems to have been the case in other Nordic countries as well. New songs are added, the voice is focused, some emphasize music theory, others drills and aural training etc. (Benestad and Fottland 1966: 800)

In the same article, these two authors speculate about the reasons for this lack of development with the suggestion that many contemporary music educators had a background in the singing movements and that subject content could not deviate from centrally prescribed curriculum guidelines. This could well be part of the explanation, but can it fully explain why, during the first half of the twentieth century – a time of rich educational debate internationally as well as in Norway – there was so little influence from these developmental perspectives on music education in compulsory schooling? It could reasonably be thought that authors of textbooks and designers of school curricula would be among the educational elite and that they would therefore have been able to influence music education in schools to a large degree.

A different way of explaining this phenomenon could be to focus on the many extra-curricular aspects of singing as a school subject. Throughout the nineteenth century and well into the twentieth century, education authorities regarded singing as a 'scaffolding' for other subjects such as language and religious education. Certainly, the close relationship between the school and the church was weakened in the twentieth century, but it was nevertheless still a strong one. In school textbooks, psalms occupied an equal position with other songs and this was also set out in the 1939 ministerial guidelines (KUD 1939). These guidelines also stressed the importance of teaching songs about the Norwegian homeland and countryside. As part of the emergence of Norway as an independent nation in 1905, there was a need to establish its national identity and accordingly songs of nationalistic character constituted a great part of the school song repertoire. Consequently, one of the main aims of compulsory schooling during this period was to initiate young children into the Norwegian nation and its state religion (Espeland 1974: 20).

It seems reasonable to conclude that as long as the focus for singing as a school subject was dictated by religious and nationalistic aims, there would be little room left for focusing on more eclectic forms of music and aesthetic education. Jørgensen (1982: 10) explains the lack of international influence on singing and music teaching in this period by referring to the fact that innovative ideas take time to travel and develop and that a broader perspective on the role of music in education based on progressive education principles did not suit the Norwegian emphasis on singing.

However, explanations other than those advocated by Jørgensen might be more important and carry greater weight. The Norwegian political situation, with the rebirth of the nation in 1905 and the whole nationalistic movement leading up to it, meant that singing had a much wider and more significant role than merely to support the church liturgy. Singing was central to the building of a new nation as well as in the celebration of national values and historical events. Around the turn of the century this coincided with similar movements in continental Europe – for example, the Jugendbewegung,[6] in which Fritz Jöde soon became a leading figure (Varkøy 1993: 62ff.). Add to this the fact that music and singing *outside* the public schools played an important part during the Second World War in sustaining resistance and national feelings.

The explanations outlined in this chapter for the lack of progressive educational thinking can be characterized as a kind of educational stasis, especially in the case of music. By 1939 the ideas underpinning progressive education seem to have been accepted at a general level and for all other subjects (Årva 1987: 229), but in the case of music, there was little evidence of such progress. Even as late as 1955 prominent educators fighting to establish 'music' as a new subject in schools complained that:

> Most of our textbooks for school subjects have undergone radical changes for a long time. But with regard to 'song' there has been a standstill for a long time. Equipment, melodies, and texts are for the most part unchanged. But there must be an end to how long we can nurture our youth on nationality and chauvinism. (Benum 1955: 22)

Ivar Benum became an important postwar figure in the movement to improve the standing of music in schools. His forthright criticism of the lack of any progressive educational reform of singing and music was one of several attempts at creating a new expanded role for music in education. Benum was deeply influenced by American as well as British educational thinking (Mork 2008: 162). Together with Egil Nordsjø, another prominent advocate for music as an aesthetic subject in Norwegian public schools, Benum led the fight to establish music as a mandatory aesthetic subject in the public school curriculum in the 1950s. Nordsjø was not an educator, but a professional singer, who wrote his first article in favour of a new subject called 'music' as early as in 1935; however, his attempts at reform and those of others were not taken seriously and failed to generate any real debate (Årva 1987: 232). Nevertheless, Nordsjø continued with his advocacy for music after the Second World War and this time his ideas gained ground. In an article in *Norsk Skuleblad*[7] in 1947 he sketched a broad platform for a new subject, which could provide for a comprehensive aesthetic education – including music – for all (Årva 1987: 241). In the late 1940s and the 1950s Nordsjø and Benum emerged as the informal leaders of a number of teacher educators, internationally and nationally, who introduced contemporary ideas about music education from Sweden, Denmark, Germany, England and the USA. Some of these influences can easily be linked to the Orff movement, the Kodály system and the Music Appreciation Movement. This activity laid the ground for the creation of a new mandated curriculum subject called 'music' in 1959 and its inclusion in the new 1960 school curriculum.

The main elements of 'music' can be described as a combination of the 'old' singing content and new ideas including listening and instrumental activities. Although the new activities were strongly conceived, they did not reflect creative and multi-genre approaches to music education that had been central in the Orff movement and in some experimental music practices in Nordic countries – for example in Denmark. According to Jørgensen, the new curriculum was influenced more by a scientifically based musicological thinking than by progressive educational thinking. Even so, in comparing the newly conceived subject to the 200-year-old 'singing' tradition, he characterized the change as a 'revolution' (Jørgensen 1982: 29).

However, there was a considerable gap between the new music curriculum as a written document and its implementation. Norway was still a predominantly rural society with a large number of small schools in small communities. The existence of music as a newly mandated subject influenced both the structure and content of teacher training courses. Three initiatives played a particularly important role and deserve mention. First, the formation of a national organization for music in schools in 1956 – *Landslaget Musikk i skolen* – which published a music education journal; second, the institutionalizing of a 3-year teacher education programme with an integrated music specialization – *Musikklinja* – in Bergen 1958; and third, the formation of a special body to provide in-service courses in music funded by the Ministry of Education – *Statens lærerkurs*. Between them, these initiatives shaped the implementation of the new subject by giving teachers and prospective teachers the competence required to implement the ideas and philosophy of the national curriculum.

From 1960 until the present

Although singing in the 1960 curriculum was still important, the new focus was on music listening and instrumental activities. However, through the 1960s the new subject progressed so that by the following decade, Norwegian music education was further influenced by other international developments such as an emphasis on classroom composition and 'creative music' – based on the work of Murray Schafer and John Paynter – as well as developing its own system for instrumental teaching through a comprehensive system of 'music schools' outside the school system, something that is now a vital part of the overall music education endeavour in Norway.

Today school music is well established in every stage of primary and secondary public schooling as a mandatory subject for pupils between the ages of 6 and 15. The curriculum consists of performing, listening and composing, with dance and drama as integrated elements. The national curriculum reforms of 1974, 1987, 1997 and 2006 have allowed music as a subject to have developed considerably from its early foundations as 'singing' and its reformation during the 1960s to become a creative, reflective and educationally progressive subject. Music as a school subject has changed its emphasis on classical music to a wider array of musical genres, i.e. contemporary popular music (see Jørgensen 2001). Even so, music as an aesthetic subject for all students – together with a number of related practical and aesthetic subjects – is presently, under pressure from the PISA[8]-driven accountability and back-to-basics movement, but that is outside the present focus of this chapter. However, it is hoped that the recent focus on creativity and the importance of arts and culture in society – as demonstrated by the designation of 2009 as the European Year of Creativity and Innovation – will better promote music as a school subject than has hitherto been the case.

Conclusion

This chapter opened with a question that addressed the reasons why music in the public school system seemed to have developed more slowly in Norway up to 1960 than in other comparable countries. Although it may seem unjust to characterize music education in Norway as having been in stasis, explanations can be found in the more gradual emergence of Norway as an independent nation than in some other European countries, the foreign occupation of Norway during the Second World War, which accounts for the lack of development of music education during this period, and the prevailing notion of music and singing as scaffolding activities for the building of identity and the support of religious education rather than as an intrinsically valuable subject in its own right.

Notes

[1] The research approach we apply can be described as 'hermeneutic content analysis' (Kjeldstadli 2000). Our work here is part of *Ideoskosa*, an acronym for a Nordic cross-institutional research project about ideology in songbooks for primary schools in Norwegian history.

[2] The etymological meaning of *klokker*, plural *klokkerne*, is associated with the Norwegian word *klokke* and the German *Glocke* (bell). In addition to assisting with the singing, the *klokker* was also responsible for calling the people to service by sounding the church bells.

[3] The second paragraph of King Christian's 1739 decree also contains detailed regulations as to the removal of *klokkere* in case of educational incompetence or leading an ungodly life with 'drinking and swearing'.

[4] The numeral notation in Norway might be based on a later revision in 1817 of Rousseau's system known as the Galin-Paris-Chevé method. In Norway, the numeral system is called *ziffer* notation (from the German).

[5] From the Greek '*stenein*', to groan, make noise – i.e. a Greek herald of the Trojan

war who, according to Homer, had a voice as loud as that of 50 men (*Webster's New Twentieth Century Dictionary*, 1979).

6 *Jugendbewegung* was a movement for children and youth established by the music pedagog Fritz Jöde in Germany after the First World War. He wanted a singing society and based his work on ideas from the philosophers J. J. Rousseau and F. Fröbel.

7 *Norsk skuleblad* was and still is a major magazine for primary and secondary teachers in Norway.

8 PISA is the acronym for 'Programme for International Student Assessment', an OECD initiative that has been very influential on school policies globally as well as in specific countries. The influence PISA has in many countries led to a focus on the so-called 'basics', namely reading, writing and science.

References

Behrens, J. (1868), *Sanglære for Skoler*. Kristiania: privately published.

Benestad, F. and Fottland, I. (1966), 'Musikk i 9 årig skole, fra sangtime til musikkfag', in R. Ness (ed.), *Skolens årbok*. Oslo: Johan Grundt Tanum forlag, pp. 791–810.

Benum, I. (1955), *Musikk Som Personlighetsdannende Fag i Skolen*. Hamar: Norsk skoletidendes boktrykkeri.

Bergheim, I. (1974), 'Lærebøker i musikk for barneskolen' (unpublished dissertation, University of Oslo).

Bjørnstad, F. O. (2001), *Frå Munn og Flatfele*. Kristiansund: KOM.

Espeland, M. (1974), 'Lærebøker i musikk for barneskolen. Ein analyse' (unpublished dissertation, Norges Lærerhøyskole).

Hole, B. (1999), 'The birth of the Psalmodikon: North American Psalmodikonforbundet', www.psalmodikon.com/history/birth_of_the_psalmodikon.htm (accessed 20 June 2008).

Jørgensen, H. (1982), *Sang og Musikk*. Oslo: H. Aschehoug & Co.

Jørgensen, H. (2001), 'Sang og musikk i grunnskole og lærerutdanning 1945–2000', *Studia Musicologica Norvegica*, 27, 103–31.

Kirke-og undervisningsdepartementet (KUD) (1922), *Normalplan for Landsfolkeskolen, Kirke-og Undervisningsdepartementet*. Kristiania: J. M. Stenersens forlag.

Kirke-og undervisningsdepartementet (KUD) (1939), *Normalplan for Byfolkeskolen. Utarbeidd ved Normalplankomiteen Oppnevnt av Kirke-og Undervisningsdepartementet*. Oslo: Aschehoug & Co.

Kjeldstadli, K. (2000), *Fortida er Ikke Hva den Engang Var (En Innføring i Historiefaget)* [The past is not what it used to be: an introduction to history], 2 vols (2nd edn). Oslo: Universitetsforlaget.

Mork, N. (2008), 'The fate of innovation. A social history of creativity and curriculum control' (unpublished dissertation, University of Brighton).

Norsk Skolemuseums Venner (1960), *Skolehistoriske Aktstykker nr. 9*. Oslo: Norsk Skolemuseums Venner.

Stålmarck, T. (ed.) (1962), *Natur og Kulturs Musikhandbok*. Stockholm: Natur och Kultur.

Storækre, J. T. (1965), *Kristen Sang og Musikk*. Oslo: Runa forlag.

Tønnesen, H. O. (1966), *Tekster og Aktstykker til den Norske Skoles Historie*. Oslo: Fabritius og sønner forlag.

Varkøy, Ø. (1993), *Hvorfor musikk?* Oslo: Ad Notam Gyldendal.

Årva, Ø. (1987), *Musikkfaget i Norsk Lærerutdannelse 1815–1965*. Oslo: Novus forlag.

7

Spain: A journey from a nominal towards a universally implemented curriculum

Gabriel Rusinek and Susana Sarfson[1]

Historical background

A serious attempt to codify the educational system in Spain took place in 1857 with the promulgation of the *Law of Public Instruction* (Ministerio de Fomento 1857). In order to solve the then major problem of illiteracy among the rural population, compulsory schooling was introduced for children aged 6 to 9, and was free for those whose families 'could not afford it'.[2] Music was not initially stipulated, but two decades later a subject called 'music and singing' was incorporated into the curriculum of the Madrid teachers' colleges (Ministerio de Fomento 1878) and in most teachers' colleges elsewhere some time later, so that by the end of the nineteenth century classroom teachers were expected to teach singing to the children in their classes. Singing was mentioned for the first time in an educational regulation in 1884 when it was included within the 'essential knowledge' to be acquired by children aged 3 to 7 (Ministerio de Fomento 1884). Although there is little evidence of this regulation being applied during this early period, two examples serve to indicate at least some teaching of music in schools. First, singing was taught from 1844 to 1911 in a school in the Canary Islands, a Spanish province off the northwest coast of Africa (Marrero Henning 1997). The second example of music teaching was in the model secondary school established by the Free Institution of Teaching (*Institución Libre de Enseñanza*) in Madrid, a highly influential educational and intellectual institution founded in 1876 that criticized contemporary restrictions to academic thought in official institutions. Singing at this school was considered to be an important means of transmitting moral values (Sánchez de Andrés 2005) and from 1882 the song repertoire comprised songs from the classical and folk traditions. Interestingly, the folksongs were collected and compiled by teachers and students during their field trips to rural areas.

Singing was formally introduced as a subject in public primary schools in 1901 with the liberal reforms to the education system, which also extended compulsory education to the age of 12 and assigned the responsibility for teachers' salaries to the state (Ministerio de Instrucción Pública y Bellas Artes 1901). There is evidence that music was being taught in school to a far greater extent by the beginning of the twentieth century including the following instances:

- some private and public schools in Girona from 1902 and 1908 respectively (Brugués i Agustí 2008)
- the public schools in Barcelona that were established after 1914 and influenced by the ideas of many progressive educators and *renovation* movements
- the 'graded schools'[3] in Madrid, where singing was taught for up to one hour per week in the 1910s and 1920s (Pozo Andrés 1996)
- the Home and Professional School for Women in Madrid, a secondary school for the vocational training of girls from the age of 12, where music was included as a 2-year general subject (Ministerio de Instrucción Pública y Bellas Artes 1911).

The teaching of music in schools was recognized as being important from the very beginning of the Second Republic (1931–1939), even though the main educational challenge was eradicating illiteracy – an ever present problem. Music was included in an ultimately unsuccessful proposal for primary and secondary teaching (Molero Pintado 1991) that was presented to parliament in 1932 by Fernando de los Ríos (Delgado Criado 1994). This was a time of all sorts of progressive educational ideas, including 'pedagogical missions' organized from 1931 when teachers who were sent to remote villages principally to improve literacy, also took phonographs and recordings of classical music with them for educational purposes. Such innovations were inspired by the work of the *Institución Libre de Enseñanza* and the advocates of the 'new school' – such as Luzuriaga (1927) – and by the ideas of music educators such as Manuel Borguñó (1933, 1938). Among the few reports about school music activities at the time were details of a teacher at a 'graded school' in the province of Soria who demonstrated how the ideas of the 'active school' were being carried out (Gómez Lozano 1933). The school had a choir of 100 children who rehearsed twice each week. The teacher provided a three-part arrangement of a lullaby as an example of the choir's repertoire and he was keen for his pupils to be recorded so that the discs could then be taken into schools by these 'pedagogical missions'. During the Second Republic, the government undertook a series of ambitious reforms of the education system despite severe economic restrictions and violent political conflicts – one of which was a result of their decision to ban religious orders from teaching.

Although exiled to Valencia because of the Civil War (1936–39), the republican government created a Central Music Council (Ministerio de Instrucción Pública y Sanidad 1937b) among whose responsibilities was the organization of music teaching in primary and secondary schools. The Ministry of Public Instruction sanctioned a primary curriculum that included 'singing and rhythmics'[4] (Ministerio de Instrucción Pública y Sanidad 1937a). But these efforts were doomed because of the ongoing Civil War and were eventually dismantled by the regime of General Franco, which remained in power until Franco's death in 1975.

In 1945 the *Law of Primary Education* (Jefatura del Estado 1945) established a Catholic fundamentalist and gender-segregated educational system whose fascist principles were thoroughly exposed in its preface. This law made primary schooling compulsory for children aged 6 to 12 – free only for those who 'could not afford it' as 100 years before – in a country that was suffering extreme poverty. 'Music and singing' were included in the curriculum as part of a 'complementary knowledge group'. A contemporary report by a German teacher (Rude 1952) records that singing was taking place in schools, although the songs were mainly of a religious and patriotic nature. Singing was also evident in religious schools run by Jesuits and at lay private schools. Manuel Borguñó (1946) organized a school choir festival in Tenerife and María Dolors Bonal – who in 1967 would establish the Catalan Children's Choirs Movement – was working from 1951 at two private schools in Barcelona, teaching Catalan songs at a time when the Catalan language was being repressed (Roche 2000).

The nominal music curricula

Spain's political isolation ended with its incorporation into the United Nations in 1955 and with the transfer of the national administration to a Catholic liberal elite, which started to displace the fascist organizations that had predominated during and immediately after the Civil War. A comprehensive music curriculum was formulated for the first time[5] that sequenced the musical content into three stages and provided an officially approved song repertoire – again, a mix of folk, religious and fascist songs (Dirección General de Enseñanza Primaria 1953).

By the end of the 1950s, the economy was slowly beginning to develop, and this favoured the extension of compulsory education to the age of 14 in 1964. Some teachers gained scholarships to study in Salzburg at the Orff Institute and were afterwards hired as specialists by private schools that incorporated music as a distinctive element of their curriculum (López-Ibor 2003; Oriol 2008; Roche 2007). One of these teachers, Monserrat Sanuy, co-edited an adaptation of the Orff Schulwerk incorporating Spanish folklore (Sanuy and

González Sarmiento 1969a, 1969b) that became very influential in terms of popularizing music education. But in spite of a music curriculum and the tireless efforts of such music educators as Manuel Borguñó (1946, 1948, 1959, 1966), music was not widely taught but remained a privilege of urban elites in a profoundly class-conscious society.

During the final period of the Franco era, 'music and singing' were included within an area of the curriculum termed 'aesthetic education' in the *General Law of Education* (Ministerio de Educación y Ciencia 1970) – a law which also prescribed compulsory and free primary schooling for all children aged 6 to 14. Soon afterwards a detailed music curriculum was published that listed performing and individual and group creativity, clearly influenced by the Orff Schulwerk (Ministerio de Educación y Ciencia 1971).

After Franco's death in 1975 and the coronation of King Juan Carlos de Borbón, a transition process began that resulted in the enactment of the 1978 constitution and in the first democratic elections after the dictatorship. Changes in the educational system slowly began to be introduced that reflected the country's political and social progress.[6] A 'renewed' curriculum for primary schools was passed that also included music, but this time within an area termed 'artistic expression'. Written by experienced music educators, the guidelines for sixth to eighth grades (Angulo *et al.* 1981) and for third to fifth grades (Ministerio de Educación y Ciencia 1982) included recommendations about vocal and instrumental performance, ear training and movement, and sample Orff-style activities. However, neither the 1971 music curriculum nor the 1981–82 curriculum was widely implemented because generalist teachers were not adequately prepared to teach them (Oriol 1999) and perhaps also because there was no system of music inspection to enforce music teaching.[7] It seems that, as in the previous decades, music was still only being taught by a few highly motivated primary school teachers with some musical background and by music specialists employed in some private schools.

From 1970 to 1989 secondary education remained non-compulsory and comprised a 3-year stage that started at the age of 14, followed by a one-year 'pre-university course'. In 1975 a one-year course called 'music' was introduced as a mandatory subject (Ministerio de Educación y Ciencia 1975). However, this was initially taught by teachers of other subjects largely to fill their teaching time allocations. This was because a bachelor's degree was required for a teacher to teach in secondary schools and conservatoire-based qualifications held by musicians were not considered equivalent to university degrees.[8] Conservatoire graduates applied pressure until they managed to attain an official matching of the degrees (Peiteado Rodríguez 1983) and in 1984 competitive examinations for employment as music teachers for public schools began. This proved to be crucially important in raising the status of music as a subject because its teachers achieved parity with the civil servant status of other specialist teachers – this step resulted in the incorporation of music into the secondary curriculum as irreversible. However, as the initial teaching of the subject had been undertaken by non-musicians and the fact that the curriculum content was heavily historical with an emphasis on declarative knowledge, this resulted in a negative image of the subject that persisted for many years.

The 1990 reform

After the 1982 elections a series of gradual but determined changes in key social issues – including education – began. A long period of public debate and experimentation was promoted by the Ministry of Education (Ministerio de Educación y Ciencia 1984) that led to a white paper on educational reform (Ministerio de Educación y Ciencia 1987) and eventually to the enactment of the *General Organic Law of the Educational System* [LOGSE] (Ministerio de Educación y Ciencia 1990). This law completely restructured the educational system and extended compulsory schooling to the age of 16, reducing primary to 6 years and extending secondary to 6. Most importantly, it established that the first 4 years of secondary education would at last be compulsory and could be followed by 2 years of post-compulsory secondary schooling or by vocational training.

Besides extending compulsory schooling, the 1990 reform aimed at transforming the previous technical model into a constructivist model, informed by contemporary psychological research and publications (e.g. Coll 1988; Palacios *et al.* 1984, 1985). There was also a belief that access to a basic arts education should be available to all children, backed by increasing social demands in a country that was rapidly developing and had just been incorporated to the European Union.

With the restoration of democracy in 1978 after decades of uncertainty, Spanish music educators had began to experience an optimistic time.[9] Many conferences were held during the 1980s to support the universality of music education – in Cáceres in 1981 (AAVV 1981) and 1982, in Madrid in 1984 (Oriol 1984), in El Escorial in 1986, in Valladolid in 1988 and in Alicante in 1989. Eventually, the concerns of music educators were being seriously considered. Most significantly, the ensuing reforms made the teaching of music in primary schools by specialists mandatory, which was also extended in secondary schools.

The primary music curriculum (Ministerio de Educación y Ciencia 1991a) advocated that children's musical activity in the classrooms should be undertaken through singing and playing instruments, through improvising and composing and through participating in active listening activities. To that end, music rooms started to be designated in all primary schools and musical instruments were allotted. All public schools were provided with pitched and non-pitched percussion instruments, electronic or acoustic pianos and hi-fi audio equipment.

Eventually, competitive examinations to fill music education posts in public primary schools were instituted[10] and music teachers were also hired in private schools. This led to an effective and universal implementation of a primary music curriculum for the first time. The key factor in this implementation was not the *enactment* of another official curriculum but, as with secondary music in the previous decade, the new 'civil servant' status of music teachers. Music education in primary schools was now firmly established.

The 1990 reform also extended the teaching of music in secondary schools to 3 years as a mandatory academic subject and as an optional subject in succeeding years. The secondary curriculum (Ministerio de Educación y Ciencia 1992) advocated active engagement with music making as a continuation of the experience in primary schools.[11] The content was organized in six blocks: singing, playing, movement and dance, music theory, music history and music in mass media (Ministerio de Educación y Ciencia 1991a), each being divided into concepts, procedures and attitudes.[12] The attainment targets included not only aural recognition of musical elements or a contextual understanding of classical music (as was previously expected for secondary music) but also skills such as group singing, group instrumental performance, group dance, melodic improvisation, reading of staff notation and basic accompaniment of songs with tonic, dominant and subdominant chords.

Training of teachers

Teachers' colleges (*escuelas normales*),[13] modelled on the French 'école normal' model, were established from 1838 in different Spanish cities. Forty years later in 1878 the subject of 'music and singing' (Ministerio de Fomento 1878) appeared for the first time in the teachers' colleges in Madrid. The subject was taken over 2 years and focused on music theory and sight singing. Different approaches to musical training emerged at the beginning of the twentieth century. Juan Vancell Roca (1902), a music lecturer at Barcelona Teachers' College, promoted an active methodology that connected theory with musical practice through ear training and the singing of Spanish folksongs (Sarfson 2007). Miguel Arnaudas and Manuel Soler (1911), music lecturers at Zaragoza and Madrid respectively, employed a more conservative approach and relied solely on teaching sight singing without pedagogical adaptations.[14] Tomás Sobrequés, music lecturer at the teachers' colleges of Girona from 1914 to 1945, published an article advocating the addition of two courses on choral singing, a music entrance examination at the teachers' colleges and even a music examination within the competitive examinations to hire primary teachers (Sobrequés 1917). Although he subsequently met with the Minister of Public Instruction, his requests were not acceded to (Brugués i Agustí 2008).

A major effort was made during the Second Republic to improve the training of teachers, but most of the colleges were eventually closed during the Civil War. Following their reopening in 1942, a purge took place to eliminate any progressive ideas and coeducation was suppressed. The Catholic Church and the Falange – the fascist organization that predominated during the Civil War and the first years of the dictatorship – assumed a dominant role in educational matters. Musical training was kept to a minimum at teachers' colleges, but the Falange soon realized the possibilities for singing as an indoctrinating medium. To this end, after the war its 'women's section' undertook the musical preparation of the female instructors who would teach the so-called 'home skills' to girls in schools (Lizarazu de Mesa 1996). During the 1960s this preparation became a 2-year course for 'music instructors' (Alonso Medina 2002; Luengo Sojo 1998), which was implemented in Madrid and many other cities, providing intensive music education training, including the Orff method, by invited foreign instructors and later by Spanish educators who had studied at the Orff Institute in Salzburg.

There was much discussion at the end of the 1980s about who should teach music in primary schools, which culminated in a conference held in Alicante in 1989. Various viewpoints were expressed about whether it should be taught by conservatoire music education graduates, by conservatoire music graduates with an additional training in education or by primary teachers with an extra training in music and music education (Oriol 1988). Following these discussions, music education workshops started to flourish nationwide. Universities and government agencies in several Spanish regions also offered non-academic in-service training programmes of 500 to 800 hours' duration to provide primary teachers with training in music education. For instance, in 1986 the programme 'Música a l'escola' (Pastor i Gordero *et al.* 1990) started in Valencia to train infant and primary teachers and in 1989 2-year training programmes were offered in Madrid by the Royal Conservatoire of Music, coordinated by Elisa Roche, and by the Complutense University, coordinated by Nicolás Oriol. Under likely pressure from trade unions, the Ministry of Education eventually decided that only those holding a 'maestro' [primary teacher] 3-year degree[15] would be entitled to teach in primary schools.[16] It also established teaching specialties, but specialist teachers were also to train as generalists and teach in that capacity if required (Ministerio de Educación y Ciencia 1991b). Music education was included among the teaching specialties and, accordingly since 1992, most universities have offered 3-year academic programmes for students wanting to become primary music teachers (*maestro, especialidad: educación musical*). In addition to a third of the training being assigned to music education, students undertook 320 hours of supervised teaching practices in schools (see Sustaeta and Oriol 1996).

The training of secondary teachers was rather different. Secondary teachers were required to hold only a bachelor's degree and, after 1971, a 'certificate of pedagogical aptitude' as well. Pre-service training for the 'certificate of pedagogical aptitude' was organized nationally through a series of short courses – in some universities, even as distance learning evaluated with multiple-choice exams – and non-supervised teaching practices. The system was clearly inadequate as a preparation for teachers to cope with the inclusion of seventh and eighth graders in secondary schools after the 1990 reform – it could not prepare them to understand early adolescence. Neither did it help them to cope with the presence of numerous disaffected learners, who would have been excluded from schooling in previous educational systems and with the increasingly conflicting classroom interactions that occurred due to social changes (Defensor del Pueblo 2006; Hernández and Sancho 2004).

Relating the past to the present

Thus far, this chapter has outlined how music was integrated into compulsory schooling in Spain. Despite a musical tradition that can be traced back to the Middle Ages, it was a long journey, highly polarized by political stances and determined by historical conflicts and socio-cultural changes. Following the introduction of music to the training of classroom teachers at the end of the nineteenth century, singing seems to have only sporadically taken root in a relatively small number of Spanish schools. There was an increasing interest in music education at the beginning of the twentieth century and even specific proposals during the Second Republic, but all progressive endeavours were dismantled after the Civil War. Education suffered a significant regression during Franco's regime and music was deliberately used as an ideological medium. Music curricula were introduced in 1953, 1971 and 1981, but essentially they existed in name only because they were implemented in so few primary schools. The 1975 secondary music curriculum was the first to be effectively taught, eventually by music specialists, but secondary education was still not compulsory. Only in 1990 did the universal teaching of music become a reality after the first democratic educational reform. Only with the mandatory appointment of specialist teachers in primary school was the primary music curriculum properly and universally implemented. The 1990 reform extended compulsory schooling to secondary schools and also extended the teaching of music as a mandatory subject taught by specialists.

In retrospect, the 1990 reform achieved success but within limits. Despite considerable enthusiasm and hard work, many changes were limited by bureaucratic processes. The extended application of its child-centred pedagogical principles was hindered by insufficient funding for a generalized in-service training of teachers[17] and by the reluctance of a great number of teachers to change their classic teacher- and subject-centred approaches to teaching. Nevertheless, there have been encouraging innovations, including work with individual composition (Murillo 2006), collaborative composition (Rusinek 2007), composition with computers (Alegret 2004), *inclusive* students' concerts (Rusinek 2008), school choirs (Sotelo 2002) and school orchestras (Murillo and Bravo 2005).

However, after the change of government with the 1996 elections, progress was somewhat hindered by limited funding for the public educational system in favour of a considerable and largely concealed subsidy for private schools. Increasingly difficult teacher–student interactions and a consistent 30 per cent school dropout rate were then attributed by teachers and the public opinion to the 1990 reform, rather than to shortfalls in funding or to the inadequacy of teacher training. A conservative counter-reform resulted (MECD 2000, 2002), which returned classic historicist approaches to teaching (Coll 2004). However, the government elected in the 2004 elections overturned this counter-reform with a new national curriculum (Ministerio de Educación y Ciencia 2006a). Regrettably, these recent educational reforms in Spain have been driven by the pressures of political parties, religious groups, trade unions, lobbies and even university departments, rather than being informed by pupils' needs, by teachers' demands or by educational research.

In summary, the position of school music in Spain has been under threat for a considerable time. This is still the case. For example, the most recent secondary curriculum requirements (Ministerio de Educación y Ciencia 2006c) have reduced the presence of music in secondary schools and the most recent primary curriculum requirements (Ministerio de Educación y Ciencia 2006b) have maintained the status quo, where music is not a discrete subject but merely a component of 'arts education' – even after 16 years of effective teaching by specialists. Perhaps even more detrimental are the regulations for the reform of higher education studies (Ministerio de Educación y Ciencia 2007). Due to the Bologna Declaration, designed to make the higher education systems in Europe converge towards a more transparent system by 2010,[18] subject specialisms within pre-service primary teacher training courses have been removed, thereby opening the possibility of a situation similar to the 1970s and 1980s when the primary school music curriculum reverts to effectively becoming nominal once more. Nevertheless, school music has proved to be resilient. Countless Spanish children and adolescents in the last two decades have experienced music as a living force in their school education, independently of their families' social status or of their economic circumstances.

Notes

1   We are indebted to Nicolás Oriol, Lluís Brugués, María Martorell and the late Elisa Roche for sharing their first-hand knowledge and to Julio Hurtado, José Luis Aróstegui and Steve Dillon for their suggestions and careful reading of the manuscript.

2   Note that this and the subsequent reforms applied only to public schools that had a charitable mission and that they educated only a fraction of the children attending schools, who were themselves only a small fraction of all Spanish children. Most private schools were religious but early in the nineteenth century, lay private schools had also been founded.

3   The *escuelas graduadas* were public primary schools in which, since 1898, teaching was organized according to age grades and where subjects had a detailed timetable.

4   Dalcroze's eurhythmics had been promoted in Barcelona by Joan Llongueras since 1911 (for a further development, see Llongueras 1942). Llongueras was awarded a scholarship by the Council for Scholarships and Scientific Investigations (*Junta para la Ampliación de Estudios e Investigaciones Científicas*) to study in Genève (López Casanova 2002).

5   These curricula, called 'questionnaires', were the first attempt to officially regulate teachers' instructional activities. However, they were 'compulsory for public and advisory for private [schools]'.

6   This was one of the few music education dissertations at the time and showed, from a positivist perspective, the contemporary preoccupation with the underdevelopment of Spanish music education. Dionisio del Río (1982) administered a Spanish version of Seashore's test (Seashore *et al.* 1977) to a wide sample of school children to confirm the hypothesis that the underdevelopment was not caused by the Spanish population's musical aptitudes being below standard, but rather by the country's general underdevelopment.

7   There were not – and there *are* not – specialist inspectors and specifically there is no inspection of school music. Moreover, the evaluation of the quality of the teaching in schools was not – and *is* not – included among Spanish education inspectors' duties.

8   The Spanish section of ISME was founded by Rosa María Kucharsky in that year.

9   For a report about teachers' perspectives of the hiring system and of the professional profile it fosters, see Rusinek (2004). For a biographical study of primary music teachers' careers, see Ocaña (2006).

10   Note that Spanish secondary schools do not provide teaching of orchestral instruments or the possibility of participating in a wind band. Such experiences are provided by private or community-based 'schools of music' for amateurs or by elementary/intermediate conservatoires for those aspiring to become professionals. Thus, Spanish secondary music is equivalent to 'general music' in the USA.

11   Inspired by contemporary notions about a 'hidden curriculum' (Torres Santomé 1991), the reform provided a curriculum frame that opposed previous technical conceptions of education as non-value-laden transmission of information.

12   Men and women studied in separated colleges until coeducation was established in 1931 during the Second Republic. Throughout Franco's regime teacher training was again gender segregated, until coeducation was re-established with the new democracy. Teachers' colleges became university colleges after 1970.

[13] Both manuals used the fixed-doh method for sight singing.

[14] The Spanish university system included, until the changes due to the Bologna Treatise, 3-year degrees (*diplomatura*) and 5-year degrees (*licenciatura*) equivalent to bachelor degrees. There were no academic master's degrees and the 'third cycle' of higher education studies were doctoral degrees. Primary teachers were required to hold 3-year degrees (*diplomatura*) in order to be employed, and were paid less than secondary teachers, who were required to possess 5-year degrees. There was, first, an intention to reduce costs and, second, to have all-purpose specialist teachers who could complete their timetables as generalists.

[15] It has to be noted that within the Spanish system, people with higher degrees – even with postgraduate degrees – are not allowed to teach in primary schools if they do not hold the 'maestro' degree. Contrariwise, those holding a 'maestro' degree are not allowed to teach in secondary if they do not hold a bachelor's degree (*licenciatura*).

[16] A major part of the funding was devoted to building more secondary schools and to extend existing buildings. This was necessary because of the massive influx of students with the incorporation of seventh and eighth graders into secondary schools and because 15 and 16 year-olds were previously excluded from schooling.

[17] See www.ond.flanders.be/hogeronderwijs/bologna/.

References

AAVV (1981), *La formación humana a través de la música: II Congreso Nacional de Pedagogía Musical*. Cáceres: Institución Cultural 'El Brocense'.

Alegret, M. (2004), 'La creación musical a través de la información: Estudio de un caser en primer cicio de secundaria' (unpublished doctoral dissertation, Universidad de Barcelona, Barcelona).

Alonso Medina, J. A. (2002), 'Cursos de formación musical para instructoras de la Sección Femenina y para el profesorado en general', *El Guiniguada*, 11, 11–21.

Angulo, M., Sanuy, C., Sanuy, M. and Roche, E. (1981), 'Programas renovados de la E.G.B. Educación Artística (I). Música. (Documento de consulta)', *Vida Escolar*, 211, 1–48.

Arnaudas, M. and Soler, M. (1911), *Tratado de música para las escuelas normales*. Leipzig: Breitkopf & Haertel.

Borguñó, M. (1933), *La música, el cant i l'escola*. Barcelona: Librería Bastinos.

Borguñó, M. (1938), 'Elementos para la organización de la pedagogía musical escolar', *Música*, 4, 33–9.

Borguñó, M. (1946), *Educación musical escolar y popular*. Santa Cruz de Tenerife: La Tinerfeña.

Borguñó, M. (1948), *La música, los músicos y la educación*. Santa Cruz de Tenerife: Instituto Musical de Pedagogía.

Borguñó, M. (1959), *Cincuenta años de educación musical*. Santa Cruz de Tenerife: Instituto Musical de Pedagogía.

Borguñó, M. (1966), *¿Ha fracasado la educación musical?* Santa Cruz de Tenerife: Galarza.

Brugués i Agustí, L. (2008), *La música a Girona. Història del Conservatori Isaac Albéniz*. Girona: Diputació de Girona.

Coll, C. (1988), *Psicología y Currículum: Una Aproximación Psicopedagógica a la Elaboración del Currículum Escolar*. Barcelona: Laia.

Coll, C. (2004), 'La revolución conservadora llega a la educación', *Aula de Innovación Educativa*,130, 7–10.

Defensor del Pueblo (2006), *Violencia Escolar: El Maltrato entre Iguales en la Educación Secundaria Obligatoria 1999-2006 (Nuevo Estudio y Actualización del Informe 2000)*. Madrid: Defensor del Pueblo.

del Río, D. (1982), 'Aptitudes musicales de la población escolar española' (unpublished doctoral dissertation, Universidad Complutense de Madrid, Madrid).

Delgado Criado, B. (ed.) (1994), *Historia de la educación en España y América*. Vol. 3: *La Educación en la España Contemporánea (1789–1975)*. Madrid: Fundación Santa María – SM – Morata.

Dirección General de Enseñanza Primaria (1953), *Cuestionarios Nacionales para la Enseñanza Primaria*. Madrid: Servicio de Publicaciones del Ministerio de Educación Nacional.

Gómez Lozano, P. (1933), *Mi escuela activa*. Madrid: Compañía de Artes Gráficas.

Hernández, F. and Sancho, J. M. (2004), *El clima escolar en los centros de secundaria: Más allá de los tópicos*. Madrid: Centro de Investigación y Documentación Educativa – Ministerio de Educación y Ciencia.

Jefatura del Estado (1945), *Ley de Educación Primaria*. Madrid: Boletín Oficial del Estado.

Lizarazu de Mesa, M. A. (1996), 'En torno al folklore musical y su utilización: el caso de las Misiones Pedagógicas y la Sección Femenina', *Anuario Musical: Revista de Musicología del CSIC*, 51, 233–46.

Llongueras, J. (1942), *El ritmo en la educación y formación general de la infancia*. Barcelona: Labor.

López Casanova, M. B. (2002), 'La política educativo-musical en España durante la Segunda República', *Música y Educación*, 50, 15–26.

López-Ibor, S. (2003), 'Entrevista con Montse Sanuy', *Orff España*, 3, 10–12.

Luengo Sojo, A. (1998), 'La pedagogía musical de la Sección Femenina de F.E.T. y de las J.O.N.S. en Barcelona: Escuela de Especialidades "Roger de Lauria"', in X. Aviñoa (ed.), *Miscellània Oriol Martorell*. Barcelona: Publicacions de la Universitat de Barcelona, pp. 333–43.

Luzuriaga, L. (1927), *La educación nueva*. Madrid: Museo Pedagógico Nacional – J. Cosano.

Marrero Henning, M. d. P. (1997), *El Colegio de San Agustín en la enseñanza secundaria de Gran Canaria*. Las Palmas de Gran Canaria: Unelco.

MECD (2000) *Real Decreto 3473/2000, de 29 de diciembre, por el que se modifica el Real Decreto 1007/1991, de 14 de junio, por el que se establecen las enseñanzas mínimas correspondientes a la educación secundaria obligatoria*. Madrid: Boletín Oficial del Estado.

MECD (2002), *Ley Orgánica 10/2002, de 23 de diciembre, de Calidad de la Educación*. Madrid: Boletín Oficial del Estado.

Ministerio de Educación y Ciencia (1970), *Ley 14/1970, de 4 de agosto, general de educación y financiamiento de la reforma educativa*. Madrid: Boletín Oficial del Estado.

Ministerio de Educación y Ciencia (1971), 'Segunda etapa de la Educación General Básica. Nuevas orientaciones pedagógicas', *Vida Escolar*, 128–130, 4–66.

Ministerio de Educación y Ciencia (1975), *Decreto 160/1975 de 23 de enero de Plan de Estudios de Bachillerato*. Madrid: Boletín Oficial del Estado.

Ministerio de Educación y Ciencia (1982), *Programas renovados de la Educación General Básica. Ciclo medio. 3er, 4º y 5º curso*. Madrid: Escuela Española.

Ministerio de Educación y Ciencia (1984), *Hacia la reforma: Documentos de trabajo*. Madrid: Servicio de Publicaciones del Ministerio de Educación y Ciencia.

Ministerio de Educación y Ciencia (1987), *Proyecto para la reforma de la enseñanza: Educación infantil, primaria, secundaria y profesional*. Madrid: Centro de Publicaciones del Ministerio de Educación y Ciencia.

Ministerio de Educación y Ciencia (1990), *Ley Orgánica 1/1990, de 3 de octubre, de Ordenación General del Sistema Educativo*. Madrid: Boletín Oficial del Estado.

Ministerio de Educación y Ciencia (1991a), *Real Decreto 1007/1991, de 14 de junio, por el que se establecen las enseñanzas mínimas correspondientes a la educación secundaria obligatoria*. Madrid: Boletín Oficial del Estado.

Ministerio de Educación y Ciencia (1991b), *Real Decreto 1440/1991, de 30 de agosto, por el que se establece el título universitario oficial de Maestro, en sus diversas especialidades, y las directrices generales propias de los planes de estudios conducentes a la obtención de aquel*. Madrid: Boletín Oficial del Estado.

Ministerio de Educación y Ciencia (1992), *Secundaria obligatoria. Música*. Madrid: Ministerio de Educación y Ciencia.

Ministerio de Educación y Ciencia (2006a), *Ley Orgánica 2/2006, de 3 de mayo, de Educación*. Madrid: Boletín Oficial del Estado.

Ministerio de Educación y Ciencia (2006b), *Real Decreto 1513/2006, de 7 de diciembre, por el que se establecen las enseñanzas mínimas de la educación primaria*. Madrid: Boletín Oficial del Estado.

Ministerio de Educación y Ciencia (2006c), *Real Decreto 1631/2006, de 29 de diciembre, por el que se establecen las enseñanzas mínimas correspondientes a la educación secundaria obligatoria*. Madrid: Boletín Oficial del Estado.

Ministerio de Educación y Ciencia (2007), *Orden ECI/3857/2007, de 27 de diciembre, por la que se establecen los requisitos para la verificación de los títulos universitarios oficiales que habiliten para el ejercicio de la profesión de Maestro en Educación Primaria*. Madrid: Boletín Oficial del Estado.

Ministerio de Fomento (1857), *Ley de Instrucción Pública*. Madrid: Gaceta de Madrid.

Ministerio de Fomento (1878), *Real Decreto de 24 de agosto de 1878*. Madrid: Gaceta de Madrid.

Ministerio de Fomento (1884). *Real Decreto de 4 de julio de 1884*. Madrid: Gaceta de Madrid.

Ministerio de Instrucción Pública y Bellas Artes (1901), *Real Decreto de 26 de octubre de 1901*. Madrid: Gazeta de Madrid.

Ministerio de Instrucción Pública y Bellas Artes (1911), *Real decreto disponiendo que en la Escuela del Hogar y Profesional de la mujer, se cursen las enseñanza que se indican*. Madrid: Gaceta de Madrid.

Ministerio de Instrucción Pública y Sanidad (1937a), *Decreto fijando el plan de estudios que ha de regir en la escuela primaria española*. Valencia: Gazeta de la República.

Ministerio de Instrucción Pública y Sanidad (1937b), *Orden de creación del Consejo Central de la Música*. Valencia: Gaceta de la República.

Molero Pintado, A. (ed) (1991), *Historia de la educación en España*. Vol. 4: *La Educación Durante la Segunda República y la Guerra Civil*. Madrid: Ministerio de Educación y Ciencia.

Murillo, A. (2006), 'Atrapando los sonidos: experiencias compositivas en el aula de música de secundaria', *Eufonía. Didáctica de la Música*, 37, 112–118.

Murillo, A. and Bravo, V. (2005), 'Com sona L'ESO: un encuentro musical en la ESO', *Eufonía. Didáctica de la Música*, 34, 106–111.

Ocaña, A. (2006), 'Desarrollo profesional de las maestras de educación musical desde una perspectiva biográfico-narrativa', *Revista Electrónica Complutense de Investigación en Educación Musical*, 3, (3), 1–14.

Oriol, N. (ed.) (1984), *I Simposio Nacional de Didáctica de la Música: Escuela Universitaria de Formación del Profesorado María Díaz Jiménez de Madrid*. Madrid: Editorial Complutense.

Oriol, N. (1988), 'Las escuelas universitarias y la formación musical del profesorado de educación básica', *Música y Educación*, 1, (1), 17–31.

Oriol, N. (1999), 'La formación del profesorado de música en la enseñanza general', *Música y Educación*, XII, (1), 49–68.

Oriol, N. (2008), personal communication.

Palacios, J., Marchesi, A. and Carretero, M. (eds) (1984), *Psicología evolutiva*. Vol. 2: *Desarrollo Cognitivo y Social del Niño*. Madrid: Alianza.

Palacios, J., Marchesi, A. and Carretero, M. (eds) (1985), *Psicología evolutiva*. Vol. 3: *Adolescencia, Madurez y Senectud*. Madrid: Alianza.

Pastor i Gordero, P., Porta Navarro, A., Equipo de Monitores a l'Escola and Rocamora Martínez, M. J. (eds) (1990), *Música a l'escola. Formación del profesorado de educación infantil y del primer ciclo de primaria. Guía del programa*. Valencia: Consellería de Cultura, Educació i Ciéncia.

Peiteado Rodríguez, M. (1983), 'La reforma de los programas de música en la enseñanza media', *Aula Abierta*, 37, 57–65.

Pozo Andrés, M. d. M. (1996), 'La escuela graduada madrileña en el primer tercio del siglo xx: ¿Un modelo pedagógico para el resto del Estado Español?', *Revista Complutense de Educación*, 7, (2), 211–74.

Roche, E. (2000), 'Entrevista: María Dolors Bonal', *Orff España*, 3, 3–9.

Roche, E. (2007), personal communication.

Rude, A. (1952), *La Escuela Nueva y sus procedimientos didácticos*. Mexico City: Labora.

Rusinek, G. (2004), 'The profile of the music teacher in Spanish primary schools, according to the teachers themselves', *Proceedings from the 26th International Society for Music Education World Conference*, Tenerife. CD-ROM.

Rusinek, G. (2007), 'Students' perspectives in a collaborative composition project at a Spanish secondary school', *Music Education Research*, 9, (3), 323–35.

Rusinek, G. (2008), 'Disaffected learners and school musical culture: an opportunity for inclusion', *Research Studies in Music Education*, 30, (1), 9–23.

Sánchez de Andrés, L. (2005), 'La música en la actividad educativa institucionista', *Boletín de la Institución Libre de Enseñanza*, 57, 7–18.

Sanuy, M. and González Sarmiento, L. (1969a), *Orff Schulwerk: Música para Niños*, vol. 1. Madrid: Unión Musical Española.

Sanuy, M. and González Sarmiento, L. (1969b), *Orff Schulwerk: Música para niños. Introducción.* Madrid: Unión Musical Española.

Sarfson, S. (2007), 'Juan Vancell y Roca. Teoría y práctica musical en la formación de maestros', *Música y Educación*, 70, 37–46.

Seashore, C. E., Lewis, D. and Saeveit, J. G. (1977), *Tests de aptitudes musicales de Seashore*. Madrid: TEA.

Sobrequés, T. (1917), 'Deficiències del pla de l'ensenyança de la música a les escoles normals', *Scherzando: Revista Catalana Musical*, 75, 49–50.

Sotelo, C. (2002), 'Los encuentros de corales de enseñanza secundaria de Cataluña', *Eufonía. Didáctica de la Música*, 26, 115–20.

Sustaeta, I. and Oriol, N. (1996), 'La especialidad de Educación Musical en la Facultad de Educación de la Universidad Complutense de Madrid', *Música y Educación*, 9, (1), 45–54.

Torres Santomé, J. (1991), *El currículum oculto*. Madrid: Morata.

Vancell Roca, J. (1902), *El libro de música y canto*. Barcelona: Fidel Giró Impresor.

Part 2

The Americas

A *North America*

Canada: Diverse developments across the decades

Nancy Vogan

Early education in Canada was influenced by various groups of immigrants – particularly those from Britain and France – and usually reflected the beliefs and heritage (including the musical heritage) of these settlers, as well as those of missionaries, members of the clergy and military personnel.

The fact that the British North America Act, which created the Dominion of Canada in 1867, made education a provincial responsibility has had a profound influence on education. This delegating of responsibility to the provinces has resulted in a lack of uniformity of standards for all subject areas including music. In 1867 there were just four provinces (Ontario, Quebec, New Brunswick and Nova Scotia) but by 1873 three more had joined – Manitoba (1870), British Columbia (1871) and Prince Edward Island (1873). Saskatchewan and Alberta did not become provinces until 1905 and the most easterly province, Newfoundland and Labrador, remained a separate British colony until 1949. There are also three northern territories that are part of Canada – Yukon, Northwest Territories and Nunavut. Canada today covers a large geographic area but has a relatively small population that is primarily spread out along the southern border from coast to coast.

During the early years of European settlement music instruction was included in several of the private and religious schools in the various regions that are now part of Canada. Private instrumental instruction and choral training for religious services were offered to both young men and women by various Roman Catholic orders. Hymns, simple songs and 'national airs' were prevalent in those parts of Canada which were settled by Protestants – English, Scottish and Irish immigrants and the United Empire Loyalists from the United States following the Revolutionary War. For several of the Protestant denominations, singing schools such as those in the American colonies provided an early form of music instruction during the late eighteenth and nineteenth centuries. With the emergence of more formal systems of public education in various regions of the country during the second half of the nineteenth century, music was included more frequently, but this was still sporadic in many places. It was usually little more than casual singing, often taught by individuals outside the school system – private music teachers, church choir directors and bandmasters. This instruction was primarily available in the larger urban centres (see Kallmann 1960; Keillor 2006).

As school enrolments increased and support for music instruction grew, many of these special instructors became music supervisors. This meant that the elementary school teachers were expected to provide the music instruction for their own classes but frequently they had had little or no training in music themselves. Early instructional programmes in music usually consisted of rote singing and a study of the rudiments of music. Support for music instruction in the schools was often obtained by mounting massed children's choirs for special occasions such as Royal Visits or Empire Day celebrations. The introduction of music in rural schools followed later in a pattern somewhat similar to that of the urban centres, but standards were rarely as high. Music's importance as a subject in the school curriculum was slight in many regions until at least the 1920s and 1930s; major advances were made in the period following the Second World War.

Establishment of free public education

Free public schools were established in Ontario in 1846; they were established in most other regions of Canada during the second half of the nineteenth century. Most of these schools were non-sectarian. However, the education situations in Quebec and Newfoundland differed from those in the rest of Canada. In addition to the private religious schools in Quebec, public schooling was also divided along religious lines until the mid-twentieth century. This resulted in Catholic schools for most of the French-speaking children and Protestant schools for most of the English-speaking. Consequently, developments in education, including those in music, evolved along entirely different paths. Similarly, in Newfoundland, schools were organized along religious lines with separate schools and school boards for the Roman Catholic and the various Protestant denominations until the late twentieth century. The three Maritime provinces on Canada's east coast – New Brunswick, Nova Scotia and Prince Edward Island – although small in both area and population, have always had separate governments, including their own departments of education.

In Ontario, vocal music was listed in the first programme of studies for schools and music instruction for classroom teachers was begun at the provincial Normal School by 1848. This reflected the influence of Egerton Ryerson, Chief Superintendent of Education for Upper Canada or Canada West (Ontario) from 1844 until 1876. Ryerson was very supportive of music instruction, partly because of his interest in the education theories of Pestalozzi, which had spread throughout parts of Europe, Britain, and the United States. He had visited many schools whose practice was based on these theories during his travels to more than 20 countries in the British Empire and Europe while he was developing his plans for a public school system for Ontario. Ryerson subsequently brought Henry Francis Sefton from Britain to teach the Wilhem-Hullah music method in the schools and at the Normal School. This method was based on fixed doh. Sefton worked in Toronto from 1858 to 1882 and created the earliest music books in Ontario intended specifically for school use; some of these materials were later used in other provinces as well including his *Three-part Songs* (1869) and *A Manual of Vocal Music* (1871) (see Trowsdale 1962, 1970).

Music appeared in the programme of studies in other provinces at various times – Nova Scotia in 1855, Quebec in 1871, New Brunswick in 1872 and Prince Edward Island in the late 1870s (see Green and Vogan 1991; Vogan 1979, 1986, 1988). In British Columbia, the first superintendent of education was appointed in 1872. He had arrived from England via Ontario where he had worked with Ryerson whom he admired greatly, so the educational policies established in British Columbia bore a close resemblance to those advocated by Ryerson in Ontario with a strong emphasis on music in the schools. In the schools of Winnipeg, music was taught before 1900 but the first detailed music curriculum for the province of Manitoba did not appear until 1928.

Much of the land that formed the provinces of Saskatchewan and Alberta in 1905 consisted of pioneer settlements, many with new immigrants. There were musical activities in some regions but generally not in rural areas. There was limited support for music instruction in the early days of establishing schools. However, inspectors encouraged the singing of patriotic songs in areas where students were of European ancestry in order to develop English-language skills and patriotism for their new country.

Music has played an important role in the life of Newfoundland both in the folk tradition and in music instruction. The major influences on education in Newfoundland have been English and Irish, in music as in general education. Several members of the English-speaking Roman Catholic orders (many of them from Ireland) played an important role in music instruction as did teachers from the various Protestant denominations. The differences between private and public school music teaching were not as clear in Newfoundland as in other provinces because the two types of music instruction already co-existed at denominational institutions: 'Though some private teachers maintained studios in their homes, a large number of them

worked in institutional settings with church affiliations. The music departments in these schools functioned almost as small conservatories' (Green and
Vogan 1991: 298; see also Woodford 1988).

Lobbying for instruction came from different sectors – sometimes from an
official within the education system, sometimes from a music teacher or
organist in the area and sometimes from the parents. School instrumental
ensembles were scarce and the majority were extra-curricular. In most of the
early schools in Canada, the aims of music were justified in terms of its
extrinsic values. To Ryerson, music was a powerful agent of moral culture.
Church music encouraged religious participation. Tomkins (1986: 90) sums
up the situation:

> Singing 'national airs' promoted patriotism. Fireside melodies, including
> 'moral songs' had leisure value in displacing questionable social
> amusements such as drinking. For some educators, music reinforced
> classroom discipline and had positive physiological effects that assisted all
> teaching. Music gained its strongest acceptances as a mental discipline;
> where it was promoted for 'relaxation' it was accepted merely as an
> 'auxiliary' subject.

Influence of the tonic sol-fa movement

From the 1860s to the 1890s John Curwen's tonic sol-fa methodology for
developing music reading skills that had become so popular in Britain was
introduced in various regions of Canada. The influence of this method was
felt from St John's, Newfoundland, in the east, to Victoria, British Columbia,
in the west, as well as in several other regions of the country. Tonic sol-fa
teaching in each of these regions often developed quite independently with
little or no influence from activities in other areas.

Most of the early teachers of this approach were from Britain; prior to the
First World War, English-speaking Canadian schools relied heavily on British
music teachers, many of whom had received tonic sol-fa training prior to
emigrating to Canada. The introduction of this system had a lasting effect on
music instruction in several parts of the country. In some places it was very
well received, while in others there was great controversy regarding its use.
The use of staff notation was especially preferred by those who taught
instruments. The French-speaking programmes continued to use the fixed
doh.

During the 1870s, the Chief Inspector of Schools for Toronto, George
Hughes, was looking for a way to improve music instruction in his schools. He
expressed dissatisfaction with the situation and wanted classroom teachers to
teach music for 15 minutes every day. Through his influence, the first detailed

course of study in vocal music for Toronto schools appeared in 1876. Subsequently a new provincial course of study was issued and a new music teacher, S. H. Preston, was appointed to the Toronto Normal School. Preston was familiar with American materials and was particularly interested in the work of Hosea Holt, a leading educator from the USA and a strong advocate of note reading using traditional notation. Preston produced his own adaptation of Tufts and Holt's *Normal Music Course* (1883) for schools in Canada in 1885.

Meanwhile, Hughes had been inquiring about the tonic sol-fa system being used in Britain as it had already been introduced in parts of Ontario including Hamilton and London. In 1886 Hughes appointed a fellow Scot, Alexander T. Cringan, as music supervisor for the Toronto schools. Cringan, a strong supporter of tonic sol-fa, taught music in Toronto in a variety of capacities for the next 44 years.

Cringan became involved in a methods controversy in his very first year in Toronto and this continued for quite some time. In 1887 a special music summer school for teachers was held in Toronto. Preston arranged that Hosea Holt from the USA be invited to teach his method of music reading. At the conclusion of the course, it was recommended by the teachers in attendance that Holt's method (and Preston's adaptation of the textbook) be sanctioned for Ontario schools. The following year, Cringan taught the summer school, using the tonic sol-fa approach, and the teachers were so impressed that they recommended the use of this method in the schools. Subsequently, a controversy arose over the virtues of staff versus tonic sol-fa notation and Preston and Cringan emerged as the main protagonists in an issue that attracted much public attention. The provincial department of education did not give exclusive authorization to either of these methodologies but, as a result of Cringan's leadership, the tonic sol-fa movement was firmly established by the turn of the century. In 1895 the Ontario Department of Education issued a music syllabus for public schools that outlined two separate courses, one using tonic sol-fa and the other using staff notation. Until the 1920s the emphasis in school music in Ontario continued to be on singing and the development of reading skills. Cringan published instructional materials, including *The Canadian Music Course* (1888). In 1901 he became music master at the Toronto Normal School and in 1919 he was appointed Inspector of the Teaching of Music for Ontario schools.

In 1886 the Montreal Protestant School Board hired a Mr Dawson to give a course of 30 lessons in tonic sol-fa for their teachers; they also issued an edict requiring classroom teachers to teach singing to their own classes. The following year a new course in this method was introduced in schools and children's concerts that illustrated the method were presented. Cringan's 1888 publication was introduced as the textbook and all teachers were required to provide instruction in music using the tonic sol-fa method or have

$10 deducted from their salaries. This ruling was kept on the books until at least 1920 by which time the penalty had increased to $40.

In the Maritimes, a Presbyterian minister from Scotland, Reverend James Anderson, played an important role in the introduction of tonic sol-fa instruction throughout the region. In 1884 he took a charge in Musquodoboit Harbour outside Halifax, Nova Scotia, and was soon involved in giving lessons in this method for teachers in the Halifax area. His involvement in music increased so much that in a few years he gave up his work as a minister in order to devote his entire time to music teaching. He travelled to all three Maritime provinces, working with teachers both during the year and at summer workshops. He used some of Cringan's publications in his teaching but he also published a series of articles on tonic sol-fa in *The Educational Review*, a Maritime periodical for teachers. Anderson later moved to Ontario where he lived in several small communities before retiring to California. Two of his pupils continued his work in the Maritimes and published materials for the schools.

Expansion of music programmes after the First World War

Following the First World War there was a gradual change in music programmes in most parts of Canada (for example, see Vogan 1993). Vocal music eventually became an integral part of elementary school education in most regions, but music in the high schools was generally offered on an extra-curricular basis if at all. Even after music was introduced as a subject in Grade 9, extra-curricular music activities (both choral and instrumental) were undertaken to supplement the often insufficient time scheduled during school hours. It was a long time before music gained the status of an accredited subject at the secondary school level.

Various aspects of education in Canada were influenced by the child development movement in the USA where school administrators and teachers had adopted principles of progressive education advocating a student-centred approach focusing on motivation and individual growth. This influence led to the adoption of the song method with less emphasis on music literacy and more emphasis on music for enjoyment:

> This meant that songs were introduced by rote and the quality of the repertoire became increasingly important as a means of placing a higher priority on appreciation. Canadian music educators were attracted to song series published in the USA; a number of US companies produced Canadian editions which often contained (with the exception of two or three Canadian patriotic songs) the same material found in the US version. (Kallman and Potvin 1992: 1190c)

Most school music programmes began to expand with the impact of technology. The introduction of the gramophone and radio contributed to improved methods and materials for music education. Phonograph companies prepared music appreciation units consisting of recordings, teacher guides and student workbooks. Radio broadcasts were skilfully devised as supplements to classroom work, offering imaginative presentations that were as beneficial to teachers as they were to their students. Although some of the first radio programmes used in Canadian schools were those directed by Walter Damrosch in New York City, by 1943 the Canadian Broadcasting Corporation was producing programmes that served the special needs of Canadian education. Orchestras in several large cities also contributed to the development of music appreciation by presenting live concerts designed specifically for student audiences. The annual competitive music festival (based on the British model) became an important venue for displaying the achievements of music students in many areas of the country. Although undue emphasis on competition has been a controversial issue, many teachers and supervisors have continued to regard festival participation as a vital outlet for their performing groups. By the late 1930s most provinces had replaced the terms 'vocal music' or 'singing' with 'music' in their programmes of study for the elementary grades.

Another influence from education in the United States was a change in the structure of the school system in some provinces. The introduction of the junior high school was a major innovation in Canadian education, musically leading to a growing interest in participation in group music making. Green and Vogan (1991: 162) highlight the significance of the junior high school development:

> The junior high school was the product of an attempt to liberalize the rigid curriculum that existed before the First World War. The movement reflected a growing recognition that schools should address themselves to the motivation of students – through activities and projects which appealed to students themselves – rather than to their mastery of prescribed subjects ... To realize these objectives, teachers possessing specialized expertise were selected to develop more fully the potential of students at this level. The western provinces experimented with junior high schools long before they were introduced elsewhere ... The patterns and traditions associated with music education in the west are significantly different from those in other parts of the country. To a certain extent these differences can be attributed to the three-level structure which had its conception in the junior high movement.

Developments in music education after the Second World War

Music instruction in secondary schools expanded in the post-Second World War period, especially in the field of instrumental music, and music courses for credit were offered at the secondary level in most provinces by the 1950s or 1960s. Universities and teacher training institutions had not anticipated the need for specialized training, so many provinces had to import music teachers or certify ex-service bandsmen and other musicians in order to meet the demand for instrumental specialists. Instrumental music programmes were aided by an expansion of the competitive music festival movement. Kiwanis and other service clubs not only established new competitions but also rejuvenated a number of older ones.

Most teachers in elementary schools continued to use some form or version of the song method. The curriculum, therefore, was determined to a large extent by the textbooks (or song series) approved by the various provincial governments. In the 1960s and 1970s several new approaches such as those of Orff and Kodály were introduced into the elementary music curriculum in many areas. An interest in multiculturalism led to an expansion of repertoire to include music of other cultures as well as music of native peoples. There was also an interest in promoting creativity and music composition in the classroom, an initiative encouraged by the John Adaskin Project for Canadian music. In this connection, the late George Proctor observed: 'the most original contribution that Canada has made in music education has been through the work of R. Murray Schafer, whose approach emphasizes original creative work in developing music sensitivity and the use of all types of sound, including environmental ones, as material for musical organization' (Proctor 1980: 35).

Changes in instructional content or methodology were often initiated by those who taught music at teacher training institutions (both teachers' colleges and university departments of education and/or music) or by music supervisors in the employ of large urban school boards. Several provinces appointed directors of music to deal with the complex demands of the postwar period that included finding solutions for increasing enrolments and teacher shortages. Summer schools and in-service training sessions became popular as well as increased emphasis on pre-service training in music teaching. This pre-service training was gradually transferred to universities from the teachers' colleges or normal schools and specific programmes in music education became more common in institutions offering a bachelor's degree in music. Opportunities to obtain graduate degrees in music, including degrees in music education, were also expanded (see Davey 1977; Green 1974).

When the International Society for Music Education was formed in 1953, Arnold Walter, director of the Faculty of Music at the University of Toronto, was elected its first president. At this time there was still no national organization of music educators in Canada; the Canadian Federation of Music Teachers' Associations had been formed in 1935 but it was primarily for those who taught music privately. A few provinces had provincial music education associations and the largest of these was the Ontario Music Educators' Association (OMEA), which had its beginnings in 1919 as a group within the Ontario Education Association (see Brault 1977). There had been talk for many years about the need for a national body of music educators in the country. Finally, in the spring of 1959, over 100 music educators from various parts of Canada gathered in Toronto at the spring meeting of OMEA to form the Canadian Music Educators' Association (CMEA). This organization has played an important role in the development of music education in Canada. Subsequent formation of provincial music educators' associations was promoted by CMEA in provinces where they did not already exist.

At the time of formation of CMEA only five provinces had individuals in the government who were responsible for music, but this situation improved over the next few years. However, a few decades later, several ministries of education eliminated their provincial music supervisors and reduced the number of music consultants. Whereas ministry officials generated most of the curriculum documents in the past, more recently there has been a tendency to use curriculum committees comprised of teachers. In many provinces, the burden of writing course outlines has been shifted to local boards.

In their publication on provincial music curriculum documents, Shand and Bartel (1993) noted that, for those interested in studying music education in Canada, published curriculum documents are rich sources of information. 'While not all teachers actually *follow* the guideline set forth by provincial ministries or departments of education, the published documents *do* reveal the orientation of provincial officials and leading music educators of a given time' (p. ix). They also pointed out that the amount of leadership assumed by provincial authorities varies considerably from province to province: 'In Newfoundland, for example,' the Department of Education provides very detailed guidance for local teachers, and even publishes collections of songs for use at specific grade levels. In Ontario, on the other hand, the Ministry of Education provides guidelines and some sample approaches, but more responsibility for curriculum development is given to local boards of education, many of which produce their own curriculum documents' (*ibid.*).

Some of the large city boards have now discontinued their director of music positions and have dismantled their centralized music departments. In some cases, music supervisors have been replaced by arts coordinators or curriculum resource personnel. Typically, such changes have been implemented as part of administrative restructuring in times of financial restraint. This has led to increased lobbying for music education. In 1992 a Coalition for Music Education in Canada was founded. Members represent a wide range of national music education-based associations as well as organizations from almost every province in the country and include educators, industry representatives, artists and performers, parents and music lovers across the country.

Teachers and administrators are still interested in sharing ideas about music teaching and continue to look for opportunities to meet. CMEA national conventions played an important role in this sharing for over three decades, beginning in 1960, but have now been suspended because of budget challenges. The organization publishes a quarterly journal, the *Canadian Music Educator*, which assists in keeping teachers in touch with one another. The organization also produces a series of books containing articles on music education research and the biennial series *Research to Practice*.[1] Other specialized groups (Orff, Kodály, band and various choral organizations) hold national meetings and many Canadian music teachers take part in international meetings, including those of ISME.

In 2005 a pan-Canadian music education think tank meeting entitled *Music Education in Canada: What is the State of the Art?* was organized at the University of Western Ontario. The idea for this gathering had been discussed by Canadians attending ISME meetings in previous years who missed the opportunity to get together for national conferences as they had in the past. Music educators from across the country were invited to attend and address the question posed in the title of the gathering. Discussions involved a number of issues facing music education in Canada including curricular concerns as well as a 'cross-Canada' panel of reports of the current state of music programmes in the various provinces. Subsequent gatherings have been organized (St John's, NL, in 2007 and Victoria, BC, in 2009). *From Sea to Sea: Perspectives on Music Education in Canada* (Veblen and Beynon 2007), is an e-book that brings together several reports and articles that were presented at the first symposium (see Coalition for Music Education in Canada). Other publications, both hard copy and web based, are being planned.

Today, some type of music instruction is included in the programme of studies for Grades K–6 in most Canadian schools but who undertakes the teaching – classroom teachers or music specialists – varies from region to region. The study of music is usually optional for other grade levels but some regions have mandated music classes up to Grade 8 or 9. Many differences in music teaching continue to exist among schools in the ten provinces and three territories, particularly in budgeting, curricula, scheduling and the training and certification of teachers, as well as the kinds of activities and the quality of musical experience available to students. Although some individuals mention the negative aspects of this fact, not all agree with that opinion and some feel that it allows teachers to develop programmes that better suit their particular jurisdictions. In speaking about situations in countries in which teachers have little say in the development of curriculum for their nation, Paul Woodford (2005) comments that Canadian music teachers are fortunate 'in part because education remains a provincial and not a federal jurisdiction ... Provincial ministries of education sometimes collaborate on curriculum reform, but Canada does not have a government sanctioned national music curriculum set of standards, or standardized assessment regime for music education' (p. 65).

After discussing both the English National Music Curriculum and the National Standards for Music Education in the United States, Woodford clarifies the distinctiveness of the Canadian approach: 'Although subject to many of the same reforms as their American and British counterparts, including at the provincial level an increased reliance on standardized (and other conservative) curricula coupled with a corresponding emphasis on accountability, most Canadian music teachers remain wary of the idea of a national music curriculum or set of standards' (*ibid.*). Given the variety of school music policies and practice in Canada – from both a historical and a contemporary perspective – diversity may well be one of the distinctive aspects that has and will continue to characterize music education.[2]

Notes

[1] For more detailed information, see Canadian Music Educators' Association website, www.cmea.ca.

[2] For a more detailed discussion of the development of school music in each province and a more in-depth reference list the reader is encouraged to consult Green and Vogan's (1991) study in which the 'evolution of school music [in Canada] is portrayed within a cultural milieu which comprises many aspects of musical activity in an emerging network of national and provincial institutions, community programs, and agencies of government support' (Green and Vogan 1991: Prologue).

References

Brault, D. (1977), 'A history of the Ontario Music Educators' Association (1919–1974)' (unpublished PhD dissertation, University of Rochester).

Canadian Music Educators' Association, www.cmea.ca.

Coalition for Music Education in Canada, www.coalitionformusiced.ca/html/sec1-about/about.php.

Cringan, A. T. (1888), *The Canadian Music Course*. Toronto: Canadian Publishing Co.

Davey, E. (1977), 'The development of undergraduate music curricula at the University of Toronto, 1918–68' (unpublished PhD dissertation, University of Toronto).

Green, J. P. (1974), 'A proposed doctoral program in music for Canadian universities with specific recommendations for specialization in music education' (unpublished PhD dissertation, University of Rochester).

Green, J. P. and Vogan, N. F. (1991), *Music Education in Canada: A Historical Account.* Toronto: University of Toronto Press.

Kallmann, H. (1960), *A History of Music in Canada, 1534–1914.* Toronto: University of Toronto Press.

Kallman, H. and Potvin, G. (eds) (1992), *Encyclopedia of Music in Canada* (2nd edn). Toronto: University of Toronto Press.

Keillor, E. (2006), *Music in Canada: Capturing Landscape and Diversity.* Montreal and Kingston: McGill-Queens University Press.

Proctor, G. (1980), 'Canada', in Sadie, S. (ed.), *New Grove Dictionary of Music and Musicians.* London: Macmillan, pp. 35–6.

Sefton, H. F. (1869), *Three-Part Songs for the Use of Pupils of the Public Schools of Canada.* Toronto: James Campbell & Sons.

Sefton, H. F. (1871), *A Manual of Vocal Music.* Toronto: Hunter Rose.

Shand, P. M. and Bartel, L. R. (1993), *A Guide to Provincial Music Curriculum Documents Since 1980.* Toronto: Canadian Music Education Research Centre, University of Toronto.

Tomkins, G. S. (1986), *A Common Countenance: Stability and Change in the Canadian Curriculum.* Scarborough, ON: Prentice-Hall Canada.

Trowsdale, G. C. (1962), 'A history of public school music in Ontario' (unpublished DEd dissertation, University of Toronto).

Trowsdale, G. C. (1970), 'Vocal music in the common schools of Upper Canada: 1846–76', *Journal of Research in Music Education*, 18, (4), 340–54.

Tufts, J. W. and Holt, H. E. (1883), *The Normal Music Course.* Boston, MA: D. Alperton & Co.

Veblen, K. and Benyon, C. (eds) (2007), *From Sea to Sea: Perspectives on Music Education in Canada.* London, ON: University of Western Ontario e-book.

Vogan, N. F. (1979), 'A history of public school music in the province of New Brunswick 1872–1939' (unpublished PhD dissertation, University of Rochester).

Vogan, N. F. (1986), 'Music education in nineteenth and early twentieth century New Brunswick', in M. Fancy (ed.), *Art and Music in New Brunswick Symposium Proceedings.* Sackville, NB: Centre for Canadian Studies, Mt Allison University, pp. 19–33.

Vogan, N. F. (1988), 'Music instruction in Nova Scotia before 1914', in J. Beckwith and A. Hall (eds), *Musical Canada: Words and Music Honouring Helmut Kallmann.* Toronto: University of Toronto Press, pp. 71–8.

Vogan, N. (1993), 'Music education in the Maritimes between the wars: a period of transition', in G. Davies (ed.), *Myth and Milieu: Atlantic Literature and Culture, 1918–1939.* Fredericton, NB: Acadiensis Press, pp. 77–86.

Woodford, P. G. (1988), *We Love the Place, O Lord: A History of the Written Musical Tradition of Newfoundland and Labrador to 1949.* St John's, NL: Creative Publishers.

Woodford, P. G. (2005), *Democracy and Music Education; Liberalism, Ethics, and the Politics of Practice.* Bloomington, IN: Indiana University Press.

9

United States of America: Reflections on the development and effectiveness of compulsory music education

Jere T. Humphreys

This chapter consists of an overview of the history of music in compulsory schooling in the United States of America. There are sections on the colonial period, the common school movement, compulsory schooling and the modern era, followed by conclusions.

A few points should be kept in mind. First, the configuration of the British colonies in North America shifted several times before they became states after the Revolutionary War with Great Britain (1775–83). Second, jurisdiction over education transferred from the colonies to the states after nationhood was achieved, not to the federal government. Specifically, the *10th Amendment to the Constitution of the United States* reads: 'The powers not delegated to the United States by the Constitution, nor prohibited by it to the States, are reserved to the States respectively, or to the people' (*The Constitution*, 1787/1791). Third, individual colonies and states were influenced by each other's laws and practices. Finally, in most instances the term compulsory schooling is employed in this chapter rather than compulsory education, because the latter refers to educational outcomes and the former to physical attendance.

Colonial America

The roots of modern, compulsory schooling can be traced to sixteenth-century Protestant reforms in Europe. The English 'poor laws', enacted soon thereafter (1563 and 1601), became the basis for early education legislation in the British colonies of North America (see Kotin and Aikman 1980; Melton 1988; Rothbard 1974).

The colony at Massachusetts Bay (now Boston), settled by English Calvinists (Puritans) beginning in 1630, enacted the first education law in the

New World in 1642. This law compelled education for children of all social and economic strata in both academic and vocational subjects. It placed the burden of education on parents and the masters of indentured servant children and thus compelled education but not schooling. However, subsequent laws and amendments enacted in 1647 and 1648 required the provision of education and schooling, respectively, and thereby affirmed the right of the state (colony) to determine the content and scope of education and to expend public funds for those purposes (Jernegan 1918; Kotin and Aikman 1980). The laws of the colony at Boston soon prevailed throughout Massachusetts.

All the (largely Calvinist) New England colonies, except for religiously heterogeneous Rhode Island, adopted compulsory and other education and school laws within 30 years of the enactment of the 1642 law. These early New England colonial laws differed from the earlier Protestant reform and English poor laws in their provision for the education and training of all children, not just the indigent. More generally, scholars believe that the statutes and acts regarding schooling from early Reformation Germany to the Puritans in New England 'were the work of religious oligarchies' (Jernegan 1919a: 24).

Scholars could have mentioned that the first permanent British colony in North America, at Plymouth, Massachusetts (1620), was slow to enact school laws perhaps because its inhabitants were lightly educated religious separatists who had lived for a decade in Leiden, Holland (1609–20), a city then known throughout Europe for its religious tolerance. At the other end of the continuum, the larger colony at Boston was characterized by religious homogeneity and relatively high levels of education and it became the New World's early leader in universal education and compulsory schooling. More generally, Cremin (1970: 92) maintained that 'schooling' in the British colonies of North America 'was viewed as a device for promoting uniformity'.

The North American colonies outside of New England followed suit to varying degrees, including the Quaker-influenced colonies of Pennsylvania and New Jersey and the former Dutch colony of New York. Maryland and (Anglican) Virginia and colonies further south passed compulsory education legislation early on, but they neither expanded the English poor laws model to cover all children nor established public schools (Kotin and Aikman 1980).

After what had been a strong beginning for education in New England, and to a lesser extent in the middle and southern colonies (Jernegan 1919b, 1920), compulsory school laws were weakened after the protracted Indian Wars broke out in New England in 1675 and because of frontier conditions resulting from the expanding geographical perimeters of settlement and increasing religious and cultural heterogeneity. Only Connecticut retained relatively strong compulsory school laws throughout the colonial era, while the other colonies generally maintained them only for indigent children (Kotin and Aikman 1980).

Music education in colonial America

European-style music instruction in what is now the United States was begun by Spanish Catholic priests following Hernando Coronado's expedition to the present state of New Mexico in 1540. Thereafter the Spaniards taught music to Spanish and Native American children in dozens of missions in the (present) southwestern United States (Britton 1958). From that point onward, most if not all groups that settled in North America provided organized music instruction. These countless influences notwithstanding, the early British Calvinist colonists of New England played a major role in the establishment of practices in music and education.

The most common form of group musical activity in colonial New England was congregational singing in the Calvinist churches. John Calvin had directed that music play a prominent role in the church service and that the musical aspects of the service be simple enough to allow participation by ordinary churchgoers. Toward those ends, he had eschewed the use of professional musicians and musical instruments in the church service.

Calvin had also commissioned the first 'psalter', a musical setting of the biblical *Psalms of David* for use in church by lay choirs and congregations. After its publication in Geneva in 1562, the (popularly called) French Psalter was translated into several languages. The Dutch Psalter by Ainsworth, brought to the New World by the first settlers at Plymouth, and the English Psalter by Sternhold and Hopkins, brought by the settlers at Boston, were musically inferior to the original. The English Psalter was further simplified and diminished in quality when it was published in Boston in 1640, only 10 years after the first settlers arrived there – the first book published in British North America. Popularly called *The Bay Psalm Book* (after Massachusetts Bay), it contained no musical notation until the ninth edition (1698). The New England Calvinists' simple, egalitarian musical practices and frontier conditions that prevented mass instruction in music and the technological means of printing musical notation led to an alarming deterioration in the quality of congregational singing from the arrival of the first permanent settlers in 1620 throughout the remainder of that century (Birge 1966; Britton 1958, 1961, 1966).

Early in the eighteenth century the singing school arose to address the poor quality of congregational singing and to provide social outlets for the colonists. These schools were commercial classes led by amateur, largely self-taught, mostly itinerant singing masters, many of whom produced instructional materials in the form of tunebooks. The first two tunebooks appeared in 1721, both compiled by New England Calvinist ministers. These and hundreds of later tunebooks contained theoretical introductions describing aspects of notation and singing techniques, followed by 'tunes' compiled from various sources (Birge 1966; Britton 1958, 1966).

Some tunebook compilers wrote some of their own music, including the most famous composer and singing school master of the revolutionary period, William Billings (1746–1800) of Boston. One of Billings' six published tunebooks, *The New England Psalm Singer*, contained all original music composed by Billings, including his patriotic tune 'Chester'. Billings called King George of England a tyrant in the preface of the book, which was published on the eve of the revolution in 1770. Except during the revolutionary period, when there was heightened patriotism and significantly reduced immigration from Europe, most music used in the singing schools was based on simplified European folk and art music. Many other tunes used during the singing schools era were religious in nature, reflecting the original purpose of the singing schools and tunebooks: the improvement of congregational singing (Birge 1966).

The singing schools, which began in New England and eventually spread south and west, provided the basis for public school music in the first half of the nineteenth century, after which they declined in popularity. Although they were supported by participant fees, not public funds, singing schools were open to the public. The teaching methods appear to have been eclectic. One notable original teaching innovation was shape note notation, where each degree of the scale was represented by a different shaped note head. This system appeared in Boston at the end of the eighteenth century, after the revolution but well before music entered public schools, and came into widespread use before giving way to traditional notation (Britton, 1966).

The New England settlers also played instruments and sang outside the church (Britton 1966) and we cannot rule out the possibility that musically inclined teachers led school children in singing during the colonial and early federal periods. Whatever the case, substantial evidence about the poor quality of congregational singing throughout the seventeenth and eighteenth centuries suggests that any music instruction that occurred in schools, homes and churches was insufficient to maintain acceptable standards in congregational singing.

The common school movement

The number of public and private schools appears to have increased faster than the population from the late seventeenth century through the revolution in the late eighteenth century (Cremin 1970), but the number and prevalence of laws requiring schools or school attendance declined during that period. Soon after the revolution Massachusetts passed the first state-wide law requiring the establishment of schools (Rothbard 1974). After that, especially during the common (i.e. universal) school era from 1830–65 (Binder 1974), the struggle continued within what had become the traditional dual system: public schools for the poor versus (mostly church-related) private schools.

During this period most New England states established free tax-supported schools, the middle and 'western' (e.g. Ohio) states followed New England, and the southern states, except North Carolina, retained the dual system (Butts and Cremin 1953).

Free public elementary schools became the norm by the middle of the nineteenth century, due in part to the public's optimistic belief that schools and other social agencies could improve conditions and help pave the way toward a brighter future for citizens of many types. Paralleling this optimism were fears over social problems resulting from immigration, industrialization and urbanization. Industrialization provided jobs for millions of new immigrants, huge numbers of whom had arrived not from the traditional origination countries of England, Scotland, Germany and Holland, but from Eastern and Southern Europe. These new immigrants tended not only to be poor and uneducated, but they looked and acted differently too (Everhart 1977). Other immigrants were viewed with suspicion due to their Roman Catholic religion (Greenbaum 1974), including the large numbers who emigrated from Ireland during the famine years in that country (1846–51).

Ultimately 'it took alliances of educators, Protestant ministers, social reformers, businessmen, politicians, and even concerned parents to take this strange mixture of hopes, fears, contradictions, and paradoxes, and meld it into legislative action resulting in the evolution of state-supported school systems' (Everhart 1977: 510). Advocates, led by Horace Mann, overcame huge obstacles in their quest to promote the development of universal schooling (see Binder 1974).

Music in the common schools

Beginning in the 1820s, when the common school movement was gaining momentum, various individuals, some of whom had observed successful music teaching in Europe by followers of the Swiss pedagogue Heinrich Pestalozzi, began to advocate adding music to the common school curriculum. Some of the strongest promotion efforts occurred in Boston, led by school reformer William Woodbridge, musician/educator Lowell Mason and the Boston Academy of Music and its president, Samuel Elliot, who became mayor of Boston (Birge 1966).

Lowell Mason began teaching music on a formal basis in an upper elementary school in Boston on 30 August 1838, an event celebrated today as the beginning of permanent public school music instruction in the United States. Among the many justifications for adding music to the curriculum, religious motives appear to have predominated (Miller 1989). Thereafter, music spread gradually until it became a required subject in many American cities by the end of the Civil War (1865) and in most American elementary schools (Grades 1–8) by the end of the century. Regular classroom teachers provided most of the music instruction, but increasingly in larger cities this instruction was overseen by trained music supervisors. The acquisition of sight singing skills was the primary objective because many music supervisors were former singing school teachers and because little live music was available to the largely rural populace before the invention of electronic reproduction devices. The focus on sight singing notwithstanding, nineteenth-century school music education was what today would be called general music because it was for general students (Birge 1966; Humphreys 1995).

The first music instruction book intended for public school use was co-authored by Lowell Mason and published in 1831 in anticipation of regular public school music instruction. Progressively-graded music textbook series began to appear in the second half of the nineteenth century. The most prominent series were dedicated to one side or the other of the 'note versus rote' controversy, which had begun in Calvinist churches in the seventeenth century and contributed to the emergence of singing schools and tunebooks (Birge 1966).

Many of the first school music supervisors continued the singing masters' practice of teaching simplified European-style folk and art music. Also like the singing masters, early school music supervisors were self-taught and or trained in singing schools and some had attended summer 'musical conventions' such as those offered by Lowell Mason at the Boston Academy of Music. Although Mason and other early leading music educators advocated Pestalozzian methods, like their singing master predecessors they generally eschewed European methods such as tonic sol-fa in favour of eclecticism. Most classroom teachers were trained in normal schools, first private and then public, in which music was a required and often popular subject (Heller and Humphreys 1991).

The common school movement provided universally-available schools, some of which offered music instruction, but many children did not attend school or enrolled for only short periods of time. Music instruction in schools was preceded and then paralleled by other types of musical experiences, such as vocal and instrumental lessons and classes in conservatories, music academies, colleges and private homes and studios; as well as community choirs, choral societies, orchestras and brass bands (Humphreys 1995).

Compulsory schooling

Colonial and common school legislation had provided for some forms of education, but neither had stipulated specific attendance requirements nor sufficient freedom from labour to permit regular attendance (Kotin and Aikman 1980). By the mid-nineteenth century, however, laws and agencies aimed toward social control were emerging as a result of immigration, industrialization and urbanization. These phenomena contributed to growing social problems such as crime, poverty and general social chaos, which many immigrants had sought to leave behind them, and to the enactment of truancy (i.e. anti-vagrancy) laws in many states, which established a legal basis for compulsory school laws (Everhart 1977; Kotin and Aikman 1980). All these factors contributed to the 'increasing centralization and bureaucratization of school systems, particularly ... in large urban areas' (Everhart 1977: 511). The centralization of school systems was probably the biggest single impetus for new compulsory school laws (see also Katz 1971; Tyack 1966).

First the common non-compulsory and then compulsory schools were 'viewed as a means of shaping the right character and implanting the right morals for the responsible exercise of freedom – in other words, to produce citizens for the state' (Spring 1974: 140; see also Friedenberg 1965). Also important were a 'majoritarian mood' (Burgess 1976: 202) and the popular concept of a 'melting pot' nation that would 'Americanize' immigrants with 'compulsory school attendance laws' intended as 'means to standardize American behavior' (Richardson 1980: 155). Compulsory schools fulfilled what some today call 'custodial' functions (e.g. Cremin 1980; Ensign 1969; Jorgensen 1997; Kotin and Aikman 1980). Other institutions and legislation aimed toward social control began to appear as well, including child labour laws, which went hand in hand with compulsory school laws. Thus, fears over rapidly increasing immigration, industrialization and urbanization resulted in shifts in the motivations behind compulsory schools and other agencies: from religious to those of social control.

For all these reasons, states began to enact new compulsory schooling statutes in 1852, with Massachusetts once more leading the way. All persons responsible for children aged between 8–14 were required to send them to school for at least 12 weeks each year (6 of them consecutive) (Cook 1912). These statutes were one manifestation of the public's growing confidence in the power of education to ensure the continuation of democracy and reduce social problems, confidence that lasted from the mid-nineteenth century until well into the twentieth (Everhart 1977; Kotin and Aikman 1980). All states and territories outside the south and Alaska passed compulsory school legislation between 1852 and the end of the nineteenth century and all southern states did so by 1918 (Department of Education 2004).

Despite their rapid spread, the new compulsory school laws were conspicuously ineffective in most instances (Everhart 1977). For example, before the Civil War, African-Americans generally had not been permitted to attend school in the south (see Binder 1974; Bullock 1967). Other formal exceptions to the laws were common, particularly when a child's family pleaded poverty, but more often the laws were simply ignored (Ensign 1969). In 1890, by which time the majority of states and territories had passed compulsory legislation, Connecticut became the first to enact a full-time compulsory school attendance law with enforcement provisions; by 1900, 30 states had enacted laws that required attendance for specified periods of time for certain age groups. The southern states did likewise between 1900 and 1918, although some of those statutes included local 'opt-out' provisions for towns and counties (Kotin and Aikman 1980). Also beginning in the second half of the nineteenth century, in situations in which federal laws prevailed, the federal government required school attendance for Native Americans (Handel and Humphreys 2005).

At no time in the history of the colonies or states was compulsory schooling supported enthusiastically by all segments of the population, but over time the public's faith in education had gradually shifted to the school as an institution (Everhart 1977). John Dewey's (1916) belief that universal schooling was crucial to democracy was shared by many, and the surprisingly low levels of literacy among conscripted soldiers in the First World War led to increased enforcement of compulsory school laws (Everhart 1977; Kotin and Aikman 1980).

Music in compulsory schools

Music instruction during the common school era (1830–1865) was compulsory in the minority of schools where it was part of the curriculum, at least for the small percentage of children who attended school regularly. As compulsory school attendance laws and their enforcement became more prevalent and as music instruction spread to most of the nation's schools, music became a *de facto* compulsory subject, albeit unevenly in different states and localities.

School music changed significantly around the beginning of the twentieth century for two major reasons. First, general music changed as a result of new technology: initially the player piano, next the phonograph, then the radio. These inventions made feasible the teaching of 'music appreciation' through music-listening activities and they provided ready access to music for people who lacked access to live music. From about 1910 the phonograph played a particularly important role in general music's shift from a nearly exclusive focus on sight singing to a mixed approach that included listening and performing, vocally and with newly available toy instruments (Humphreys 1995).

The second factor was the powerful progressive education movement, which evolved in Europe and North America in response to the industrial revolution. Progressives sought to make the schools 'levers of social reform' and to prepare students for what they foresaw as an adult life with copious amounts of leisure time. The movement led to expanded ideas about the purposes of schooling and thus to an expanded curriculum, in part to serve the increasing numbers of students attending high schools (Humphreys 1988).

Music education benefited from this public confidence and belief in the public schools during the progressive era, a period when 'devotion to education was strong' (Everhart 1977: 521). Specifically, during this period general music took on its modern forms; the most distinctive form of music education in North America, the ensembles, entered the schools and flourished; and both general music and ensembles developed stronger roles in school and community life. These changes occurred during a period of major educational reform, much like vocal music instruction was added to the curriculum during the common school movement (Humphreys 1995).

While classroom teachers continued to receive musical training in normal schools, during the late-nineteenth century some music supervisors began to receive specialized training in summer institutes sponsored by music textbook publishers. A specialized normal school for music educators was founded by Julia E. Crane at Potsdam, New York, in 1882. By the early decades of the twentieth century, when states were partially enforcing their compulsory schooling laws, 'public school music' departments were cropping up in many teachers' colleges and some universities. These departments supplanted textbook publishers' institutes in the production of general music teachers by the end of the First World War. The earliest orchestra and band directors in the schools were vocal music teachers, teachers of other subjects, professional performers, and students. However, the college- and university-based music departments began to turn out trained instrumental teachers during the 1920s (Humphreys 1989, 1995).

The modern era

Direct federal initiatives in education began during the late 1950s after the launching of the Soviet space satellite Sputnik. Federal initiatives in the arts, including arts education, began in 1962 under the Kennedy administration (see Gauthier 2003). Most of the responsibility and resources continued to derive from the states, but federal legislation and judicial rulings helped bring about changes in specific aspects of education. Among the most significant changes were the US Supreme Court's decision outlawing racially segregated schools (1954) and Congressional legislation that provided for students with special needs (1975). Other influences, such as accrediting agencies and subject matter organizations (e.g. the Music Educators' National Conference), contribute to the enterprise in many ways and the states continue to influence each other.

Music education in the modern era

Currently, ongoing educational reforms are under way in all 50 states. Federal legislation called 'No Child Left Behind', through which funds can be awarded or withheld based on various criteria imposed at the state level, emphasizes standardized test scores and is generally seen as detrimental to school music programmes.

All 50 states compel school attendance, typically through to age 16. All states also require music instruction for at least a portion of the time in Grades K–6, but for an average of less than one hour per week, with some also requiring it for portions of Grades 7–8. Most secondary schools offer ensembles – sometimes orchestras, usually choirs and almost always bands, and, in some cases, other types of group as well – but ensemble participation is virtually never required. Approximately 25 per cent of secondary students participate in elective ensembles. Thus, general music is compulsory, whereas ensemble participation is not.

Most public school music teachers hold university degrees and state-issued certificates aimed toward the teaching of music. Some 84 per cent of American elementary schools are served by credentialed music teachers, by far the largest percentage in history, and nearly all public high schools employ one or more credentialed ensemble directors. General music series books, and to lesser extent band method books, include music from wider, more diverse geographical, ethnic and cultural sources than ever before. School and university music ensembles also perform a wider array of music of higher quality, much of it written by competent and in some cases even prominent composers (Humphreys 1995; Wang and Humphreys 2009).

Surveys show that the American public overwhelmingly supports music in schools, but consistently ranks music at or near the bottom in importance among school subjects. This means that the public wants music in the schools, but not too much of it, much like the often quoted dictum paraphrased from Aristotle's writings: 'All gentlemen play the flute, but no gentleman plays it well' (for related writing by Aristotle, see *Politica*, Book VIII (Mark 1982)). There is also evidence that students, especially boys, are more favourable toward their general music classes in the lower elementary grades than in the higher grades.

Conclusions

Today, the vast majority of American elementary schools offer general music; a majority of secondary schools offer elective ensembles and a few offer other specialized secondary music courses; and many middle schools offer both general music and ensembles, sometimes required and sometimes not. Therefore, it could be said that music is compulsory only in the lower grades, for an average exposure of slightly less than one hour per week, whereas music is not compulsory in the upper grades despite the fact that young people are compelled to attend school, until age 16 in most states. Thus, music is offered in compulsory schools but in the upper grades it is not a compulsory subject.

Questions remain, however, about the effects of compulsory education and music education. For example, there is evidence that compulsory attendance legislation may not have increased school attendance in the nineteenth century, at least not before the laws were enforced (Landes and Solmon 1972). More troubling are questions about the results of compulsory schooling aside from actual school attendance. Early critics worried about the loss of privacy and individualism inherent in universal, compulsory schooling (see Cremin 1961) and since the 1940s sociologists have seen the schools as perpetuators of existing social classes (Spring 1972). Indeed, studies in political socialization have shown that children learn in elementary school to equate good citizenship with obeying the law – that is, with passivity and obedience as opposed to active citizenship (Hess 1968; Spring 1974; Tyack 1966). Studies also show that local school boards tend to be dominated by the upper classes, again often in the interests of the status quo (Counts 1969; see also Spring 1972).

In addition to problems that can result from people being compelled to do things against their will, most schools still utilize an industrial-era paradigm. Because the nation has long since moved beyond industrialism and into the information age, this outdated paradigm might be working against student achievement in and of itself. In music, one could argue that the ensemble format itself is a conservative paradigm taken from military (band), church (choir) and elite cultural (orchestra) traditions (Britton 1958; Humphreys 1995, 1999).

There is little solid evidence about the outcomes of the approximately 10 years of compulsory schooling on American students, or on society as a whole, except that it is probably fair to credit schools with the nation's very high rate of reading and writing literacy. However, tests of knowledge of subjects other than reading and writing show increasingly dismal results. Whereas public schools were once seen as equalizers for less fortunate elements of society, later commentators began to see them as part of the problem. Some see education as being not about what children need, but instead about the perceived needs of society – that the current system of schooling has been helpful to some children, but 'its long-range effect has been to restrict the options by which most children can be educated' (Everhart 1977: 526). For example, Small (1977) believes that the university music major curriculum limits students' musical options.

Surviving evidence does not permit comparisons in musical achievement among children or the general populace before and after the advent of music in compulsory schooling. We cannot determine how many people learned music or much about what they learned or how they learned it beyond the contents of the singing school tunebooks (Britton 1966). However, much like many children learned to read and write and a few to 'cipher' before the passage of compulsory attendance laws, some children and adults learned to sing and play instruments without the benefit of formal schooling. Judging from the increasing instrument and sheet music sales, number of magazines devoted to musical topics (Fellimger and Shepard 1986), and other indicators, including the plethora of singing schools, choral societies, bands, orchestras and widespread parlour piano and organ playing and singing and other musical activities, we can conclude that music learning outside the schools was ubiquitous during the eighteenth and especially the nineteenth centuries (Birge 1966; Humphreys 1995).

In the modern era, results from the three nation-wide assessments of achievement in general music are extremely discouraging (National Assessment of Educational Progress 1974, 1981; Persky, Sandene and Askew 1998). Documented contributing factors include too little class time and, in the case of classroom teachers teaching music, inadequate teacher qualifications. What has not been discussed as a possible factor in these dismal results is compulsory schooling itself (including most general music), with its emphasis on middle and lower achieving students and therefore minimal standards of achievement (Humphreys 2006).

Perhaps not surprisingly, the elective ensembles are a different story. On the negative side, the ensembles serve only a minority of students, deal with limited types of music and focus primarily on performance skills, not composition, arranging, conducting, listening or other musical activities. Furthermore, school music experiences do not seem to extend into adulthood for most participants (Humphreys, May and Nelson 1992). On the positive side, ensembles offer one of the relatively few truly challenging experiences in schools for students with high levels of ability and motivation (Humphreys 2006) and there is ample evidence that the performance quality of school performing ensembles has improved markedly over the century of their existence. Many teachers and some scholars also attribute significant extra-musical benefits to ensemble participation (Humphreys, May and Nelson 1992).

As for repertoire, it was the colonial singing school masters who began the non-working practice of trying to 'reform' the musical tastes of the American public (Britton 1958). Unfortunately, recalcitrant music teacher education institutions have continued the practice as evidenced by their failure to train pre-service teachers in popular and non-Western music (Humphreys 2002, 2004; Wang and Humphreys 2009). Despite these failures, however, persistent attempts by individual teachers, professional organizations and the profession at large to improve the musical repertoire in schools have met with some success.

The American public has lost confidence in the nation's public schools and a few alternatives to the current system of schooling and education are being promoted, such as charter schools and home schooling. However, no serious attempts to discontinue compulsory education or schooling loom on the horizon today. On the contrary, the national standards (actually curriculum guides) and various forms of legislation are attempts to impose even more stringent 'top-down' control over the education enterprise than existed in the past (Humphreys 2002), a phenomenon that continues as of this writing.

It is probably fair to say that compulsory general music exhibits many of the same failings of compulsory education as a whole, including minimal standards of expectations and achievement and lack of student motivation, problems that become worse at successively higher grade levels. Secondary school music ensembles, by way of contrast, are not compulsory even in compulsory schools. Due at least partially to their voluntary, non-compulsory nature, the ensembles appear to be more successful in fulfilling their purposes.

References

Aristotle (1982), 'Politica, book VIII', in M. L. Mark (ed.), *Source Readings in Music Education History*. New York: Schirmer Books, pp. 9–17.

Binder, F. M. (1974), *The Age of the Common School, 1830–1865*. New York: John Wiley & Sons.

Birge, E. B. (1966), *History of Public School Music in the United States*. Reston, VA: Music Educators National Conference. [First published in 1928, revised in 1937.]

Britton, A. P. (1958), 'Music in early American public education: a historical critique', in N. B. Henry (ed.), *Basic Concepts in Music Education, Fifty-Seventh Yearbook of the National Society for the Study of Education*, Part I, Chicago: University of Chicago Press, pp. 195–207.

Britton, A. P. (1961), 'Music education: an American specialty', in P. H. Lang (ed.), *One Hundred Years of Music in America*. New York: Grosset & Dunlap, pp. 211–29.

Britton, A. P. (1966), 'The singing school movement in the United States', in *International Musicological Society, Report of the 8th Congress*, vol. I. Kassel: Bärenreiter, pp. 89–99.

Bullock, H. A. (1967), *A History of Negro Education in the South: From 1619 to the Present*. Cambridge, MA: Harvard University Press.

Burgess, C. (1976), 'The goddess, the school book, and compulsion', *Harvard Educational Review*, 46, 199–216.

Butts, R. F. and Cremin, L. A. (1953), *A History of Education in American Culture*. New York: Henry Holt & Co.

Constitution of the United States (adopted 17 September 1787), *Bill of Rights, Amendment 10–Powers of the States and People* (ratified 15 December 1791).

Cook, W. A. (1912), 'A brief survey of the development of compulsory education in the United States', *The Elementary School Teacher*, 12, 331–35.

Counts, G. S. (1969), *The Social Composition of Boards of Education*. New York: Arno Press. [Reprint from original, Chicago: University of Chicago Press, 1927.]

Cremin, L. A. (1961), *The Transformation of the School: Progressivism in American Education, 1876–1957*. New York: Alfred A. Knopf.

Cremin, L. A. (1970), *American Education: The Colonial Experience, 1607–1783*. New York: Harper & Row.

Cremin, L. A. (1980), *American Education: The National Experience, 1783–1876*. New York: Harper & Row.

Department of Education, National Center for Educational Statistics (2004), *Digest of Education Statistics*. Washington, DC: US Department of Education.

Dewey, J. (1916), *Democracy and Education*. New York: Macmillan.

Ensign, F. C. (1969 [1929]), *Compulsory School Attendance and Child Labor*. New York: Arno Press & The New York Times.

Everhart, R. B. (1977), 'From universalism to usurpation: an essay on the antecedents to compulsory school attendance legislation', *Review of Educational Research*, 47, 499–530.

Fellinger, I. and Shepard, J. (1986), 'Periodicals', in S. Sadie and H. W. Hitchcock (eds), *The New Grove Dictionary of American Music*. New York: Oxford University Press, pp. 505–535.

Friedenberg, E. Z. (1965), *Coming of Age in America: Growth and Acquiescence*. New York: Random House.

Gauthier, D. R. (2003), 'The arts and the government: the Camelot years, 1959–1968', *Journal of Historical Research in Music Education*, 24, 143–63.

Greenbaum, W. (1974), 'America in search of a new ideal: an essay on the rise of pluralism', *Harvard Educational Review*, 44, 411–40.

Handel, G. A. and Humphreys, J. T. (2005), 'The Phoenix Indian School Band, 1894–1930', *Journal of Historical Research in Music Education*, 27, 144–61.

Heller, G. N. and Humphreys, J. T. (1991), 'Music teacher education in America (1753–1840): a look at one of its three sources', *College Music Symposium*, 31, 49–58.

Hess, R. D. (1968), 'Political socialization in the schools', *Harvard Educational Review*, 38, 528–36.

Humphreys, J. T. (1988), 'Applications of science: the age of standardization and efficiency in music education', *Bulletin of Historical Research in Music Education*, 9, 1–21.

Humphreys, J. T. (1989), 'An overview of American public school bands and orchestras before World War II', *Bulletin of the Council for Research in Music Education*, 101, 50–60.

Humphreys, J. T. (1995), 'Instrumental music in American education: in service of many masters', *Journal of Band Research*, 30, 39–70.

Humphreys, J. T. (1999), 'On teaching pigs to sing', www.maydaygroup.org/php/resources/colloquia/VII-humphreys-reenergizing.php.

Humphreys, J. T. (2002), 'Some notions, stories, and tales about music and education in society: the coin's other side', *Journal of Historical Research in Music Education*, 23, 137–57.

Humphreys, J. T. (2004), 'Popular music in the American schools: what the past tells us about the present and the future', in C. X. Rodriguez (ed.), *Bridging the Gap: Popular Music and Music Education*, Reston, VA: MENC, The National Association for Music Education, pp. 91–105.

Humphreys, J. T. (2006), '2006 Senior Researcher Award Acceptance Address: "Observations about music education research in MENC's first and second centuries"', *Journal of Research in Music Education*, 54, 183–202.

Humphreys, J. T., May, W. V. and Nelson, D. J. (1992), 'Music ensembles', in R. Colwell (ed.), *Handbook of Music Teaching and Learning*. New York: Schirmer Books, pp. 651–68.

Jernegan, M. W. (1918), 'Compulsory education in the American colonies: I', *The School Review*, 26, 731–49.

Jernegan, M. W. (1919a), 'Compulsory education in the American colonies: I (continued)', *The School Review*, 27, 24–43.

Jernegan, M. W. (1919b), 'Compulsory education in the southern colonies', *The School Review*, 27, 405–425.

Jernegan, M. W. (1920), 'Compulsory education in the southern colonies: II', *The School Review*, 28, 127–42.

Jorgensen, E. R. (1997), *In Search of Music Education*. Urbana, IL: University of Illinois Press.

Katz, M. B. (1971), *Class, Bureaucracy, and Schools*. New York: Praeger.

Kotin, L. and Aikman, W. F. (1980), *Legal Foundations of Compulsory School Attendance*. Port Washington, NY, and London: National University Publications, Kennikat Press.

Landes, W. M. and Solmon, L. C. (1972), 'Compulsory schooling legislation: an economic analysis of the law and social change in the nineteenth century', *Journal of Economic History*, 32, 54–91.

Melton, J. V. H. (1988), *Absolutism and the Eighteenth-Century Origins of Compulsory Schooling in Prussia and Austria*. Cambridge: Cambridge University Press.

Miller, D. M. (1989), 'The beginnings of music in the Boston Public Schools: decisions of the Boston School Committee in 1837 and 1845 in light of religious and moral concerns of the time' (unpublished PhD dissertation, University of North Texas).

National Assessment of Educational Progress (1974), *The First Music Assessment: An Overview*. Denver, CO: Educational Commission of the States.

National Assessment of Educational Progress (1981), *Music 1971–79: Results from the Second National Music Assessment*. Denver, CO: Educational Commission of the States.

Persky, H., Sandene, B. and Askew, J. (1998), *The NAEP 1997 Arts Report Card* (NCES 1999–486). Washington, DC: US Department of Education.

Richardson, J. G. (1980), 'Variation in date of enactment of compulsory school attendance laws: an empirical inquiry', *Sociology of Education*, 53, 153–63.

Rothbard, M. N. (1974), 'Historical origins', in B. A. Rogge (ed.), *The Twelve-Year Sentence*. LaSalle, IL: Open Court Publishing Company, pp. 11–32.

Small, C. (1977), *Music, Society, Education: An Examination of the Function of Music in Western, Eastern and African Cultures with its Impact on Society and its Use in Education*. New York: Schirmer.

Spring, J. H. (1972), *Education and the Rise of the Corporate State*. Boston, MA: Beacon Press.

Spring, J. H. (1974), 'Sociological and political ruminations', in J. F. Rickenbacker (ed.), *The Twelve-Year Sentence*. LaSalle, IL: Open Court Publishing Company, pp. 139–59.

Tyack, D. (1966), 'Forming the national character: paradox in the educational thought of the revolutionary generation', *Harvard Educational Review*, 36, 29–41.

Wang, J. C. and Humphreys, J. T. (2009), 'Multicultural and popular music content in an American music teacher education program', *International Journal of Music Education: Research*, 27, 19–36.

Part 2

The Americas

B *Latin America*

10

Argentina: From 'música vocal' to 'educación artística: Música'

Ana Lucía Frega, with Alicia de Couve and Claudia Dal Pino

Introduction

From colonial times music education in Latin American territories was associated principally with the Roman Catholic Church, for which music played an important liturgical role. Jesuit and Franciscan priests in the missions and chapel masters in the cities, together with independent music educators, employed music as a means of reinforcing religious and cultural concepts (de Couve, Dal Pino and Frega 1997, 2004; de Couve and Dal Pino 1999).

During the nineteenth century, Spanish colonies in the Americas – from Mexico in the north to those in Central and South America – underwent political revolution which led to their independence. In Argentina, the revolutionary process began in 1810 and culminated with the promulgation of successive national constitutions in 1853 and 1860. Thus a representative, republican and federal system of government was established. Although the role of education was emphasized, by 1869 only 20.2 per cent of children attended school and 77.9 per cent of the population was illiterate.

Music accompanied the revolutionary process and soon after the first patriotic government took charge on 25 May 1810, several songs were composed in order to promote patriotic feelings. Although music was not conceived as a school subject, students sang this repertoire at public celebrations. For example:

[T]he 'Patriotic Song' by López and Parera (the National Anthem) was intoned for the first time in public, the 25th of May 1813 at the Victory Square, near the Pyramid of May, by the pupils of Don Rufino Sanchez' school. (Gesualdo 1961: 133)

In 1822 Antonio Picassarri (1769–1843) and Juan Pedro Esnaola (1808–1878) founded the first music teaching institution in Buenos Aires, the *Escuela de Música y Canto*. Local authorities supported this private enterprise and provided a public building for teaching to take place.

During the nineteenth century, intellectual figures encouraged music education and pointed out its values. For example, in 1832 Juan Bautista Alberdi (1810–1884) lawyer, politician and composer, published *Ensayo de un método nuevo para aprender a tocar el piano con mayor facilidad* (Essay on a new method of learning to play the piano easily) and the *Espíritu de la música a la capacidad de todo el mundo* (The spirit of music within the reach of everybody), both of which promoted the value of musical knowledge. Domingo F. Sarmiento (1811–1888) teacher, politician, journalist, writer and Argentine President, affirmed that:

> Music teaching at school instills discipline. Without music, that is if they do not sing during the marches, there is lack of order. It is important to teach children at an early stage how to memorize sounds, to listen to the intervals and to sing accurately. In order to achieve these aims all pupils must begin each music lesson with the following exercises: the scale, the scale with notes accompanied by manual signs, vocalizing the scales, singing the scale in quavers, and learning the songs that are associated with marching. (Sarmiento 1848: 196, quoted in Sarmiento 1938: 43–4)

Music was taught in several schools around this time. For example, the *Colegio de Pensionadas de Santa Rosa* was opened at San Juan City in 1839 and its programme stated that there were daily music lessons devoted to learning musical notation, playing the piano, applying the methods designed by Muzio Clementi and Juan Bautista Alberdi. Pupils of the *Colegio Filantrópico Bonaerense*, founded in 1843, presented a concert in 1848 playing arrangements of pieces by Carulli, Bellini and Rossini for piano, guitar, violin and flute. There were similar performances by the students of the *Colegio de Niñas de Montserrat* in Buenos Aires in 1848 and of the *Colegio de la Independencia* in Salta City in 1849 (Gesualdo 1961: 323–5).

Compulsory education

Despite Argentina having been conceived as a federation of provinces, a centralized system of government administration emerged in which the politicians looked to European and North American models to consolidate and modernize the country. The government increasingly recruited European immigrants to work in the fields, but many of them decided to settle in the cities. In under 50 years between 1870 and 1915, the population quintupled with considerable diversity of linguistic and cultural backgrounds.

In this context, the First National Pedagogical Congress was organized in 1882 with 250 delegates including the most prominent political and intellectual figures of the time. They debated the ideas and principles that should inform public education. Religious issues generated political conflict; some members of the Congress wanted to include Catholic education in public schools, while others maintained the principle of secular schooling.

As a result of the Congress, legislation approved in 1884 provided compulsory, free and graded primary education for all children between the ages of 6 and 14 (Ley No.1420, www.bnm.me.gov.ar/giga1/normas/5421. pdf). Singing was included as a mandatory subject: '[D]aily lessons at public schools will alternate with breaks, physical training and singing' (Art. 14). Religious education, by way of contrast, could only be provided 'before or after the hours of class' (Art. 8). It was also stipulated that a teacher's diploma would be granted by national or provincial normal schools. Foreign teachers had to revalidate their credentials and had to be competent in Spanish if they wanted to teach in primary public schools (Art. 25). The first normal school had been founded in 1870 in Paraná city in Entre Ríos province under the direction of the American educator George A. Stearns. The training generally lasted for 4 years, and 'song' or 'music' was included in the curriculum.

Introduction of music into compulsory schooling 1884–1920s

Vocal music and its repertoire

Although the official syllabi and training programmes did not include specific objectives for music education at the primary level, it appears from other documentary sources that music was conceived as a means of promoting national identity:

> School singing helped to revive patriotic feeling ... some patriotic songs that had been sung by the people and the Argentine armies in the struggles for freedom arose from their memories. (Consejo Nacional de Educación [CNE] 1913: 10)

But this intention was not always achieved in practice:

> Music, that so important factor for the education of the feelings, was also neglected in primary education. In some schools they sang pieces of operas, in others foreign songs, generally badly translated, and in the rest,

worthless songs that each professor adopted according to his own criterion. As I have personally checked, there were many of these teachers who did not know the National Anthem. (CNE 1913: 10)

In addition to promoting patriotism, music education was highly valued because of its beneficial influence on child development and because it strengthened Spanish as the national language. José María Torres, a well-known educator of the time, pointed out that:

> The song is offered in the schools as a way to vary and to animate the occupations of the children, and exerts a healthful influence on the lungs and the chest. Giving fullness, clarity and extension to the voice, it helps to perfect the choral expression; it prepares the vocal organs to later produce the sounds and the inflections of the foreign languages; and, forming the habit of free and prolonged breathing ... it facilitates elocution, and it tends to correct the defects of the pronunciation. A musical ear, that is the faculty to distinguish and to imitate musical notes, can be cultivated in almost all children ... If vocal music spreads like a branch of obligatory teaching in all the schools of primary education, it would modify with time the unpleasantness of the provincial accent, it would contribute to the homogeneity of the intonation in the national pronunciation, and it would give more melody to our language. (Torres 1887: 23–4)

As far as vocal repertoire was concerned, the National Anthem was the cornerstone. It had been approved by the General Assembly in 1813 but, by the end of the nineteenth century, it had become somewhat problematic. The original manuscript of 1812 by Blas Parera (1778?–1838?) had been lost and so there were several versions of it. But, as José André pointed out in 1927:

> Combined public performances became impossible because the schools under the jurisdiction of the National Council of Education and the Normal Schools of the Ministry of Justice and Public Instruction sang different versions. (*La Nación*, 26 June 1927, in Mondolo 2005)

These problems notwithstanding, the practice of singing the National Anthem became compulsory in all schools, especially in the celebration of the patriotic anniversaries: 'All the schools of the Capital should sing the National Anthem on the morning of May 25th (anniversary of the assumption of the first patriotic government) at 9 a.m. in the squares or avenues in the jurisdiction of each district' (CNE 1913: 36). Moreover: '[I]t was set down that the headmasters should give lectures to the children on diverse topics related to May Week, including ... the origin and adoption of the National Anthem: its poet and its composer' (CNE 1913: 35).

Furthermore, in 1909 the National Council of Education specified that in order to pass Grade 3 of primary school the pupils should know the National Anthem by heart (Circular Nº 31 in Mondolo 2005). It was not until 1944 that the score by Juan Pedro Esnaola (1808–1878), originally published in 1860, was approved as the official version of the Argentine National Anthem.

The National Council of Education approved a number of textbooks and music scores as a syllabus and published the corresponding listing in the periodic government report *El Monitor de la Educación Común* (The monitor of common education). Several musicians composed school songs with particular attention to the range of children's voices. The lyrics were based on moral, national or poetic precepts. For example:

> [T]he credited professor of music of some of the public schools, Mr. Orestes Panizza, has sent us a book containing several school songs ... Those that we have now received are titled 'A la noche' [To the night], 'El canto del Cisne' [The swan song] and 'Vals' [Waltz]. (CNE, *El Monitor de la Educación Común* 1891/92: 271)

An example of a female contributor was Manuela Cornejo de Sánchez (1854–1902) who composed and taught 'El sol de Julio' (The sun of July) – a reference to Argentine Independence Day – at Normal School No. 1 of Salta City in the north of the country in 1900 (Frega 1994). Other composers, such as Gabriel Diez, also made adaptations and arrangements for voice and piano of works by composers such as Donizetti, Handel, Haydn, Verdi and Weber.

These vocal practices in schools appear to have generally achieved satisfactory results, as was stated in this official report: 'In all the schools pupils sing in one or more *parts* ... this was evidence of the good quality of teaching which resulted in the pupils' public performances' (CNE 1938: 57).

As far as musical accompaniments for singing in schools were concerned, it was debated in the National Council of Education in 1893 whether the piano or the harmonium was more appropriate. The opinions of music educators and composers were sought, including Alberto Williams (1862–1952) and Julián Aguirre (1868–1924). They stated that:

> Considering the numerous advantages that the harmonium has over the piano for elementary music teaching, such as the greater prolongation of the sound, the most exact and durable tuning, the reduced cost and size, and, finally, its adoption in the schools of the more advanced countries in Europe, we do not hesitate in indicating to you, as beneficial, the substitution of the pianos of the common schools by the harmonium. We must also add that the execution is easier and less subject to inaccuracies in unskillful hands. (CNE, *El Monitor de la Educación Común* 1893: 143–4)

Although music had not previously been a compulsory subject for adult and rural schools, it was included in their programmes from 1905 to 1911. They provide an interesting listing of vocal activities and repertoire:

> 1) The students will daily sing suitable songs learnt by ear, during such a time so as not to interfere with the instructional subjects. The practice of the National Anthem is compulsory. 2) The National Anthem and the songs 'Saludo a la Bandera' [Greeting to the flag], 'Viva la Patria' [Long live our country], 'El Viejo Hogar Argentino' [Old Argentine home], 'La Canción Nacional' [The national song], 'Himno a Sarmiento' [Hymn to Sarmiento], 'Himno al Árbol' [Hymn to the tree], 'Himno al Trabajo [Hymn to labour] and every other song approved by the National Council of Education are obligatory. (Consejo Nacional de Educación 1938: 119)

Finally, it is remarkable that no evidence has been found of school repertoire based on Argentine folk music or of the use of the guitar in the classroom during the first decades of compulsory music education.

Textbooks and methods

The music curriculum at the turn of the twentieth century, while emphasizing singing, also included musical theory. The approved text books utilized the fixed-doh system of sol-fa, following the tradition of the Italian and French conservatories. The following texts, approved by the National Council of Education in 1889, give some indication of the method: *Abecedario musical* (J. G. Panizza), *Tratado de música* (Saturnino Berón), *Método de solfeo* (Hilarión Eslava), *Método de solfa* (J. G. Guido), *Carteles y método de solfeo* (Gabriel Diez) (CNE, *El Monitor de la Educación Común* Año XI Nº 151 1888/89: 522).

The *Nuevo Método Teórico Práctico de Lectura Musical y de Solfeo* (New theoretical and practical method for music reading and sol-fa) (1877) by Juan Grazioso Panizza (1851–1898) was not only approved by the National Council of Education but also by the Conservatoire of Milan and was used in the choral classes at the Metropolitan Cathedral of Milan as well as in normal and common schools in Buenos City and in the Province of Buenos Aires. In the preface, the author pointed out that:

> [T]he lack of a theoretical and practical treatise on Musical Division and Solfa both easy and suitable to be adopted in the classes of the Normal and Common schools of the Province has induced me to publish this Method. (Panizza 1877: n.p.)

He based his work on those by Hilarión Eslava,[1] Fétis[2] and Panseron[3] and stated:

In this book I attempt to put science within the reach of infants' intelligence, simplifying the study and trying to make it pleasant to the student, to simultaneously follow theory and its application, to induce the pupil to proceed progressively from the first rudiments of music to the theoretical principles of harmony, to be clear and concise. (Panizza 1877: n.p.)

Its contents included the staff, tonalities, enharmonic scales, the *seticlavio* or table of the seven keys, major, minor, perfect, diminished and augmented intervals and their inversions. Panizza maintained that sol-fa should comprise the basis of all branches of musical art (Panizza 1877: 21).

In a later publication by Panizza, *Método de Lectura Musical y Solfeo* (Music reading method and sol-fa) (1885), he suggested singing in unison applying dynamics (piano, crescendo and forte) with piano accompaniment in unison or at the octave in order not to tire children's ears. Sol-fa practice should take 15 or 20 minutes every day and the remaining time should be spent on singing songs. The study of musical theory should begin at the third grade:

Each pupil will have a slate with a [musical] staff. The teacher will first write on the blackboard what his pupils have to write on their slates. Music reading will begin by reading from the blackboard, then copying on the slates writing the names of the notes up to the moment they may read them easily and with confidence. Pupils should learn every rule by heart. (Panizza 1877: n.p.)

The *Gramática Musical arreglada especialmente para el uso de los colegios donde se enseña canto sin previo estudio de un instrumento* (Musical grammar especially arranged for use in those schools where singing teaching does not follow the previous study of an instrument) (1882) was written by Josefina B. de Farnesi, Professor of Song at the Normal School of Paraná. She advocated attention to musical dictation:

My work does not include useless details nor sol-fa as other books do ... In my opinion the quickest way to teach musical theory is to make the pupil write, analyze and read the combinations of signs and parts of the dictated musical pieces. This method has another advantage: all pupils no matter their number may be simultaneously engaged in the task. (Farnesi 1882: n. p.)

The book contains no exercises or melodies for singing.

The most unusual pedagogical method was proposed by Pablo Menchaca (1855–1924), a stenographer by profession, who created a notational system that facilitated both reading and writing music. It consisted of a chromatic musical alphabet in which each sound was called by an invariable syllabic name: la, se, si, do, du, re, ro, mi, fa, fe, sol, nu. A petal-like symbol represented each note by its angle and position on a single line staff. There was much else besides.

Menchaca promoted his system internationally. He presented a lecture on his system at the Sorbonne in Paris in 1889 where it was positively received and subsequently made promotional tours to Belgium, Britain, Germany, Italy and the United States. In 1903 he carried out a pilot test, applying his system at the Boys' School No. 1 in La Plata City with the approval of the local school council and a year later published his proposal as *Nuevo sistema teórico gráfico de la Música* (New system of musical notation) (see Menchaca 1912). By 1907 his system was being used at the normal schools of Buenos Aires and La Plata cities. Between 1911 and 1913 he continued to promote his system in the hope that it would be applied in general education. He estimated that his system was being followed by 5000 students throughout the country (*ibid.*). However, the Inspector for Music, Rosendo Bavío, rejected Menchaca's petition arguing that it was not a universally accepted code. (Fernández Calvo 2001a, 2001b).

Teacher training

In the early years of music being introduced in compulsory schooling it was expected that classroom teachers would teach the subject as there was no provision for specialist teachers. Graduates from the normal schools were expected to have taken at least two subjects in music education. The following comprised the syllabus:

First Grade. 1. Music. Sound. Musical characters. 2. Staff. Notes. Treble clef. Additional lines. 3. Notes, their values. Rests, their values. 4. Metre. C (Common) or 4/4 time. Bar lines. 5. Dot and double dot. 6. Even and odd metres. Simple and compound metres. 7. Tie and syncopation. 8. Triplet and sextuplet. 9. Accidentals: sharp, flat, natural, double sharp and double flat. 10. Whole step and half step. Diatonic and chromatic half step. 11. Bass clef. The position of notes in this clef. 12. Conventional symbols and marks. 13. Diatonic and chromatic scales. 14. Major scales with sharps: key signatures. 15. Major scales with flats: key signatures. 16. Differences between major and minor scales. How to find the relative minor of a major scale. 17. Major scales with sharps and their relative minor scales. 18. Major scales with flats and their relative minor scales. 19. Reading and division in treble and bass clefs.
Second Grade. 1. Conventional symbols. Ornaments. 2. Diatonic major scales. Diatonic minor scales. 3. Intervals. Intervals in the major and minor diatonic scales. 4. Mode. Key signatures. Major tonalities and their

relative minor tonalities. 5. Musical metres. (CNE, *El Monitor de la Educación Común* 1883: 80–81, 94)

School inspectors, having detected unequal musical achievements in classrooms, gradually promoted the appointment of specialist music educators: 'At first elementary schoolteachers conducted children's singing practices, but in a short time the authorities appealed to *specialized* teachers, resulting in a standardization and intensification of teaching' (CNE 1938: 56).

In the 1870s and 1880s music educators had usually studied abroad or had taken private lessons with local professors as there had been very few and often short-lived institutions at which to study music. Such as there were included the *Escuela de Música y Declamación de la Provincia de Buenos Aires* founded in 1874 and presided over by Juan Pedro Esnaola, and the Conservatoire of Music, opened in 1880 by Juan Gutiérrez (1840?–1906?).

Alberto Williams (1862–1952), who had won a grant to study in the Paris Conservatoire, founded the *Conservatorio de Música de Buenos Aires* in 1893 where the most distinguished musicians of the time taught sol-fa, piano, violin, violoncello, flute and singing. By the 1900s the institution had almost 50 professors and more than 1,000 students. Intent on spreading music education, Williams established branches all over the country (Roldán 1999: 86). This private enterprise obtained state subsidies and its qualifications received official recognition. These privileges were lost when the state opened its own conservatories.

In 1919 the Buenos Aires Town Hall Band conductor, Galvani, promoted the foundation of several town hall music schools that by 1927 had became a unified organization – the *Conservatorio Municipal de Música Manuel de Falla*. A parallel development was the establishment in 1924 by the National Ministry of Public Instruction of the *Conservatorio Nacional de Música*, which took the Paris Conservatoire as its model. Both institutions offered degrees in several instruments and singing and were the main training ground for school music educators in Buenos Aires city. In the same year the Departments and Superior Schools of Music of the National Universities of La Plata, Córdoba, Tucumán, Mendoza, San Juan and Santa Fe were established. These developments notwithstanding, there were never enough music specialists to teach in the primary schools, and non-graduate, often amateur musicians took on the teaching positions.

Conclusion

During the twentieth century, compulsory music education in primary schools was influenced by international and local pedagogical developments.

During the 1940s Émile Jaques-Dalcroze's ideas gained the approval of the Music Inspector Athos Palma, during the 1950s Guillermo Graetzer promoted Carl Orff's method and during the 1960s Edgar Willems lectured in Argentina and Maurice Martenot's method was translated into Spanish. During the following decades, several books by John Paynter, R. Murray Schafer, Brian Dennis and François Delalande were published in Argentina. Local music educators such as Susana Espinosa, Ana Lucía Frega, María Inés Ferrero, Silvia Furnó, Violeta Hemsy de Gainza, Silvia Malbrán and Juan José Valero became prominent through their pedagogical ideas and trained new generations of music teachers. This process resulted in an increasing number of musical activities in the classroom, such as playing musical instruments (mainly recorder, guitar and Orff instruments) and improvising.

Public and private conservatoires and universities provided courses in preparation for traditional performing careers and added subjects in composition, choral conducting, orchestral conducting, ethnomusicology, early music, popular music, electroacoustics and so on to their programmes.

Following contemporary trends, the subject, *música* (music), became *educación musical* (music education) in primary schools in 1972. In 1993 a new law, *N° 24.195*, established 10 years of compulsory education from kindergarten to the age of 15 and confirmed a system of administrative and pedagogical decentralization. In 1995 the Federal Council of Culture and Education approved a basic common curriculum that each province and Buenos Aires City had to take into consideration when designing their own curricula. Although *educación artística* (artistic education) remained as a mandatory area of study, *música* was no longer a compulsory subject, but just one of the artistic options that each jurisdiction could include in its own curriculum. Although many provinces maintained primary school music education, some did not include it in all grades of basic education.

In 2006 a new law (N° 26.206) prescribed that in 13 years of compulsory education 'every pupil should have the opportunity to develop his sensibility and creative capacity in at least two artistic disciplines' (Art. 41) and that the training of music teachers was to be supported at high-level institutes (Art. 39). Nowadays both the Ministry of Education and the Federal Council have to approve the new basic common curriculum and each jurisdictional educational authority has to reform its own curricular documents accordingly.

To conclude, the historical progression of school music education in Argentina can be summarized as shown in Table 10.1.

It will become apparent that the history of music education in Argentina has incorporated some highly distinctive features, including the influence of the Roman Catholic Church, nineteenth-century political revolution and the development of a network of music conservatoires. Only by acknowledging such influences can we come to appreciate something of the complexity that

Table 10.1 History of school music education in Argentina

Date	Subject description	National documentary sources
1884	*Música vocal* (Singing [literally: vocal music])	Law of Common Education N° 1420
1887	*Canto y Música* (Singing and music)	*Plan de estudios* Curriculum/syllabus for primary school. Consejo Nacional de Educación
1903	*Música* (Music)	*Plan de estudios para las escuelas normales de la nación* Curriculum/syllabus for normal schools. Ministerio de Justicia e Instrucción Pública
1972	*Educación musical* (Music education)	*Lineamientos curriculares de 1 a 7 grados* Curriculum/syllabus for first to seventh grades. Ministerio de Cultura y Educación de la Nación
1995	*Educación artística: música* (Artistic education: music)	*Contenidos básicos comunes* Basic common curriculum contents. Consejo Federal de Cultura y Educación
2006	*Educación artística: música* (Artistic education: music)	National Law of Education N° 26.206

underpins the achievement of music educators in providing a musical education for the majority of children in the schools of Argentina today.

Notes

[1] Miguel Hilarión Eslava y Elizondo (1807–1878) was a Spanish priest, musician and composer who wrote a *Método de Solfeo* (Method of sol-fa) (1846).

[2] François Joseph Fétis (1784–1871) was a Belgian musicologist, composer, critic and teacher who wrote *Biographie universelle des musiciens* (1966).

[3] Auguste Matheu Panseron (1796–1859) was a French composer and singing teacher who wrote a *Méthode complète de vocalisation* (Complete vocalization method) (1855) and *Abc musical ou solfège* (Sol-fa musical rudiments) (n.d.).

References

Alberdi, J. B. (1832), *El espíritu de la música a la capacidad de todo el mundo*. Buenos Aires.

Alberdi, J. B. (1832), *Ensayo sobre un método nuevo para aprender a tocar el piano con la mayor facilidad*. Buenos Aires.

Consejo Nacional de Educación (1883), *El Monitor de la Educación Común*, 2, 21–40.

Consejo Nacional de Educación (1888–1889), *El Monitor de la Educación Común*, 9, 141–160.

Consejo Nacional de Educación (1891–1892), *El Monitor de la Educación Común*, 12, 201–220.

Consejo Nacional de Educación (1893–1894), *El Monitor de la Educación Común*, 13 221–240.

Consejo Nacional de Educación (1913), *La Educación Común en la República Argentina. Años 1909–1910, presidencia del doctor don José María Ramos*. Buenos Aires: Penitenciaría Nacional.

Consejo Nacional de Educación (1938), *Cincuentenario de la Ley 1420. Tomo II. Memoria sobre el desarrollo de las escuelas primarias desde 1884 a 1934*. Buenos Aires: Consejo Nacional de Educación.

de Couve, A. and Dal Pino, C. (1999), 'Historical panorama of music education in Latin America: music training institutions', *International Journal of Music Education*, 34, 30–46.

de Couve, A., Dal Pino, C. and Frega, A. L. (1997), 'An approach to the history of music education in Latin America', *Bulletin of Historical Research in Music Education*, XIX, (1), 10–39.

de Couve, A., Dal Pino, C. and Frega, A. L. (2004), 'An approach to the history of music education in Latin America. Part 2: Music education from the sixteenth to eighteenth centuries', *Journal of Historical Research in Music Education*, XXV, (2), 79–95.

Eslava y Elizondo, M. G. (1846), *Método de Solfeo* (Method of Sol-fa). Madrid.

Farnesi, J. B. de (1882), *Gramática Musical arreglada especialmente para el uso de los colegios donde se enseña canto sin previo estudio de un instrumento*. Buenos Aires: Imprenta Porvenir.

Fernández Calvo, D. (2001a), 'Reformas a la notación tradicional. Una propuesta argentina: Ángel Menchaca', *Boletín de Investigación Educativo Musical*, 8, (24), 23–8.

Fernández Calvo, D. (2001b), 'Una reforma de la notación musical en la Argentina: Ángel Menchaca y su entorno', *Revista del Instituto de Investigación Musicológica 'Carlos Vega'*, XVII, (17), 61–130.

Fétis, F. J. (1866), *Biographie universelle des musiciens* (12th edn). Paris: Librairie de Fermin Didot Frères, Fils et Cie.

Frega, A. L. (1994), *Mujeres de la Música*. Buenos Aires: Planeta.

Gesualdo, V. (1961), *Historia de la Música en la Argentina. III. La Época de Rosas. 1830–1851*. Buenos Aires: Libros de Hispanoamérica.

Ley de Educación Nacional Nº 26.206 (Law of National Education No. 26.206) (2006) Buenos Aires: Ministerio de Cultura y Educación.

Ley Federal de Educación Nº 24.195 (Federal Law of Education No. 24.195) (1993) Buenos Aires: Ministerio de Cultura y Educación.

Ley Nº 1420 de Educación Común (Law of Common Education No. 1420) (1884), www.bnm.me.gov.ar/giga1/normas/5421.pdf.

Menchaca, A. (1912), 'New music notational system', in *Report of the Fourth Congress of the International Musical Society*. London: Novello, pp. 267–78.

Mondolo, A. M. (2005), 'Siglo XX: Leyes, decretos, resoluciones y fallos judiciales', in C. Vega, *El Himno Nacional Argentino*. Buenos Aires: EDUCA, Apéndice Quinto, pp. 1–19.

Panizza, J. G. (1877), *Nuevo Método Teórico Práctico de Lectura Musical y de Solfeo*. Buenos Aires: Hartmann.

Panizza, J. G. (1885), *Método de Lectura Musical y Solfeo*. Manuscript.

Panseron, A.M. (1855), *Méthode complète de vocalisation* (Complete vocalization method). Paris: Brandus, Dufour et Cie.

Panseron, A. M. (n.d.), *Abc Musical ou Solfège* (Sol-fa musical rudiments). Paris.

Roldán, W. A. (1999), *Diccionario de Música y Músicos*. Buenos Aires: El Ateneo.

Sarmiento, D. F. (1938), *Ideas Pedagógicas*. Buenos Aires: Consejo Nacional de Educación.

Torres, J. M. (1887), *Primeros Elementos de Educación*. Buenos Aires: Imprenta de M. Biedma.

11

Cuba: Music education and revolution

Lisa M. Lorenzino

With a history marked by foreign domination, racism, centuries' long struggles for independence and the eventual attainment of self-government, the journey to implement music education in Cuban public schools has paralleled the country's battle for compulsory education and, in turn, nationhood itself.

It was but 50 years ago, after Fidel Castro's Revolution of 1 January 1959, that Cuba gained independence and began establishing a nationwide system of schooling (Johnston 1995). Building on existing institutions, as introduced by the Spanish and the Americans, Cuba took education-related matters into her own hands, developing a unique and highly effective system (Breidlid 2007; Carnoy 2007; Johnston 1995). Today Cuba is recognized as having developed one of Latin America's most successful national education programmes, recognition that gives the country a great sense of national pride (Breidlid 2007; Carnoy 2007). Most notable within this system is Cuba's ability to provide free, high-quality, child-centred music education to all of its citizens from pre-school through to Grade 7. The country also operates an impressive specialized stream of music education, offering free professional music training nationwide for students aged 8–18 (Moore 2006).

Historical beginnings of music education in Cuba

Whereas informal music education in Cuba most likely took place among the Taino and Siboney tribes prior to the arrival of Columbus (Rodríguez and García 1989), it is believed that the first formal music educator in Cuba was an Iberian named Ortiz (Alvarez 1982). Shortly after the arrival of the Spanish in 1492, Ortiz opened a dance school in the Cuban city of Trinidad where he began teaching melodies to the local inhabitants to accompany their movements. With the Spaniard's actions began a tradition of European-born and trained musicians of the highest quality being involved in music education in Cuba (*ibid.*).

In ensuing years, as seen in the development of public education, the Roman Catholic Church was the first institutionalized setting for music education in Cuba. In 1544 Miguel Vélazquez, the first church organist at the Cathedral of Santiago (founded in 1514), began to teach children to sing the church offices (*ibid.*). In 1612, when the organ was installed in Havana Cathedral, the capital city took over as the economic, ecclesiastic and musical centre of the nation. Throughout the seventeenth century, musical life was focused on these two institutions and, each year, highly trained professionals arrived from Europe to strengthen the islanders' musical skills.

Hailed as the country's first native composer of Western European art music, Esteban Salas (1725–1803) initiated the tradition of locally-trained music educators in Cuba. In the second half of the eighteenth century, Salas developed the Santiago Cathedral into a centre of high-quality music teaching, expanding classes to include strings, voice, winds and a small orchestra (Carpentier 2001). Despite his efforts, however, Havana reigned as the cultural capital of the country, a position that it maintains to this day (Alvarez 1982).

At the beginning of the eighteenth century, Cuban music education expanded beyond church walls into the realm of private business. Havana violinist Bousquet is believed to have been one of the first private studio teachers in the nation, whereas shortly afterwards, in Santiago, Juan Parés began teaching lessons at his home (*ibid.*). With the French influx following the Haitian slave revolt, private piano teaching flourished in the nation (Vega 2002).

Throughout the nineteenth century, studio teaching expanded, both in homes and in institutions. In 1814 Santiago became home to Cuba's first private music academy. Like the public schools of the time, the conservatory's clients were primarily Iberian – unlike the public schools, which were restricted to Spanish-born men, the conservatory catered predominantly for women, with lessons focused on singing, piano and the violin (Alvarez 1982). Within 2 years (1816), a similar institution, the *Academía Santa Cecilia*, opened in Havana. Staffed by Spanish-born teachers, this conservatory also was restricted to the Iberian population.

Expansion of music teaching institutions, both private and public, flourished throughout the nineteenth century as Spanish and Cuban musicians opened studios and schools in Camagüey, Santa Clara, Remédios, Cienfuegos and other municipalities throughout the island (*ibid.*). Just over a century later, Cuba boasted the highest number of private music academies per capita in Latin America (Gramatages 1982). By 1929 Havana alone was home to 35 conservatories and more than 160 smaller music schools. The census of that same year listed 1,850 music teachers nationwide, most of whom taught piano, violin and singing (Calero Martín 1929).

Racism and early Cuban music education

The first Africans to arrive in Cuba in 1515 began the process of radically altering the racial makeup of the nation (Delgado 2001). By 1811 over 320,000 black slaves had been transported to Cuba, accounting for 54 percent of the nation's inhabitants (Moore 1995). Because public schools and music academies restricted their clientele to those who were Iberian born, the imported African population had to rely on other sources for music education. Ironically, the opportunities for their music education were available only through organizations designed to control and inhibit their actions.

Beginning as early as 1598 in Havana, slave owners began promoting the establishment of lodge-like organizations called *cabildos* or *cofradías*. For the *cabildos* members, the groups served as centres for drumming, singing, dancing and the preservation of culture and religion (Delgado 2001). Organized by place of origin, these social outlets also served as havens of respite from the harsh daily reality of slavery and assisted blacks with their social adjustment to life in the New World (*ibid.*).

The *cabildos* served a different purpose for the masters. For the Iberians, these tribally based groups prevented blacks from gathering on a large scale, thereby restricting revolts and uprisings. The groups also assisted in indoctrinating the Afro-Cuban population with respect to the Spanish crown and the Catholic Church (*ibid.*).

Learning within the *cofradías* differed greatly from that of the Iberian music institutions. Rather than focusing on note reading and literacy skills, the Afro-Cuban institutions were aurally based, using imitation and rote learning. Music performed was rhythmically complex and polyphonic in texture and was taken from the traditional folk music of the various tribes. In contrast to the individual study of piano and violin, the *cofradías* focused on the fusion of drumming, singing and movement. Organizations were also communal and multigenerational in nature (Moore 1995).

With the abolition of slavery in 1870, Cuban blacks were officially free to choose a profession (Carpentier 2001). In reality, however, racism regarding which jobs blacks could engage in was rampant, thereby limiting their range of employment. Because the white population had access to a range of financially stable and upwardly mobile professions, the social climate encouraged blacks to become professional musicians, a job considered financially 'unstable' at the time. As a result, instruments became 'secured in the hands of people of colour' (*ibid.*: 153).

With money to pay for lessons, blacks began enrolling in music schools, becoming skilled in counterpoint, opera, piano and symphonic instruments. No longer restricted from becoming professors and private music teachers, blacks now became involved in institutionalized music education (Alvarez

1982). The black *maestros* made an impact on the teaching of European art music in Cuba, introducing pedagogical components influenced by their traditions of rhythmically complex music, movement and rote learning. Unfortunately, despite this progress in music, blacks continued to suffer from racist attitudes in many areas of society (Moore 1995).

Cuban independence and the roots of public schooling

Because education was, by and large, aligned to the Iberian Catholic religious orders, Cuban schools were elitist, racist and urban based throughout the duration of Spanish imperial rule (Johnston 1995). It is notable, however that forward-thinking laws on the part of the Spanish did make primary schooling compulsory as early as 1842 (Epstein 1987). However, in practice this did not happen. Further, the *conquistadores* did pass administrative policies in an effort to nationalize education, but the 'social and economic conditions of colonialism precluded any significant educational impact on the island' (Epstein 1987: 7). As a result, the poor, black, rural and female populations remained marginalized in Cuban schooling through to the beginning of the twentieth century (Johnston 1995).

Following the Liberation War of 1895–1898, Cuba was granted independence from Spain. Due to substantial economic losses, the nation was left vulnerable and shortly thereafter became occupied by the United States Army (1906–1909). Following a brief period of military control, Cuba was again declared 'independent' and self-governing (Milbrandt 2002). In reality, the nation was now privy to the 'supervision' of her North American neighbour, the United States. This supervision developed into governmental control akin to that of the Spanish *conquistadores* (Bethell 1993; Galeano 1997).

The change in the political climate of Cuba did have some benefits, however. With the American military occupation of 1906–1909 came attempts to establish a national system of public education through the creation of the Cuban Ministry of Education. Unfortunately, as with the Spanish, the new Ministry did not have the resources to fulfil its mandate of nationwide public education and, as decades ensued, public schooling experienced minimal growth (Johnston 1995).

Under the new 'imperialism' of the United States, the early years of the twentieth century became a time of bloodshed, political tyranny and unrest (Moore 1995). From abroad, the nation was viewed as an island paradise, resplendent with beaches, music, dance and prosperity. In truth, however, at home, Cuban citizens were developing deeply seated anti-American sentiments as the administrations of General Machado (1925–1933) and General Batista (1933–1944 and 1952–1959) developed into hotbeds of graft, corruption, absenteeism and tumult (Galeano 1997; Moore 1995). Unfortunately, public schools, music academies and Cuban society at large became subject to these vices (Johnston 1995).

Reacting to the violent leadership of General Batista in the 1930s, public confidence in the government reached a point of crisis. Batista aggressively squelched citizen protests by closing schools and withholding teachers' salaries (*ibid.*). As dissatisfaction escalated, the General lashed out by dismissing or deporting teachers and imprisoning students. A small elite private school sector, funded by American companies and religious denominations, managed to survive the upheaval. As in previous centuries, only the smallest minority of the nation's population was able to access these facilities (*ibid.*).

The founding fathers of Cuban music education

At the turn of the twentieth century, a parallel struggle to the struggle for nationhood began as music teachers aligned themselves in an effort to organize free, compulsory, non-racist, non-elitist public music programmes in Cuba. Spearheaded by Havana pedagogues, from both the music academies and the private studio sector, these educators' efforts were a direct response to the failing social mores of the times. With a few notable exceptions, the music academies, like their public school equivalents, had become renowned locations of corruption (Alvarez 1982). Complaints about the selling of music diplomas and prizes and the exploitation of student artists proliferated throughout both the Machado and Batista regimes as staffing and administration became indelibly linked to local political parties. In Havana, mayoral elections alone brought about wide-sweeping faculty and adminis-trative changes in music institutions. Again, citizens' displays of dissatisfac-tion with these changes, as found in the public school sector, resulted in teacher deportations, imprisonments and school closures (*ibid.*).

Within these tumultuous times emerged three of Cuba's most influential pioneers of music education. Working simultaneously to incorporate music into the public school curriculum as well as to expand the clientele of the nation's music conservatories, the efforts of Hubert de Blanck, Guillermo Tomás and César Pérez Sentenat laid the foundation for Cuba's current system of public school music.

Hubert de Blanck (1856–1932)

Born in Holland and educated in Europe, Hubert de Blanck quickly distinguished himself as a professional pianist, composer, conductor and pedagogue of the highest degree on his relocation to Havana in 1883 (Diez 1982). In 1885, along with violinist Anselmo López, de Blanck made his first contribution to the development of music education in Cuba by opening his *Conservatorio Nacional*. An institution providing classes for students aged 12 to 20, the *Conservatorio* was the first Cuban music school to receive government support (*ibid.*). Using the somewhat limited funds provided, de Blanck was able to award eight scholarships annually to promising young black music students, a first in the nation (Alvarez 1982).

The curriculum of de Blanck's conservatory expanded on those of other institutions on the island. Setting rigorous standards, de Blanck developed an academic programme that focused on the development of *solféo* (*solfège*) skills, the study of harmony, training in composition, along with individual instruction on an instrument (*ibid.*). Employing the best musicians of the time, de Blanck's conservatory initially specialized in the teaching of piano, singing, violin, flute and guitar. In the passing decades, instrumental choices expanded to include most orchestral instruments.

Passionate to develop musical skills nationwide, de Blanck established music academies in the interior of the country that were incorporated with the Havana conservatory (*ibid.*). Curriculum offerings in these provincial institutions were similar to those found in the Havana school. With the development of these institutions, de Blanck distinguished himself as the first to attempt to nationalize music education in Cuba.

De Blanck was also a seminal figure in establishing a music publishing industry, creating the nation's first music education publication. He also authored numerous books and articles on music pedagogy, many of which are still in use today (Diez 1982). Active in many realms, his achievements have caused him to be recognized as one of the most important figures in the development of culture in Cuba (*ibid.*).

Guillermo Tomás (1856–1933)

Guillermo Tomás' *Conservatorio Municipal de la Habana*, founded in 1903, became the nation's first fully state-sponsored music school to provide free lessons to students of any race (Alvarez 1982). Unlike existing conservatories and music academies of the time, the *Conservatorio Municipal* did not concentrate on teaching piano, violin or singing. Instead, the school was aligned with the Municipal Band of Havana providing free lessons on winds, brass and percussion for students aged 10 to 20 capable of passing the rigorous entrance examination (*ibid.*). Existing music academies did not perceive the *Conservatorio* as an economic threat as it catered to an entirely different clientele – poor, often black, working-class students.

Military bands had developed in several Cuban communities throughout the late 1880s, the most notable being in Havana, Remédios, Sancti Spíritu and Cienfuegos (Alvarez 1982). Along with the development of the bands were associated schools for winds and percussion that provided lessons for children and youth wishing to become instrumentalists. In addition to learning *solféo* and theory, student musicians were apprenticed to a military musician with the objective of taking over their position in the band. Like de Blanck's *Conservatorio* that was known for its high standards, Tomás employed the best musicians associated with the Havana Municipal Band (*ibid.*).

For the initial years of the conservatory's existence, teachers taught on a *pro bono* basis, motivated by the inclusive nature of the school but as the institution developed, teachers received suitable remuneration for their services (*ibid.*). The conservatory went on to expand its classes to include courses in theory, harmony and music dictation. After a brief closure from 1930 to 1932 due to student revolts against the Batista government, the conservatory prospered under the new leadership of Almadeo Roldán, Tomás' protégé. The conservatory later went on to develop into one of the nation's most influential music schools (*ibid.*).

César Pérez Sentenat (1896–1973)

A contemporary of Roldán, César Pérez Sentenat was integral to the development of music education in Cuba (Ponsoda 2002). A pianist and composer who had trained with Debussy and Ravel, Sentenat was active in Cuban music education for over 30 years. One of his most notable contributions was to spearhead a movement to create a national teacher training institute in Cuba – the *Escuela Normal de Música* (*ibid.*).

Following the 1909 lead of Saint-Saëns, Massenet and Dubois, who were developing an institute of piano pedagogy in Paris, in 1910 Sentenat approached politicians with the intent of creating a school for music pedagogy in Cuba (Barreras 1928; Rodríguez 2004). With goals of protecting the public from corruption and graft and ensuring the development of quality music teaching in Cuba, Sentenat's request was not approved by the Machado government. In 1917 the maestro again proposed his plan to the government; however, it, too, fell idle in the hands of a government preoccupied with societal unrest (Ponsoda 2002).

In 1931 Sentenat, along with Roldán, focused his energy in a different direction. On this occasion, the government supported the proposal, the result being the foundation of the *Conservatorio Municipal de la Habana*. Cuba now had its first fully funded music school (*ibid.*). It was not until 1961 however that a state-funded music teacher training institution came into being in Cuba. In the interim, music professors continued to be tied to the whims of the government. So, too, did political unrest remain a factor hindering the development of publicly funded compulsory music education (Alvarez 1982; Ponsoda 2002).

Primary music education and Cuba's first music pedagogue

De Blanck, Tomás and Sentenat, while making significant contributions to the Cuban conservatories, also had an effect on elementary music classrooms. In 1901 their efforts led to the addition of music into the primary school programme of studies. Using a curriculum designed in part by de Blanck, Tomás and colleague Emilio Agramonte (1844–1916), the programme emphasized unison and part singing. There was also a curricular emphasis on *solféo* and music theory (Ortega 2004).

Gaspar Agüero Barreras (1878–1951)

The work of de Blanck and his colleagues was carried on by Gaspar Agüero Barreras. With a career spanning over six decades of involvement, Barreras was seminal in developing compulsory music education in Cuba to the point that he was considered the nation's first music pedagogue (Rodríguez 2004). As an academic well versed in psychology, philosophy and pedagogy, Barreras worked in teacher training and this went on to impact generations of Cuban music educators.

A child prodigy of sorts, Barreras was playing the piano professionally by the age of 14, moving on to become a conductor of operettas and *zarzuelas*[1] shortly thereafter. Beginning in 1893 the pedagogue began a 58-year tenure as professor of the *Asociación de Dependientes del Comercio*. With his 1902 decision to leave conducting, Barreras began working at Hubert de Blanck's conservatory teaching *solféo* and piano. Adding to his professional duties, the maestro later began one of his most influential roles at the *Escuela Normal de Maestros de la Habana* in 1915, a post he held until 1946 (*ibid.*).

As a pedagogue, Barreras was considered forward thinking for his time. He was well trained in philosophy, especially the work of Leibnitz, Descartes and Herbart and he was well informed of global movements in music pedagogy. In addition, Barreras had a profound knowledge of European and Latin American schools of thought, especially those of France, Switzerland, Germany, Argentina, Mexico and the United States (*ibid.*). Specifically, he was impressed by the writings of the Argentinian Greppi (on modal systems), along with those of Chevé and Pestalozzi. Barreras' greatest influence in the area of general education was Dr Alfredo Aguayo, an important figure in the New School movement in Cuba.

A philosophy reaching its period of greatest influence between 1930 and 1950, the New School movement in Cuba was based on the French post-revolutionary concepts of liberty, equality and fraternity, as well as the tenets of Darwinism and Gestalt theory (*ibid.*). Philosophically, the movement supported the ideals of vitalization, spontaneous activity, childhood, literacy and community, focusing on the concept of the child as a 'subject' as opposed to an 'object' of learning (*ibid.*). Along with Aguayo, the primary influences on the New School movement who also made an impact on Barreras included Rousseau, Froebel, Dewey and Montessori.

Basing his own philosophy on these global influences, Barreras went on to develop a music pedagogy that integrated theory with practice. The pedagogue placed great attention on the concept of the spontaneous and natural process of children's singing (Barreras 1928). Owing to his work with the *zarzuela* companies, where roles were taught by rote, Barreras also gave great importance to singing by imitation. Foremost in his philosophy, however, was the need to teach music in a manner that was instinctual to children, that related to their world of sounds and that was sensitive to their natural curiosity and inquisitiveness (Rodríguez 2004).

Barreras incorporated this child-centred philosophy of music education into his professional activities, going on to train classroom generalist teachers in the Havana Normal School, as well as some of the city's greatest conservatory and studio music teachers (*ibid.*). Providing the philosophical basis for future generations, Barreras set the stage for innovative, child-centred music teaching in Cuba that is well informed by cognitive and psychological theory.

Developments in school music

Beginning in the 1920s the fledgling elementary school music programmes in Cuba added a new dimension into their classes – movement (Ortega 2004). Curricular requirements now mandated teaching music with physical education. In 1926 the link between the two subjects was strengthened by additional curricular reforms. Whereas these reforms were implemented into teacher training programmes in Havana through Sentenat and his contemporaries, progress in other provinces remained slow (*ibid.*). At the same time specialist training for elementary music teachers remained virtually non-existent with the government reporting only one music specialist or maestro for every 691 public students in Havana in 1931 (Pichardo 1973).

A decade later, in 1943, amidst severe political turmoil, the Ministry of Education organized the Department of Music Education with the goal of introducing music into the public schools nationwide (Menendez 1944). Philosophically, the department aspired to integrate theoretical work and singing in all the nation's classrooms. In 1943 the Ministry invited Margarita Menendez of New York University to present music pedagogy courses to interested school music teachers. A valid attempt to increase pedagogical training on the island, the programme was flawed – with no Spanish songbooks available, workshop participants sang and conducted American folksongs in English! Despite this lack of suitable materials – a perennial concern for Ministry officials – Menendez noted that 'Cubans are exceptionally musical and ... there is much eagerness to cultivate this art and to participate in all kinds of instruction in it' (*ibid*.: 28).

Simultaneously, provisions were made for the training of specialist teachers and curricular materials were expanded to include hymns, songs, exercises, elementary theory, *solféo*, music appreciation and a limited number of rhythmic bands into Cuban elementary schools (Ortega 2004). The existence of quality school music programmes in this decade, however, was uneven, with urban areas possessing the most comprehensive offerings. Rural populations, suffering from governmental neglect for education, did not receive the benefits that Havana and, to a lesser degree, Santiago schools enjoyed.

Throughout the 1950s political tensions reached their pinnacle and education, especially in rural areas in Cuba, was given little attention. Although improvements had been effected in terms of teacher education and administrative policy, even in the nation's capital, only one new school had been built during the first half of the century (MacDonald 1985). As political tensions rose, Fidel Castro used the battle cry of public education to fuel his 1 January Revolution of 1959 (Castro 1961).

The Cuban Revolution

Some argue that the Cuban Revolution was fought primarily for the right to universal education (Breidlid 2007; MacDonald 1985). In 1959 Cuba's literacy rate stood at 23.6 per cent. In addition, over 64 per cent of school-age children were not attending classes with only 3 per cent completing the required 6 years of compulsory schooling (Bérubé 1984). To thank the largely agrarian population that had assisted in his triumph, Castro began, immediately after his transfer to power, a complete restructuring of the nation's public education system.

Indeed, many of the decisions made by the newly formed government in the months immediately following the Revolution were not well planned (MacDonald, 1985; Moore 2006). However, what was eminently clear were Castro's specific goals for public schooling. Placing literacy and national pride at the forefront, Castro immediately began making policy changes to establish a system of national public education based on the writings of Jose Martí, Cuba's national poet, and Karl Marx (Breidlid 2007; Figueroa, Prieto and Gutiérrez 1974). Castro set out to formulate a public school system for Cuba, inclusive in nature, that:

> Integrated productive work with school work, the school community with the rural community, educational development with the country's

economic, social and cultural development, the formation of intellectual faculties with that of moral, social, physical and aesthetic faculties, the adolescent age group with the adult one, all this in a comprehensive vision of the new man and of a society confident in its future. (Figueroa, Prieto and Gutiérrez 1974: iv)

Funded in part by Russia as part of its new alliance with Cuba, the first effort of the new government was to eliminate illiteracy. In 1961 Castro began training a force of over 200,000 volunteer teachers to move into the countryside to educate the largely illiterate rural population (Bérubé 1984). Within the year, education and specifically literacy became the focus of the nation as volunteering for the Literacy Campaign became equated with furthering the cause of the Revolution (Breidlid 2007). Soon the peasants 'discovered the word, the volunteers discovered the poor, and all discovered their own *patria*' (Gumbert 1988: 122). By 1962 literacy had risen to 95 per cent and UNESCO declared Cuba illiteracy free (*New Internationalist*, 1998).

Castro continued to make sweeping changes to the education system in ensuing years. With the opening of hundreds of schools across the nation, the previously marginalized portions of the population were now able to access free quality public education (Eckstein 1997). As Castro went on to open universities and technical schools, students were given greater access to high-quality post-secondary education. By 1986 Cuba boasted 268,000 university graduates, a substantial increase from its 1958 count of 19,000 (*ibid.*).

Castro's new system of education, rather than being based on material incentives, encouraged the development of a new morality emphasizing solidarity, self-sacrifice, honesty, nationalism and internationalism 'built in an atmosphere of commitment, collective effort and mutual support' (Breidlid 2007: 627). Students were taught to work collectively together and programmes were established to foster an environment stressing the cause of the Revolution as opposed to individualism and competition. As a result, biases on race, gender and geographic location were essentially eliminated within the school system (Breidlid 2007; Gasperini 2000; Lutjens 1996).

Into this new system of public education Castro began embedding Cuba's existing music academies. Starting with conservatories in Santiago and Havana, later adding those in Piñar del Rio, Matanzas, Santa Clara and Camagüey, Castro nationalized music schools, turning them into free music conservatories open to any student passing the audition (Moore 2006). With the 1961 opening of *La ENA* (the *Escuela Nacional de Artes* in Havana), the country now offered a nationalized programme for children aged 8 to 18 interested in becoming professional musicians (Moore 2006; Schwartz 1979). This professional stream programme expanded to include schools in every province, thereby allowing citizens access to free, high-quality professional music instruction (Moore 2006).

Building on the curriculum of the private conservatories existing in Cuba prior to 1959, the music schools provided advanced training in *solféo*, music theory, music history, complementary piano and individual instrument training (Alvarez 1982). As the specialized programme developed, the conservatories began to offer matriculation subjects as mandated by the Ministry of Education (*ibid.*). These professional music schools have gone on to produce some of the nation's finest musicians and music teachers for both the specialist and general education stream, a role that they continue to serve today (Alvarez 1982; Ortega 2004; Sublette 2004).

Post-Revolutionary public schools and compulsory music

Widespread changes also were implemented in public school music following Castro's triumph in 1959. Controlled by the Ministry of Education, the process of establishing a nationwide programme of compulsory music education was highlighted by a commitment to high standards; quality, locally produced materials; innovative teaching practices; and reforms linked to teacher education and professional development (Carnoy 2007; Gasperini 2000).

Attempts to implement a nationwide compulsory music programme began with the preparation of music appreciation teachers. Trained in a manner similar to that of the Literacy Campaign volunteers, the teachers were sent out to inform children about the history of Cuban music. Linked with the work of important Cuban musicologists, materials used were locally produced and of the highest quality (Ortega 2004).

At the end of the 1960s the country underwent another revolution – in pre-school programmes and teacher training. Based on the methodologies of Dalcroze, Kodály, Orff and Stokoe,[2] a programme was implemented that further employed indigenous materials (*ibid.*). With resources written by María Antonieta Henríquez, a specialist in music, and Elfrida Mahler, a specialist in dance, the nation began implementing the locally produced texts into Cuban classrooms. The materials – which featured traditional games and folklore – followed a nationally based curriculum that combined music and kinesthetic expression together in one activity (*ibid.*). Shortly thereafter, pre-service teachers began to receive music instruction in their professional training to incorporate into the 80 minutes per week mandated for the arts education at the pre-school level (Gasperini 2000).

Curricular reform at the elementary school level now meant an 80-hour per year requirement for arts training in Grades 1–6 with 70 hours per year in Grade 7 (*ibid.*). In 1974 innovative elementary music programmes, following a reformed national curriculum, were implemented beginning with Grade 1. To expedite the implementation of the curriculum, programmes were offered through radio broadcasts, thereby reaching all areas of the nation (Ortega 2004).

Beginning in the later years of the 1980s innovative music education programmes were developed by the Ministry for use in upper elementary grades. Curricular content highlighted the study of the music and dance of Cuba as well as European art music via vocal, rhythmic, creative expression, corporal expression and dance (*ibid.*). Unfortunately, difficulties occurred in implementing the curriculum and programmes were perceived as lacking a 'continuous and homogenous nature for the eight grades, from pre-school through to the 7th grade' (*ibid.*: 47). There were also incongruencies in the 'relationship between program content and methodological strategies used' (*ibid.*: 47).

To overcome these deficiencies, once again in 2001, reforms in keeping with worldwide trends in music pedagogy were introduced for primary music education (Ortega 2004). This time the changes were more successful in their implementation. Curricular requirements for music now focused on perception, exploration and sound expression. The content of the revised programme consisted of songs, games, corporal expression, sound perception, listening activities and the creative process with students being encouraged to reflect, explore, listen, sing, describe, annotate, read, observe and compare. Curriculum reforms were based on the work of Orff, Dalcroze, Kodály, Villa-Lobos, Hemsy de Gainza and Frega along with Cuban pioneers such as Sentenat and de Blanck (*ibid.*).

Music education in contemporary Cuban schools

Today, over 500 years after Ortiz' humble start in Trinidad, Cuba operates a highly effective dual stream system of music education. In the generalist stream, all Cuban children are taught music 70–80 hours per year from pre-school through to Grade 7. Embedded in a public school system that is recognized as being among the most successful in Latin America (Breidlid 2007; Gasperini 2000), generalist teachers are well trained and dedicated to high academic achievement for all social groups (Breidlid 2007; Carnoy 2007; Gasperini 2000; Moore 2006). Curriculum materials are of the highest quality, locally produced and linked to the cultural context of Cuban society. Lessons involving creativity, movement and singing are presented using pedagogical methods that are grounded in current cognitive and psychological theory (Carnoy 2007; Gasperini 2000).

In the specialist or professional stream, Cuban music schools are internationally renowned for producing some of the world's greatest musicians – a disproportionately high number for a population of 11 million (Levinson 1989; Moore 2006). Students aged 8 to 18 receive free professional music instruction of the highest quality along with their regular matriculation subjects. Teachers, though less innovative in their methodology, are well trained, setting high standards as based on a nationally mandated curriculum (Rodríguez 2004).

Without any financial support from outside institutions – for example, UNESCO or the World Bank – Cuba offers a unique system of music education. The system is one that bears additional study from a global perspective. Known for a focus on inclusion and equality of opportunity, Cuban schools appear to 'to undermine the conventional wisdom that only well-functioning countries in the north can provide quality education for the majority of their pupils' (Breidlid 2007: 619).

Notes

[1] A *zarzuela* is a Spanish lyric-dramatic genre that alternates between spoken and sung scenes, the latter incorporating operatic and popular song, as well as dance.
[2] Patricia Stokoe (1929–1996) was an Argentinian dancer and pedagogue known for her work and writings related to corporal expression.

References

Alvarez, M. (1982), 'La enseñanza de la música en Cuba' (diploma dissertation, Faculdad de Música, Instituto Superior de Artes, Havana, Cuba).

Barreras, G. (1928), 'La enseñanza de la música,' *Pro Arte Musical*, reprinted in *Educación*, 111, (enero–abril, 2004), 52–3.

Bérubé, M. (1984), *Education and Poverty: Effective Schooling in the United States and Cuba*. Westport, CT: Greenwood.

Bethell, L. (ed.) (1993), *Cuba: A Short History*. New York: Cambridge University.

Breidlid, A. (2007), 'Education in Cuba – an alternative educational discourse: lessons to be learned', *Compare – A Journal of Comparative and International Education*, 37, (5), 617–34.

Calero Martín, J. (ed.) (1929), *Cuba Musical: Album-resumen Ilustrado de la Historia y de la Actual Situación del Arte en Cuba*. Havana: Imprenta Molina y Cía.

Carnoy, M. (2007), *Cuba's Academic Advantage: Why Students in Cuba Do Better in School*. Stanford, CA: Stanford University Press.

Carpentier, A. (2001), *Music in Cuba*. Minneapolis, MN: University of Minnesota Press.

Castro, F. (1961), *History Will Absolve Me*. New York: Lyle Stuart.

Delgado, K. (2001), 'Iyesá: Afro-Cuban music and culture in contemporary Cuba'. *Dissertation Abstracts International*, 62, (09), 292. (UMI No. 3026270).

Diez, A. (1982), 'Hubert de Blanck: Baluarte de la pedagogía musical en Cuba (1856–1932)' (diploma dissertation, Faculdad de Música, Instituto Superior de Artes, Havana, Cuba).

Eckstein, S. (1997), 'The coming crisis in Cuban education', *Assessment in Education*, 1, 1–12.

Epstein, E. (1987), 'The peril of paternalism: imposition of education on Cuba by the United States', *American Journal of Education*, 96, 1–23.

Figueroa, M., Prieto, A. and Gutiérrez, R. (1974), *The Basic Secondary School in the Country: An Educational Innovation in Cuba*. Paris: UNESCO.

Galeano, E. (1997), *Open Veins of Latin America*. New York: Monthly Review.

Gasperini, L. (2000), 'The Cuban education system: lessons and dilemmas', *Country Studies, Education Reform and Management Publication Series, The World Bank*, 1, (5), 1–36.

Gramatages, H. (1982), 'La música culta', in Ministerio de Cultura (ed.), *La Cultura en Cuba Socialista*. Havana: Editorial Letras Cubanas, pp.124–50.

Gumbert, E. (ed.) (1988), *Making the Future: Politics and Educational Reform in the United States, England, the Soviet Union, China, and Cuba*. Atlanta, GA: Georgia State University Press.

Johnston, L. (1995), 'Education in Cuba libre, 1989–1958', *History Today*, 45, (8), 26–32.

Levinson, S. (1989), 'Talking about Cuban culture: a reporter's notebook', in P. Bressner, W. LeoGrande, D. Rich and D. Siegle (eds), *The Cuba Reader*. New York: Grove, pp. 487–97.

Lutjens, S. (1996), *The State, Bureaucracy, and the Cuban Schools*. Boulder, CO: Westview.

MacDonald, T. (1985), *Making a New People: Education in Revolutionary Cuba*. Vancouver, BC: New Star.

Menendez, M. (1944), 'Public school music in Cuba', *Music Educators' Journal*, 30, (3), 27–8.

Milbrandt, R. (2002), *History Absolves Him: Reading Package, History 291*. Camrose, AB: Augustana University College Press.

Moore, R. (1995), 'Nationalising blackness: Afro-Cubanismo and artistic revolution in Havana, 1920–1935', *Dissertation Abstracts International*, 56, (06), 2376. (UMI No. 9534899).

Moore, R. (2006), *Music and Revolution: Cultural Change in Socialist Cuba*. Berkeley: University of California Press.

New Internationalist (1998), 'Jewels in the crown', 301, 27–28.

Ortega, P. (2004), 'Tendencias pedagógica-musicales del siglo XX y su influencia en Cuba', *Educación*, 111, (enero-abril), 43–7.

Pichardo, H. (1973), *Documentos Para la Historia de Cuba III*. Havana: Editorial de Ciencias Sociales.

Ponsoda, A. (2002), 'César Pérez Sentenat y la pedagogía musical cubana', *Clave*, 4, (2), 49–52.

Rodríguez, D. (2004), 'Gaspar Agüera Barreras: Primer pedagogo musical cubano', *Educación*, 111, (enero–abril), 48–51.

Rodríguez, V. and García, Z. (1989), *Haciendo Música Cubana*. La Habana, Cuba: Pueblo y Educación.

Schwartz, C. (ed.) (1979), *Impressions of the Republic of Cuba*. Washington, DC: American Association of State Colleges and Universities.

Sublette, N. (2004), *The Missing Cuban Musicians*. Albuquerque, NM: Cuba Research and Analysis Group.

Vega, A. (2002), 'Breve historia de la música Cubana', www.contactomagazine.com/delavega2.htm (accessed 7 September 2002).

Part 3

Africa and Asia-Pacific

Australia: Recurring problems and unresolved issues

Robin Stevens and Jane Southcott

As a political entity, Australia began as a set of British settlements and colonies that were established from the late eighteenth century. As with other members of the far-flung British Empire, early colonists attempted to replicate the social institutions that they had left behind in their 'home country'. By the time of federation in 1901, all colonies had established systems of state-supported schools which, alongside the various denominational and private schools, provided elementary education for their child populations. This chapter will consider the progress in three Australian colonies (later states under a federal government) that represent the development of music as a subject within compulsory schooling in Australia. The first colony to institute compulsory school attendance was Victoria in 1872, followed by South Australia in 1875 and New South Wales in 1880. However, as a mandatory subject of the school curriculum, the status of music varied in the respective colonies. Singing was included in the required 'standards of proficiency' in New South Wales from 1867 and was a mandated subject in the Victorian 'course of free instruction' in 1874 (Stevens 1978). In South Australia, singing – at least by ear – was expected to be taught in schools from 1890, but it was not until 1900 that music became a required subject with a prescribed syllabus (Southcott 1997). These three colonies, with their differing histories, encompass all of the significant issues associated with the introduction of music to compulsory schooling in Australia. The chapter will discuss the implementation of music in elementary education – provision of music in schools, the training of generalist and specialist teachers of music and the desired curriculum content and pedagogy. The rationale for including music in the curriculum will be outlined and, lastly, the nature of the school song repertoire and the experiences of the recipients of school music – the children – will be considered. Many of the current issues identified in the 2004–2005 National

Review of School Music Education (Pascoe et al. 2005) have their origins in the past and it is not only useful, but also, as Aldrich (1996: 3) reminds us, essential to consider the past as a means of informing present circumstances and future directions in educational policy and practice.

The education of indigenous Australian (Aboriginal) children is not considered as a separate topic for two main reasons. First, during the nineteenth and early twentieth centuries, what schooling was available for Aboriginal children was left largely in the hands of missionary organizations. Second, prior to 1967 when Australian citizenship was formally granted to Aboriginal people, an essentially assimilationist policy was in place, which meant that there was no special provision for the education of those few Aboriginal children who did attend their local state school.

Colonial background and context

European settlement of Australia began in 1788 with the arrival in Botany Bay (the site of modern-day Sydney) of the 'First Fleet' – a convoy of ships bringing government officials, convicts and marines to establish the penal colony of New South Wales. Further convoys brought more convicts and, as they earned the limited freedom of their 'tickets of leave' and as free settlers began to arrive, the colony started to grow and become increasingly self-sufficient. Between 1788 and 1850 over 162,000 convicts had arrived by the time transportation ceased (Marvic n.d.). Convicts were accommodated in penal settlements principally at Port Macquarie in New South Wales, at Morton Bay (now part of Queensland), at Port Arthur in Van Diemen's Land (later Tasmania) and at Norfolk Island. Other settlements were established by free immigrants at Swan River Colony – founded in 1829 and renamed Western Australia in 1836 – and subsequently at Adelaide where the colony of South Australia was proclaimed in late 1836. In 1851 the southern Port Phillip District separated from New South Wales to become the colony of Victoria. The founding of the colonies of Tasmania and Queensland followed in 1856 and 1859, respectively. With a growing tide of nationalism towards the close of the nineteenth century, a series of referenda and an act of the British parliament in 1900 finally resulted in the proclamation of the Commonwealth of Australia in which the six previously self-governing British colonies became a federation of states on 1 January 1901.

Provision for music in colonial schools and teacher training

As separate entities under the British Crown, each colony was responsible for the provision of elementary education. This has continued to be the case to the present day with school education remaining a state issue. During the early years of the three selected colonies, schooling for the juvenile population was provided by private tutors, church organizations and proprietors of private venture schools. The establishment of schools was often a priority with the early colonists. For example, in South Australia within the first year of the colony's existence, three private schools were established (Smeaton 1927). Ten years later, a Board of Education was established to supervise the financial aid granted to licensed schools. Singing was included in their revised curriculum but was not mandatory (Southcott 1997). It was not until the *Education Act 1875* that state-supported, compulsory and secular schooling came into being in South Australia (Miller 1986). In New South Wales, given many pressing demands on government funding, it was some years before colonial authorities turned their attention to school education. In 1848 the New South Wales colonial government appointed a Board of National Education (modelled on the Irish National System) to establish a system of non-sectarian schools, as well as a Denominational Schools Board to support the efforts of the churches in providing elementary education. Much the same happened in Victoria with dual education boards being set up in 1851 (*ibid.*). However, it was not until 1872, 1875 and 1880, respectively that elementary education became compulsory for children in Victoria, South Australia and New South Wales.

Singing, or 'vocal music' as it was often called, was introduced as one of the 'subjects of ordinary instruction' at the National Model Schools established by the respective National Boards of Education in Victoria and New South Wales. In the national schools of New South Wales, it was recommended in 1851 that singing should be timetabled for half an hour each day and that generalist classroom teachers should give singing lessons (*ibid.*). Unfortunately, the vast majority of national school teachers had little background or skill in music. This is hardly surprising since most teachers at this time were inadequately trained as teachers of 'the three Rs', let alone music. Although vocal music, initially based on Hullah's method, was included in the course of study at the teacher training institutions attached to the National Model Schools in both Sydney and Melbourne, most teacher education was undertaken through a system of pupil–teacher apprenticeship. However, with supervising teachers generally lacking musical knowledge and skills themselves, this system achieved little in preparing pupil–teachers to teach singing (Stevens 1978).

Given the general lack of musical competence among teachers in all colonies, music was soon regarded as an extra subject rather than as part of the ordinary curriculum. Despite recognizing the importance of music in education, the New South Wales School Commissioners in 1855 could nevertheless 'only lament its all but universal neglect' (Stevens 1981: 68). Accordingly, vocal music was introduced to teacher education under the national school system – for example, into pupil–teacher training undertaken in schools and to courses at Fort Street Training School – as well as being included as a subject for teacher classification examinations (the means through which teachers could gain promotion). All these measures were designed to encourage music teaching by generalist teachers, but success was limited (Stevens 1978).

About the same time, educational authorities in Victoria decided to appoint itinerant singing masters to overcome deficiencies in musical knowledge and skill among generalist teachers. The first full-time singing master, George Leavis Allan (1862–1897), was appointed by the Denominational Schools Board in 1853 to give musical instruction at several of its Melbourne schools. More appointments of itinerant singing masters followed. In 1859 a gratuity of £5 per annum was offered to generalist teachers in rural areas in an effort to encourage them to give 'systematic' instruction in vocal music (*ibid.*). Local unpaid singing teachers (generally amateur musicians) were also fairly common in denominational schools at this time. The Board of National Education in Victoria decided to follow the lead of its denominational counterpart and also appointed itinerant singing masters to ensure at least some provision for music teaching in its schools. However, in New South Wales, the teaching of singing was left entirely to generalist teachers to do as best they could. Given that many teachers were still largely untrained and that those who had been through training courses had generally covered little more than the musical content stipulated in the school curriculum, the extent and quality of music teaching by generalist teachers was very limited.

All this laid the foundations for three of the major issues that have bedevilled school music education in Australia ever since:

1   the provision of music teaching in government elementary schools, specifically the issue of whether generalist or specialist teachers should teach music
2   the inclusion of music in teacher education, specifically courses of training for elementary generalist teachers who generally come to teacher education with little or no prior musical experience
3   the notion that music can be an optional inclusion in school curricula.

Nevertheless singing was still highly valued by education authorities and in New South Wales it was formally introduced to the ordinary school curriculum in 1867 by the new (consolidated) Board of Education. Under this arrangement, generalist classroom teachers were responsible for teaching singing to their pupils according to a prescribed syllabus based on the tonic sol-fa method, notation and curriculum sequence. Vocal music through tonic sol-fa was also introduced as a compulsory subject for teacher training courses as well as for the system of teacher classification examinations. With the formation of the Department of Public Instruction in 1880, music continued to be a mandatory subject of the school curriculum and, by the 1890s, virtually all children in New South Wales public schools were being taught music by generalist classroom teachers with 75 to 80 per cent pass rates being achieved at the annual school inspectors' examinations (*ibid.*). The system was supported by a superintendent of music whose role it was to train teachers in music and to assist established teachers to prepare the music requirements for their classification examinations. Initially, this role was taken by James Fisher (1826–1891), the officially appointed 'Singing Master' (Stevens 2002) and then, from 1885, by his successor, Hugo Alpen (1842–1917), the first Superintendent of Music (Stevens 1993).

In contrast to the steady progress made in New South Wales, school music in Victoria regressed during the period of the Council of Education that had replaced the dual board system of National and Denominational Boards in 1862. This was due chiefly to the introduction in 1864 of a special fee of one penny per week for children attending singing lessons. The fee scheme was designed to offset the now substantial cost of maintaining a staff of specialist teachers – the itinerant singing masters – in public schools. Under these arrangements, music effectively became an optional extra in the school curriculum and due to the extra fee involved, the number of children receiving musical instruction declined markedly (Stevens 1978).

With the coming of 'free, compulsory and secular' schooling under the Victorian Education Department in 1872, fees for singing were abolished and the subject was included in the 'course of free instruction'. Singing was to be taught 'where practicable' in what were now termed 'state schools' either by an itinerant singing master or by a generalist classroom teacher who was licensed to teach singing and who received an annual bonus of £10 for giving musical instruction. Itinerant singing masters and licensed generalist teachers were supervised by an inspector of music. Although it was intended, over time, to replace the specialists with generalist teachers properly trained in music, the economic depression of the 1890s forced the government of the day to withdraw all paid instruction in singing from state schools, retrench professional singing masters and abolish the post of inspector of music. Therefore, despite its mandatory inclusion in the school curriculum, the teaching of singing 'by note' all but ceased in Victorian state schools and, for the remainder of the century, children were generally taught only singing 'by ear' by musically untrained generalist teachers (*ibid.*). The vulnerability of music as a school subject taught by specialists rather than generalists in government elementary schools continues to be a significant factor in school music education to the present day.

In South Australia prior to the *Education Act 1875* that established state-supported education as compulsory and secular, there were several attempts to manage schooling in the colony more effectively. The first 10 years were difficult but, in 1847, financial aid was given to schools and a supervisory Board of Education was established. The *Education Act 1851* created an independent Central Board of Education. Initially, this semi-governmental body had considerable impact but the achievements of the enthusiastic but largely untrained teachers varied considerably. It was not until 1860 that the regulations for Board schools recommended the teaching of singing but it was not compulsory, nor was any method suggested. However, with the active promotion of music teaching in schools by Alexander Clark (1843–1913), initially as head teacher of the demonstration model schools in Adelaide from 1876 and then more widely in the colony as a school inspector from 1884, singing – at least 'by ear' – was prescribed in the *Education Regulations 1890*. Clark developed a school music syllabus modelled on the contemporary English code and adapted for use in South Australia that came into force in 1900 (Southcott 1997). This course was similar to the requirements of the Elementary Certificate of the Tonic Sol-fa College and also formed the basis for the music curriculum taught to students at the Adelaide Training College, which opened in 1876.

The nature of and rationale for music in colonial schools

Clearly, the colonial educational authorities in the early days had difficulty providing even a rudimentary education in 'the three Rs', let alone including music in the school curriculum. However, from the outset, there seems to have been a desire among educational authorities, parents and the general public to include music in schooling. It is reasonable to ask what the nature of and rationale for music in schools was during the colonial and subsequent federation periods. The school curriculum *per se* and its inclusion of music were part of an inherited tradition from Great Britain – the 'home country'. The system of national schools in New South Wales and Victoria, established in the early 1850s, was closely modelled on the Irish National System[1] and colonial educational authorities simply adapted the existing Irish National School Curriculum, including vocal music, to local circumstances. The introduction of school music had a strongly utilitarian basis founded on the belief that music could be of great value as a humanizing and civilizing influence on society in general and on children in particular. The social environment in which many colonial children found themselves during the mid-nineteenth century was often far from good. Most colonies were initially populated by convicts and then by free settlers, many of whom were redundant paupers or dissidents from Great Britain. The situation was aggravated by the influx of fortune seekers following the gold strikes of the early 1850s, many of whom were considered by respectable colonists as 'undesirables'. The situation on the goldfields in New South Wales and

Victoria represented a highly unstable environment for many children. According to James Bonwick, a school inspector, children on the Victorian goldfields at this time lived in a world of 'gambling, swearing, drunkenness and licentiousness' (Stevens 1981: 67). Even without the presence of convicts or the decadence of the goldfields, South Australian government authorities perceived music in schooling as an antidote to larrikinism and roughness – vocal music could be a powerful agency for refining the individual (Southcott 2004).

Colonial education authorities were anxious to imprint whatever civilizing and reforming influences they could on rising generations. Music, in the form of class singing, was widely held to be of value in this respect. For example, the New South Wales School Commissioners in reporting the 'all but universal neglect' of music in the schools during 1855 cited its ability to soften manners, prevent intemperance and civilize. In 1857 the Victorian Denominational School Board recognized the importance of school music for children living on the goldfields by appointing itinerant singing masters. Two years later, when a shortage of educational funding threatened the dismissal of singing masters, the public response was one of indignation. Petitions objecting to any withdrawal of musical instruction came flooding into the Denominational School Board. The residents of Ballarat district argued that the music teacher helped the intellectual and moral progress of lower class children (Stevens 1981). In New South Wales during the same year, Inspector William Wilkins put forward a scheme to encourage national school teachers in country districts to teach singing with much the same idea in mind and adding that it would make schools popular with parents (Stevens 1978).

By the late 1860s the recreational value of school music began to be recognized by education authorities. In advocating an extension of music teaching in New South Wales in 1867, Inspector William McIntyre maintained that school music preserved morals, offered innocent amusement and had a cheerful affect on all endeavours. A colleague, Inspector Allpass, added: '[F]ew teachers seem to understand that a burst of song acts as a safety valve to children of excitable temperament, and enlivens those who are sluggishly disposed' (quoted in Stevens 1981: 68).

In South Australia, from the 1890s, there was a vigorous campaign to improve the vocal tone of both children and teachers. In 1911 the South Australian Minister for Education gave a very clear directive to schools, stating that: 'It was felt necessary to eradicate unclear enunciation, general slovenliness of speech ... [and] Australian twang and slang' (*South Australian Parliamentary Papers* 1911: 24). Singing was seen as a major weapon in this campaign and was also perceived as a relieving break between other subjects that could both calm and enliven children. Singing could be a 'pleasant break', relieve the 'tedium' of ordinary lessons and included at 'odd moments, never interfering with the work, but just giving the necessary stimulus to classes in danger of weariness' (Southcott 1997: 84). Singing could also be an accompaniment to mechanical activities such as sewing and, particularly, drill. At this time, almost every school had a drum and fife band which could accompany drill and perform at school and community functions (Southcott 1997). There was also some recognition of the 'intellectual progress' attending the study of 'music by notes' (Stevens 1978) – in modern-day parlance, promoting cognitive skills through a study of music theory and development of music literacy.

Music curriculum content and implementation

In all colonies, there was an assumption – based on contemporary English and Irish curricula – that vocal music should be taught 'by note' rather than merely 'by ear'. In all three colonies, Hullah's fixed-doh method had been tried but found wanting. In New South Wales, William Wilkins promoted tonic sol-fa as the most effective teaching method and notational system for use in schools. Tonic sol-fa teaching was undertaken by James Fisher who was appointed as Singing Master in 1867. Although Fisher's professional conduct was later deemed unsatisfactory, the tonic sol-fa method became the basis of a 'movable-doh' staff notation method that was successfully developed and implemented by his successor, Hugo Alpen, the new Superintendent of Music. In Victoria, the 'tonic numeral' method (an application of the numbers 1 to 7 on a movable system to staff notation), based on the principles of the English clergyman John Waite (Rainbow 1967), was adapted to local needs by the senior singing master George Allan during the 1850s. The method continued to be officially endorsed and supported by the Inspector of Music, Dr Joseph Summers (1839–1917) who was appointed in 1878 (Stevens 1997). During the 1880s, however, the tonic numeral method was challenged by proponents of tonic sol-fa, led by Dr Samuel McBurney (1847–1909) who later succeeded Summers as Inspector of Music (Stevens 1986). Both methods were later put on an equal footing through the publication in 1890 of a Tonic Sol-fa Programme, which supplemented the earlier 1884 'Programme of Instruction in Singing for State Schools' (Stevens 1978). In South Australia, after an early and unsatisfactory trial of Hullah's method, tonic sol-fa was introduced by Alexander Clark (Southcott 1995) and its promotion was continued by his successor Francis Lymer Gratton (1871–1946), himself a talented product of the South Australian public school system (Southcott 1996).

By the turn of the twentieth century school attendance had been compulsory in Victoria since 1872, in South Australia since 1875 and in New South Wales since 1880 and music was now mandated in the elementary school curricula of all three colonies (from 1867 in New South Wales, from 1872 in Victoria and from 1900 in South Australia). However, with technological innovations (such as the gramophone) and new methods of manufacture (such as the mass production of fifes and other musical instruments), singing as a school subject now became known as 'music' to reflect a broadening of content and the introduction of new approaches to music education. From the 1920s school music began to include music listening and appreciation and percussion band activities. The ubiquitous school drum and fife bands that had existed in Australian schools from their inception were now acknowledged in the syllabus. Other forms of instrumental music – such as the Manby group violin teaching method in Victoria – were introduced to schools (Cameron 1969; Southcott 1993), and Dalcroze eurhythmics was introduced through radio broadcasts from the 1930s (Pope 2006). Few of these developments were uniquely Australian, most being modelled on overseas practices. This trend continued with the introduction of school recorder playing in the 1950s, the Orff Schulwerk and Kodály approaches in the 1960s and creative compositional approaches from the early 1970s.

The school music repertoire and the experiences of children

The songs chosen for class singing were, especially in the early years of the colonies, carefully selected to include moralistic and didactic texts. In 1876 James Fisher used a simple melody to carry cautionary words: 'I must not tease my mother; She loves me all the day. And she has patience with my faults, And teaches me to pray. Oh, how I'll try to please her, She every hour will see; For should she go away or die, What would become of me!' (Stevens 2002). As well as inculcating religious and moral values through hymns and other such edifying songs, the singing repertoire chosen for children could also carry texts that evinced the virtues of home and family life.

Later, particularly with contingents of colonial soldiers being sent to the Sudan War and the South African (Boer) War, songs with patriotic and nationalistic words were popular as a means of promoting imperial citizenship. For example, one of the important days on the Australian cycle of celebrations was Empire Day that was first officially celebrated in Australia in 1905. On this day children listened to stories about the Empire, sang 'God Save the Queen' and 'Advance Australia Fair', performed callisthenic and martial drill exercises, participated in patriotic tableaux and took part in march pasts and trooping the colours. One schoolgirl memory was typical of many: 'Empire Day was a very special day. I can remember being Boadicea one year, wearing a white flowing gown and the British flag and a gold-painted helmet and three pronged fork' (quoted in Hetherington *et al.* 1979: 99) (see Figure 12.1). The celebration was not complete without songs, some Australian but most British such as 'The Sea is England's Glory' and 'Ye Mariners of England' (Southcott 2002)

FIGURE 12.1 Empire Day, Mount Templeton School, South Australia. (*Children's Hour, Classes IV and V, Grades 7 and 8*, XXVII, (308), August 1915: 169)

As the colonies moved towards federation, school singing also became an important medium for imbuing children with feelings of patriotism. In 1906 it was unequivocally stated: 'to cultivate patriotism is of great importance. We have thousands of pupils who should leave our hands feeling and believing that there is no country like their own ... Songs about the national flag, the deeds of great men and women, native scenery, &c., are recommended' (*Education Gazette South Australia* 1906: 43).

Perhaps the most authoritative statements regarding the value of music in colonial education came from William Wilkins (1827–1892), chief architect of the New South Wales' education system. In 1870 he recounted the reasons for including singing in the new public school system. Wilkins cited the example of Germany, which had, by the influence of music in schools, been changed from the most drunken to the most sober nation in Europe. He reiterated his belief in 'the humanizing and civilizing influence of music as an instrument by which a child might be trained in those social feelings which frequent intercourse with his fellows nurtured' (quoted in Stevens 1978: 51). This was seen as being particularly important in sparsely populated regions where opportunities for social intercourse might be few and far between. Even more, music had a strong disciplinary influence, by which a song could render corporal punishment unnecessary.

Although a natural outgrowth of class singing, the development of choral singing festivals enabled children to experience music as a performing art in the same way as adults did in choral societies or church choirs. End-of-year and charity concerts, musical pageants and system-wide events appear to have been fairly common in colonial schools (Stevens 1978). In New South Wales, massed singing by school children was arranged for important public occasions such as in 1868 when Prince Alfred, Duke of Edinburgh visited the colony. Ten thousand children from Sydney schools, accompanied by military bands and conducted by James Fisher, sang 'God Save our Noble Queen' in apparently faultless unison and with 'glorious effect' on the lawns of Government House (*ibid.*: 98). A schools choir of a similar number performed choral and massed singing items – including Hugo Alpen's 'Federated Australia' – at the 1901 inauguration ceremony for the Commonwealth of Australia at Centennial Park in Sydney, again evincing the strong patriotic and nationalistic sentiments (Chaseling 2003). Later still there were annual choral festivals such as the South Australian Decoration Society concerts that featured the 'Thousand Voices Choir' (see Figure 12.2) and that, in modified form, continues to the present day as the Primary Schools Music Festival.

Larger performance pieces designed for school children were often constructed around didactic messages. One of the few examples of a child describing her own experience of music in school describes just such a concert work. In 1892 Luella Quarton, a student at Gawler School in South Australia, sent a letter to a school newspaper in which she wrote about her

FIGURE 12.2 Alexander Clark and the Thousand Voices Choir rehearsing for the Decoration Society Concert, 1912. (*Education Gazette* XXVIII, (312), 8 October 1912: 216)

end-of-year school concert. Although this was probably written under teacher supervision, this remains an unusual example of the child's voice. Luella Quarton described the performance of a school cantata, *The White Garland*, by children of the Fifth Class:

> The curtain rose at 8 o'clock, and disclosed the 'queen', Miss N. Beadnell, seated on a throne surrounded by the scholars. The girls were dressed in white which made a nice effect against the dark green with which the stage was decorated. The head teacher, Mr R. Burnard, made a short speech, and then we sang the opening chorus, 'Happy Hearts.' The songs were all accompanied on the pianoforte by Miss. A. Morris. Various characters such as punctuality, the tardy, persevering, quarrelsome, generous and selfish scholar, were taken by L. Quarton, P. Beadnell, E. Gartrell, S. Burnard, L. James and G. Limb. At the close of the cantata a programme of songs was carried out. Mr. R. Northy was the conductor, and thoroughly deserved the success gained for the pains he had taken. (Quarton 1893: 95)

The White Garland, a purpose-written cantata for schools, was a 'scholar's festival' with a clear moral message – the queen of the scholars rewards good, studious scholars (the punctual, the generous, the persevering) and rebukes but eventually forgives (once they have seen the error of their ways) the bad scholars (the tardy, the quarrelsome, the selfish) (Allen n.d.). There were and continue to be, many works written with such messages and for such events.

Other songs simply allowed children to enjoy singing about such aspects of their lives as games, toys, outdoor adventures and other childhood pleasures. For example, 'Paddling Song' described the experience of the Australian child running across the beach: 'Across the shining sand we fly, With naked feet and gowns pinned high' (Macrae and Alsop 1910: 1–3). One of the recurring themes in such recreational songs was that of nature, particularly the Australian bush. One of the earliest songs about Australian fauna was the 'Joey's Song' published in 1879. This was included at the back of a cautionary tale in verse form entitled 'Marsupial Bill or the Bad Boy, the Good Dog and the Old Man Kangaroo' (Stevens 1879). Another example, 'Tale of the Bellbirds', composed by Samuel McBurney in Victoria (see Figure 12.3), again has a cautionary aspect to it with words that tell of children attracted by the bellbird's call becoming lost in the bush (Stevens 2006).

The most common form of school concert was and remains the construction of a programme from a number of different items that show different classes and activities. Finding past descriptions of such events by children is often difficult. An early example is from 1879 where Mabel

FIGURE 12.3 'Tale of the Bellbirds', music by Samuel McBurney, words by Andrew Barton 'Banjo' Paterson (McBurney, S. (n.d. [c 1895]), *The Australian Progressive Songster No. 2 for Senior Classes*. Sydney: Angus & Robertson, Sydney, pp. 35–6). An excerpt from a late nineteenth century Australian children's song with both staff and tonic sol-fa notation.

Richards of the Moonta Mines School described an annual concert in which a series of smaller performances were combined:

> The first item was an overture by a member of staff, Mrs. M.C. Mitchell, after which the choir of about thirty boys and girls ... sang and acted 'A Laughing Song'. After this the infants did their part of the singing and musical drill ... after many cheers and much clapping another song by the children entitled 'A Wet Sheet and a Flowing Sail', which was followed by a boys' carbine drill to musical accompaniment ... next a tableau Cinderella in four scenes ... staff drill was next given by a number of girls, and bayonet exercises by elder boys ... last item ... song given by the girls, named 'Chinese Umbrella' and that was acted splendidly. (Richards 1879: 245)

This brief description encapsulates the range of school music activities for children at this time. Songs prepared for concert performance such as 'A Wet Sheet and a Flowing Sail' reflected Australian allegiance to England and were often performed at massed concerts, sometimes with actions or even a hornpipe. The second song, 'Chinese Umbrella', was in the tradition of a number of school concert items that reflected contemporary taste, particularly theatrical musical comedy.

From the later years of the nineteenth century it was usual for all Australian schools to have a drum and fife band of between 10 and 40 members (see Figure 12.4). Initially, these bands were extra-curricula, but they eventually became part of the school music programme. The bands, militaristic in their practices, often accompanied school drill. In 1894 Alexander Clark was one of the co-authors of the official South Australian Education Department's *Manual of Drill* that was modelled on the British Army Manual. As part of the school concerts, boys often performed their physical drills – carbine drill (with mock or real weapons) was visually impressive and particularly popular. There were other callisthenic drills for boys and girls, the latter often using apparatus such as hoops, wands and clubs.

FIGURE 12.4 Sturt Street School Band (South Australia) 1917. (Postcard in the author's possession)

The lessons of history

There are several major issues to have emerged from this review of music in compulsory schooling that remain relevant to the contemporary Australian situation and from which 'the lessons of history' may be drawn in terms of future policy decisions. There are three overriding 'lessons' to be learnt. The first is that there are inevitably economic constraints on the provision of elementary school music teaching through any system of specialist teachers. Therefore such a means of delivering elementary school music is vulnerable in times of economic recession – as occurred in Victoria in the 1890s. Moreover, when specialist teachers were again employed as the principal means of providing music in Victoria from the 1950s, history repeated itself – although more through a change in curriculum policy than for economic reasons. In the late 1970s the Music Branch of 107 specialist music educators, most of whom taught music as itinerant teachers in primary schools, was disbanded in favour of school-based music teachers (Stevens 1978). Unfortunately, the new system failed to deliver music teaching in schools due to progressively more school-based music positions being filled by specialists in other curriculum areas. The place of music in schools was and remains vulnerable, particularly during times of economic downturn.

The second 'lesson' is that there is a need for all generalist elementary teachers to receive comprehensive training in music education through both pre-service and in-service education – as was the case in New South Wales during the last decades of the nineteenth century – to ensure their ability to implement effective music programmes in elementary schools. The historical justification for this claim is the success, using an appropriate music teaching method (tonic sol-fa), of the 'generalist approach' in New South Wales where by the early 1890s nearly all children in New South Wales public schools were being taught music with 75 to 80 per cent pass rates at the annual school inspectors' examinations (*ibid.*). If more adequate provision is made for music within primary teacher education courses, the place of music in the school curriculum is more likely to be assured.

The third 'lesson' is that music educators must continue to advocate for the inclusion of music as a mandated subject in schools. Too many state school curricula have moved to make music one of the 'arts' subjects of which not all must be taught. To deny children a holistic education by abandoning such an important subject is reprehensible.

Like many other countries, Australia continues to suffer from several longstanding and unresolved problems in its provision of school music education in its public schools. Accordingly, the lessons of history should be considered in the formulation of future policies in school music education.

Notes

1   For details, see the chapter by Marie McCathy in this volume on school music in Ireland.

References

Aldrich, R. (1996), *Education for the Nation*. London: Cassell.

Allen, C. G. (n.d.), *The White Garland*. London: John Curwen & Sons.

Cameron, A. E. (1969), 'The class teaching of music in secondary schools in Victoria, 1905–1955' (unpublished MEd thesis, University of Melbourne).

Chaseling, M. (2003), 'The great public school choir', in K. Hartwig and G. Barton (eds), *Artistic Practice as Research: Proceedings of the XXVth Annual Conference of the Australian Association for Research in Music Education*. Syndey: AARME, pp. 25–43.

Education Department, South Australia (1906), *Education Gazette*, XXII, (232), 43.

Hetherington, H., Sharam, R. and Rymill, P. (1979), *Penola Primary School Centenary History*. South Australia: Penola Primary School Centenary Committee.

Macrae, D. F. and Alsop, M. (1910), 'Paddling Song', in *Some Children's Songs*. Melbourne: George Robertson, pp. 1–3.

Marvic, A. (n.d.), *[Australian] Historical Timeline*, home.vicnet.net.au/~pioneers/pppg10.htm, accessed 30 August 2008.

McBurney, S. (n.d. [c. 1895]), *The Australian Progressive Songster No. 2 for Senior Classes*. Sydney: Angus & Robertson.

Miller, P. (1986), *Long Division: Schooling in South Australian Society*. Adelaide: Wakefield Press.

Parliament of South Australia (1911), Report of the Minister of Education in *South Australian Parliamentary Papers*, No. 44.

Pascoe, R., Leong, S., MacCallum, J., Mackinlay, E., Marsh, K., Smith, B. *et al.* (2005), *National Review of School Music Education: Augmenting the Diminished*. Canberra: Australian Government.

Pope, J. (2006), 'Music through movement over the radio: a dilemma for Dalcroze', in A. Giráldez, M. J. Aramberri, F. Bautista, M. Díaz, L. Hentschke and M. Hookey (eds), *Proceedings of the 26th World Conference of the International Society for Music Education*. Kuala Lumpur: ISME. CD-ROM

Quarton, L. (1893), 'News of the month: entertainment at Gawler', *The Children's Hour*, Class 4, V, (44), 95.

Rainbow, B. (1967), *The Land without Music: Musical Education in England 1800–1860 and its Continental Antecedents*. London: Novello & Co. Ltd.

Richards, M. (1879), 'Letter', *Tonic Sol-fa Reporter*, November, 245.

Smeaton, T. H. (1927), *Education in South Australia from 1836 to 1927*. Adelaide: Rigby.

Southcott, J. E. (1993), 'Martial strains', in V. Weidenbach and J. Callaghan (eds) *The Transformation of Music Praxis – Challenges for Arts Education: Proceedings of XIVth Annual Conference of the Australian Association for Research in Music Education*. Sydney: AARME, pp. 269-286

Southcott, J.E. (1995), 'The establishment of the music curriculum in South Australia: the role of Alexander Clark', *Research Studies in Music Education*, 5, 1-10.

Southcott, J.E. (1996), 'Curriculum stasis: Gratton in South Australia', in V. Weidenbach (ed), *Proceedings of the 15th Annual Conference of the Australian Association for Research in Music Education*. Sydney: AARME, pp. 51–9.

Southcott, J. E. (1997), 'Music in state-supported schooling in South Australia to 1920' (unpublished PhD thesis, Deakin University).

Southcott, J. E. (2002), 'Songs for young Australians', in J. E. Southcott and R. Smith (eds), *A Community of Researchers: Proceedings of the XXIInd Annual Conference of the Australian Association for Research in Music Education*. Melbourne: AARME, pp. 164–71.

Southcott, J. E. (2004), 'The singing by-ways: the origins of class music education in South Australia', *Journal of Historical Research in Music Education*, XXV, (2), 116–27.

Stevens, J. B. (1879), 'Marsupial Bill: of the bad boy, the good dog and the old man kangaroo', reprinted from *The Queenslander*. Brisbane: Gordon & Gotch.

Stevens, R. S. (1978), 'Music in state-supported education in New South Wales and Victoria, 1848–1920' (unpublished PhD thesis, University of Melbourne).

Stevens, R. S. (1981), 'Music: a humanizing and civilizing influence in education', in G. Featherstone (ed.), *The Colonial Children*. Melbourne: Royal Historical Society of Victoria, pp. 63–72.

Stevens, R. S. (1986), 'Samuel McBurney – Australian tonic sol-fa advocate', *Journal of Research in Music Education*, 34, (2), 77–87.

Stevens, R. S. (1993), 'Hugo Alpen – New South Wales Superintendent of Music, 1884–1908', *Unicorn: The Journal of the Australian College of Education*, 19, (3), 93–6.

Stevens, R. S. (1997), 'George Leavis Allan', in W. A. Bebbington (ed.), *The Oxford Companion to Australian Music*. Melbourne: Oxford University Press, p. 20.

Stevens, R. S. (2002), 'James Churchill Fisher: pioneer of tonic sol-fa in Australia', in J. E. Southcott and R. Smith (eds), *Proceedings of the XXIInd Annual Conference of the Australian Association for Research in Music Education*. Melbourne: AARME, pp. 172–82.

Stevens, R. S. (2006), ' "Forward gaily together" – the school music compositions of Samuel McBurney', in J. E. Southcott and P. de Vries (eds), *Proceedings of the XXVIth Annual Conference of the Australian Association for Research in Music Education*. Melbourne: AARME, pp. 116–25.

13

China: Socio-political constructions of school music

Wai-Chung Ho

This chapter examines the effects of historical and political changes on the development of compulsory school music curricula in China and how music education has responded to those effects. As the socio-political situations of China during its long history have been complex, the chapter will mainly focus on the development of music education since the influence of Western powers after the First Sino-British War (also known as the 'Opium War') of 1839–42. During the first half of the twentieth century, Chinese music education was under the influence of Japan, Soviet Russia and other Eastern European countries. Following the founding of the People's Republic of China (PRC) on 1 October 1949 by Mao Zedong (1893–1976) and during the ensuing Cultural Revolution (1966–1976), education, including music education, continued to be an instrument for the transmission of revolutionary communist ideas. With the announcement in 1978 by Deng Xiaoping (1904–1997) of the 'open-door policy', however, the influence of Eastern European communist countries over the development of music education gave way to that of Western countries.

Historical context for the introduction of music into the education system

Traditional Chinese culture was isolated from the rest of the world by geography. Bordered by mountains to the west and by the sea to the east, China long regarded itself as the 'Middle Kingdom'. As Huang (1988) argues, Chinese culture and values have been remarkably consistent over the nation's long history, mainly due to the domination of its education system by the teachings of Confucius (or Kong Fuzi, 551–479 BCE), who lived during a turbulent period in China's history. Chinese emperors used the Confucian value system to rationalize the hierarchical structure of Chinese society, to legitimize their political leadership and to promote socio-political harmony. Confucius was mainly concerned with *ren* (moral goodness, humanity and benevolence) and *li* (ritual, rites) in education. He emphasized the 'six arts' – rites, music, archery, charioteering, writing and numbers – as curriculum subjects through which social harmony and morality are developed, with rites and music being the most important (Lau 1979: 67; Legge 1971: 155), as '[O] ne is aroused by the songs, established by ritual and perfected by music' (Thomas 1981: 36). Music and rites were used in the hierarchical society of traditional China to improve people's behaviour and to promote social harmony (see Roberts 2006: 15–6; Wang 2004). This value system was reinforced by traditional learning and examinations, which were used both to educate the people and to train officials for service in the imperial government.

The government of Imperial China adopted the Confucian view of music education, which saw it as an instrument for the management of Chinese social and political life to consolidate the rule of the emperors. Chinese music education was always associated with officialdom. The Office of the Grand Music Master was set up to formalize the music educational structure in the Zhou dynasty (1122 BCE to 256 BCE). The music education system offered 9-year courses. The teaching content was based on the *Classics of Poetry* (Shi Jing), the *Book of Documents* (Shu Jing), the *Record of Rites* (Li Chi) and the *Classics of Music* (Yue Jing), which were reportedly written by Confucius.

The Han dynasty (206 BCE to 220 CE) witnessed another peak in the development of royal court music, when an official administrative institution named *Yuefu* (the Office of Music) was established in 112 BCE for collecting and editing folksongs and ballads, composing and revising music scores and presenting performances and concerts. The Office consisted of 800 teachers, musicologists, song writers, producers, musicians, dancers, instrument makers and so on (Liang 1985: 79). *Gongche* notation, invented in the Tang dynasty (618 to 907 CE), was used to indicate musical notes and became popular in the Song dynasty (960 to 1279 CE). The Tang dynasty is described as a 'golden age' in Chinese history; and the organization for court music under this dynasty was regarded as an important educational institution (Feng 2008). Music education was viewed as a controlling factor in harmonizing human beings within the well-ordered Confucian society.

Music education after the First Sino-British War

Beginning with the First Sino-British War in 1839, China suffered repeated military defeats at the hands of other countries – first the European powers, then the Japanese and the Russians. Western powers demanded the freedom to propagate the Christian religion and the liberty to proselytize the Chinese. European music was brought to China by Roman Catholic priests and Protestant missionaries. They were probably the earliest teachers of Western music (Scott 1963). Matteo Ricci (1552–1610), an Italian missionary who came to China in 1582 to preach Catholicism, was not only the first to introduce the religious music of the West into China, but also the first to introduce the operatic and sacrificial music of China to the West. Ricci carried a primitive clavichord with him across China from 1583 until he was allowed to present it to the Ming Emperor Wanli in 1601 (see Gong 2004; Lindorff 2004). Protestant missionaries introduced congregational hymn singing to China in the nineteenth century. Hong Xiu-quan (1814–1864), who led the Taiping Revolution (1851–1864) against the Qing dynasty, became acquainted with various features of Protestant worship under the influence of a Baptist minister from Missouri. Among the hymns Hong learned was 'The Old Hundredth', which he later adopted, with a new text, as the state hymn of the Taiping Heavenly Kingdom (Wong 1984: 113).

Tonic sol-fa was introduced to the Chinese population in 1862, in association with the missionary work of James Legge (a leading sinologist and a representative in Hong Kong of the London Missionary Society) (see Southcott 2004; Stevens 2007). In 1872 John Curwen noted that this system was employed by missionaries all over the world and 'Hong Kong was the third site' to establish the method (cited in Southcott and Lee 2008: 215). The Reverend Timothy Richard, who came to China in 1882, generated two different Chinese modulators and wrote a book, in Chinese, on the history and theory of music (see Bohr 2000; Stevens 2007). The beginning of informal music education in Hong Kong was also connected with the 'missionary invasion' or 'cultural invasion' from different parts of the world, including members of various Protestant and Roman Catholic associations.

At the primary and secondary levels, Japanese school songs and songs from Western Europe and America were adopted as teaching materials in China. Luo (1991: 11) identifies Chinese school songs as a 'new cultural phenomenon' for China in the early twentieth century and a 'double cultural contact' between the Western, Japanese and Chinese cultures. He characterizes the performance of Chinese school songs as the result of the 'reception of Western culture through Japan' (*ibid.*: 12). This Western-style music education was introduced into China with the help of foreign-trained Chinese musicians and music educators and of Western musicians. Early school songs in Shanghai adopted the melodies of British and American songs (Zhuang 2005). As Zhang (1991) notes, 'the introduction of Western music into China and the exchange between Western and Chinese music represent the irresistible historical trend favorable to people which no one can change or stop' (p. 411).

However, classroom learning was still traditional and rote oriented; and teacher education received very little attention in Chinese educational reforms. In 1897 the Qing Government founded the Nanyang Public School, regarded as the first school to provide teacher education in China and to introduce the study of teaching method in formal training. In 1904 it required all student teachers to receive instruction in the teaching methods for each school subject (Cao and He 2000: 7). In the following year the Qing government abandoned traditional education with the abolition of the Civil Service Examination and the ties between the ruling social class and the dynasty were cut. Chinese music educators suggested a major restructuring of the education system by developing new areas of learning. Music educators and musicians began to adopt a numerical notation known as the *jianpu* system (literally, simplified notation or numerical notation, an adaptation of the French Galin-Paris-Chevé system) by using the Arabic numerals 1 through 7 to denote pitches. This notation was copied from Japan where it had been successfully introduced by a French musician. *Jianpu* uses numbers to replace characters, but is a natural extension and unification of the *gongche* notation. Towards the end of the Qing dynasty, *jianpu* was also promoted by Chinese students who studied music in Japan.

In 1907 music was formally introduced in girls' schools and 2 years later in boys' schools (Liu 1998: 36–7). Music as a school subject was mainly based on teaching and learning songs. Cai Yuanpei (1868–1940), the first Minister of Education of the Chinese Republic after 1911, Chancellor of Peking University and a leading figure in aesthetic studies and liberal education in the early twentieth century, acknowledged the integrity and uniqueness of each culture, while suggesting that Western cultures could be assimilated into Chinese culture (Cai 1983, 1987; Xiu 1998; Zhang 2000). According to Cai (1983), aesthetic education aimed at the provision of a moral basis for society; music was a means of accelerating the development of culture and the adoption of Western music education would improve the development of Chinese music. Xiao Yumei (1884–1940), the 'father of contemporary Chinese music education', played an important role in the promotion of Western musical learning in China and opened up the improvement of Chinese music by borrowing Western elements, particularly in the theory of composition. Significantly, he had studied at the Leipzig Conservatory.

The development of patriotic songs from the 1910s to the 1940s

After the establishment of the Republic of China in 1911, a commission on music education was formed to provide suitable music for schools and for civic and national gatherings (Wiant 1966). Between 1912 and 1919, the Ministry of Education (MoE) established policies on a range of issues, including primary school regulations and timetabling, middle school curricula and teacher education. The MoE encouraged both primary and secondary schools to implement music lessons in their curricula and music textbooks underwent a period of significant development in Chinese publishing (Cao 1996: 45).

Early reforms in school songs were led by Chinese music students who had studied in Japan. Shen Xingong (1869–1947) and Li Shutong (1880–1942), who returned from musical training in Japan in 1903 and 1910 respectively, were two of the more important composers. The texts of their songs called for patriotism, self-discipline and the strengthening of the wills of Chinese children (Ho 2003). Shen and Li, who believed that music could help to save the country, were the first 'modern' composers to synthesise Western (European/Japanese) songs with Chinese marches (Gild 1998: 111–12; also see Ho 2006: 438). The end of the First World War coincided with the advent of the 1919 May Fourth Movement, which advocated the use of the Chinese vernacular language as a written medium of communication in all areas. This influenced the development of Chinese literature and music and led Chinese intellectuals to attack Confucian values. Chinese musicians' new vision was to introduce nationalism and the struggle for democracy into their music through the use of Western compositional skills and methods.

School music education was expanded in the early 1920s. The music curriculum guidelines for primary, junior and senior high schools were implemented in 1923, 1932 and 1940 respectively (Cao and He 2000: 7). In 1923 the Chinese government renamed 'lessons on national songs' as 'music lessons' for 6-year primary and 3-year junior high schools. The guidelines for junior high schools stressed four objectives:

1   to enable students to understand the basics of music theory
2   to teach students to sing Chinese songs
3   to give students an aesthetic education and to convey to them the spirit of music
4   to arouse students' interest in arts appreciation (*ibid.*).

In 1934 the Committee for Music Education was established to plan for primary and secondary teaching materials (Zhang 1990: 445). It was now asserted that music education was a valuable component of the school curriculum. Music performance such as singing was seen as contributing to the formation of personal intelligence, ethical discernment and moral responsibility. Moreover, Huang Zi (1904–1938), a Chinese music educator and composer, and other composers were requested to edit a set of music books in June 1933 and six sets of music textbooks were published in October 1939 (see Liang 1985: 138–9; Liu 1990: 439–45).

The growth of nationalism in Chinese music education was further reinforced when the country was militarily invaded during the Second Sino-

Japanese War (1937–1945). Encouraged and promoted by the Chinese MoE, the singing of anti-war songs became a significant musical activity from 1937–1945. According to Kwok (1987), the Western diatonic tonal system influenced the melodies of Chinese folksongs, which supplemented new teaching materials aimed at countering Japanese aggression during the 1930s and 1940s. Communist musicians in China produced 'a deluge of songs', mostly published on mimeographed sheets and in pamphlets (Hung 1996: 906). Patriotic/communist composers such as Nie Er (1912–1935) and Xian Xinghai (1905–1945), who all made use of tunes in national styles, produced large numbers of songs to motivate the masses to resist the Japanese invasion and to achieve national liberation. Nie Er's 'March of the Volunteers', 'Docker's Song' and 'Female Singer under Cruel Oppression' were representative of the new popular style, which included revolutionary European elements in song writing; the 'March of the Volunteers', for example, depicted Chinese intellectuals marching bravely to the front in the War of Resistance again the Japanese. This kind of song was typically taught and learned in school. The MoE sent officers to observe music lessons, produced both Chinese and English versions of the 'Collections of Anti-War Songs' and trained pupils to sing the 'Choral Work for Thousands of People' (Liu 1998: 246); the first such mass choral singing was organized in the spring of 1941 in Chongqing, Szechwan's largest city, with participants coming from different sectors including middle schools, vocational schools, universities and workers. The Music Education Committee also promoted military music through a 3-year programme that recruited teenagers aged 15 to 18 to receive formal vocal and instrumental training (Liu 1998: 248). Owing to the anti-foreign and anti-Japanese wars of the 1910s and 1940s, musicians and music educators became primary agents of cultural transformation, encouraging the musical expression of patriotism as a socio-political tool for disciplining society through compulsory education.

Promotion of revolutionary music from 1949 to the 1970s

Following the growth of the communist movement in China, Mao Zedong delivered, in 1942, a famous speech at the Yenan Forum on the use of literature and art to serve communist ideology and on the nature of art in a class-based society. In 1949 the Kuomingtang (the Chinese Nationalist Party) led by the Chinese Nationalist Chiang Kai-shek (1887–1975), which claimed to rule China from the 1930s through the Second World War, retreated to Taiwan and the PRC was formally established on 1 October, with its national capital at Beijing. The Chinese Communist Party (CCP) promoted revolutionary music while suppressing traditional and popular music. Many of the protest and revolutionary songs supported by the party were Chinese versions of existing

Soviet songs. Values education and politics were blended with traditional Chinese thought; and role models, cultural heroes, and politically sanctioned models were used to ensure the cohesion of Chinese culture and to create a well-ordered and cordial society (Reed 1995); for example, the song 'Without the Communist Party, There Would Be No New China' was very popular with the CCP. Thus, in Communist China, music and the arts in general were governed by Marxist-Leninist-Maoist ideology and were required to serve the students, workers, peasants and soldiers, as well as to convey the messages of the government. In the mid-1950s Communist China sent groups of 'politically reliable' students and party members from diverse fields of music to the Moscow Conservatory of Music and to other musical institutions in Eastern European countries, to further their studies (Mao 1991: 109).

The First National Conference on Education was organized by the MoE in December 1949. Ma Xulun, the Minister of Education, in his opening speech to the conference, defined education in the PRC as 'national, scientific, and mass-oriented' (cited in Shen 1994: 2). The old music syllabus was criticized as not reflecting the new era in China. After the establishment of the PRC in 1949, its first regulation for primary school students declared that they should develop a new democratic ideology and an international spirit, dedicate their love to the nation, its people and its public properties, instil national morals, strive for democracy and be brave, healthy and disciplined people (Yao 2000: 32). In 1950 the MoE focused on how singing could be improved for junior elementary grades and how the music curriculum guidelines could be positively implemented in primary and secondary school education (*ibid.*: 14–15). The teaching of revolutionary songs in school was encouraged.

In 1952 the Chinese MoE announced the reform of teacher education, which should be based on the Soviet Russian model. Education studies for trainee teachers represented 18.1 per cent of total curricular time in 1952 and 23.5 per cent in 1956 (Jin 1989: 44). There were nine compulsory music courses for student teachers:

1 an introduction to the arts
2 music theory
3 a study of important musical works
4 vocal and choral music
5 instrumental learning
6 music teaching method
7 an introduction to leisure activities
8 the practice of music and singing
9 the practice of education (Ma 2002: 170).

Weekly tutorials were scheduled focusing on music teaching methods. Teaching practice was usually conducted for 6 weeks in the sixth and seventh terms. All students who would become music teachers were required to take four subjects for their graduation examinations, including the basic ideology of Marxism-Leninism and the new democracy, educational methodologies and music teaching methods, music theory and instrumental and vocal performance (*ibid.*: 170–1).

The Cultural Revolution (1966–1976) was officially launched on 8 August 1966; its slogan was 'grasp revolution, [and] promote production'. The anti-intellectual policies of the Cultural Revolution brought chaos to the music educational establishment. As the politics of music in the PRC came to be reflected in the Cultural Revolution, tensions mounted within musical circles. The anthem that typified the Cultural Revolution was 'The East is Red', an old revolutionary song that became the movement's anthem. In the song, Chairman Mao was 'deified' as the sun in heaven. Its words are: 'The east is red, the sun has risen. China has produced Mao Zedong. He works for the people's happiness. He is the saviour of the people.' Music education was regarded as a 'political commodity' and was monitored to ensure that it conformed to the state's political ideology.

The Cultural Revolution took Chinese music education into a new phase of development, while bringing about educational disorder and the loss of cultural life. Between 1966 and 1969 all music programmes in teacher education ceased on the mainland (*ibid.*: 181). Although some teacher training institutions operated their individual music education programmes between 1970 and 1976, programmes did not have shared teaching goals and materials and their operational styles depended on local practical needs. Even when music activities were carried out in these educational institutions, they were mainly based on the revolutionary content. Music teachers had diverse cultural and musical backgrounds and they were required to implement their own curricula in schools. However, the song repertoire was restricted to only a few songs under this system of political control. Lei Feng (1940–1962), a 22-year-old soldier who died in a tragic accident in 1962, was thought to exemplify the communist role model by doing good deeds or favours for people and became a symbol of China's communist spirit. On 5 March 1963 Chairman Mao initiated the nationwide 'Learn from Lei Feng' campaign as a mandatory part of the Chinese education system (Reed 1995). Songs such as 'We Have to be Lei Feng-style Good Teenagers' and 'Lei Feng: Our Friend in the War' were among the common materials learnt by students in school. Yao (1989: 25) maintained that 'singing one song' was, by impli-cation, to have one 'political education' lesson. The only extra-curricular musical activities that schools were allowed to attend were eight revolu-tionary musicals: including the symphonic suite *Shachiapang*, two ballets *The Red Detachment of Women* and *The White-haired Girl*, and five operas: *Red Lantern's Record, Capturing the Tiger Mountain by Strategy, On the Docks, Raid on the White Tiger Regiment* and *Shajiabang* (Chen 2002; Yao 1989). The themes of the eight model dramas were 'drawn from the proletarian struggles during the Civil and Sino-Japanese War' (Liang 1985:157). This small group of officially sanctioned model works (also known as the eight revolutionary model works) limited what people in China could watch, hear, perform and appreciate in the community.

With the fall of the 'Gang of Four' (the group of Chinese Communist Party leaders, including Jiang Qing, Zhang Chunqiao, Yao Wenyuan and Wang Hongwen, who played key roles in the Cultural Revolution), mainland China entered a new era, one of rapid economic growth from 1978 onwards under the leadership of Deng Xiaoping. It was a time of transition for mainland China from the revolutionary stage towards a more open and inclusive type of politics that has led to an increase in economic cooperation, trade and interdependence between countries. Deng Xiaoping criticized the effects of the Cultural Revolution on the arts and asked, 'How can eight shows [i.e. the eight revolutionary musicals] satisfy an audience of eight hundred million people?' (cited in Manuel 1988: 232). Thus traditional Chinese music and Western classical music were turned to once again. Many musicians from Europe, America and other Asian countries were invited to China to teach music or give performances and Chinese students were permitted to go abroad to study music. The development of music and music education in China underwent considerable change, with the influence of the Eastern bloc countries waning, and the influence of Western countries increasing after the 1978 declaration of the open-door policy.

Major changes to school curricula following the 1978 open-door policy

The 10 years of the Cultural Revolution had brought the Chinese education system to a virtual halt, so formal and structured music education was now very difficult to conduct. In the aftermath of the Revolution, Deng Xiaoping declared, in 1978, the nation's commitment to science and technology, and proclaimed four areas for modernization – agriculture, industry, science and technology and the military – as key means of achieving China's national goals. Deng succeeded in setting the country on the road to socialist modernization. He encouraged the creation of a market economy and his reforms lifted an estimated 170 million peasants out of extreme poverty (*CNN News*, 1999).

Openness and reform under Deng Xiaoping's leadership in the 1980s shifted the national focus away from class struggle and towards economic reconstruction; compulsory education was identified as the pathway for advancing science and technology (see Dual and Cheng 1990; Kau and Marsh 1993; Rao 1985). Current Chinese music education is guided by Deng

Xiaoping's educational principle of 'Looking for modernisation, looking to the world and looking to the future' (Ho 2004: 234). In June 1979 the MoE distributed a new music syllabus for primary and secondary schools and instruction in methods for teaching music in secondary schools was enforced in teacher training courses in December of the same year (Cao and He 2000: 8; also see Ma 2005: 153).

From the late 1970s to 2000 China enacted several major education laws and over 200 regulation changes in order to promote good educational practice, to enhance and universalize primary and junior secondary (i.e. Grades 1–9) school education, to increase the number of schools and qualified teachers and to reform education in order to enable China to compete in the global economy (see Law 1999, 2007). The Fourth Session of the Sixth National People's Congress, held in Beijing in 1986, adopted the 'Compulsory Education Law of the PRC', stipulating that the state should provide 9 years of compulsory education (i.e. Grades 1–9) for all children, and music lessons in all primary and junior high schools (i.e. up to year nine, age 15); music was introduced into senior high schools (i.e. years ten to twelve, for those aged 16 to 18) in 1994. The child-centred approach is encouraged, one in which a music teacher is not viewed merely as an instructor, but also as a facilitator who uses a variety of media and a commitment to high artistic standards in his/her teaching (see Ministry of Education 2001; Song 2007; Wang 2008; Xu 1998; Zheng and Jin 2004).

Music specialists are trained at universities, teacher training institutes and teacher training colleges, which enroll graduates from senior high schools in full-time 4-year programmes (to train senior high school teachers), and full-time 2- or 3-year programmes (to train junior high school teachers). Music teachers for primary schools, kindergartens and special education are usually generalists, graduates from junior high schools trained in 3- or 4-year programmes that include compulsory courses such as ideology and political education, basic audio-visual education, Chinese, mathematics, music, fine arts, physical education, teaching practice and extracurricular activities (see China Education and Research Network 2001). There has been a great shortage of music teachers for school education, more so in rural than in urban areas. A 1996 National Education Committee survey of eight provinces (Fujian, Beijing, Tianjin, Shandong, Shanxi, Hainan, Zhejiang and Guizhou) showed that rural areas had 0.06 music teacher per primary school and 0.63 music teacher per junior high school, while urban primary schools have 1.14 music teachers per school, and 2.51 music teachers per junior high school (see Ma 2002: 232).

The teaching materials were compiled in accordance with new compulsory education standards determined by the MoE (*China Education Daily*, 12 July 2001). Although *jianpu* is still present in Chinese school education, teachers are advised to teach students, eventually, the five-stave notation (Ma 2002:

200; Yao 2000: 37). Music textbooks in China largely present the materials using this notation. As instructed by the MoE, the People's Music Publisher issued standard music textbooks for primary and secondary school education in 1980, and its publications ended the long-term lack of music materials in China's education (Jin 2003: 4). Since then, a uniform standard for school curricula, textbooks and teacher qualifications has been established; however, provinces, autonomous regions and special municipalities retain significant autonomy and variations are allowed. The MoE suggests that the teaching contents of music lessons for junior (i.e. Grades 1–2), intermediate (i.e. Grades 3–4) and senior primary schools (i.e. Grades 5–6) should include singing, instrumental learning, music appreciation, music reading and sight singing; singing is strongly emphasized in the curriculum (see Table 13.1) (Lu 1999: 65). For music lessons in the junior high schools (Grades 7–9), there is an attempt to balance these activities evenly in the curriculum (see Table 13.1) (*ibid.*: 66).

Music teaching materials must be those accepted by the MoE, which reviews and approves the music textbooks widely used as teaching materials in primary and secondary schools in Shanghai, Beijing, Harbin and other major cities of China. The recent textbook revisions, newly published materials and recommended technological resources for teaching musical cultures are all

Table 13.1 Teaching contents and hours of music lessons as suggested by the Ministry of Education, China

Grades	Teaching contents	Teaching hours
1–2	Singing	50
3–4	Singing	50
5–6	Singing	40
7–9	Singing	30–40
1–2	Instrumental learning	20
3–4	Instrumental learning	20
5–6	Instrumental learning	20
7–9	Instrumental learning	20
1–2	Music reading and sight singing	10
3–4	Music reading and sight singing	10
5–6	Music reading and sight singing	15
7–9	Music appreciation	20–30
7–9	Learning of basic music theory and aural training	20

designed to make education truly meaningful to Chinese youth, to help them to 'break free' from the limitations of traditional education and to construct learning experiences with links not only to society and technology but also to students' lives (Guo 2005; Song 2007; Teaching Resources Editing Group for High School Teachers 2001). Interactive mass media teaching resources and learning materials involving broadcasts for schools, television and internet capabilities are regarded as creating windows to expand students' musical horizons (Ho 2007; Ministry of Education 2001; Zheng and Jin 2004).

Concluding remarks

This chapter has examined Chinese music education from the 1840s to today's rapidly modernizing society, with the main focus on state power and its ongoing efforts to incorporate values education into compulsory education. During periods of socio-political transformation in China, cultural roles were established for music that served political ideologies and state power was exercised to turn the less obviously political institution of the school into an ideal venue for music education. We have seen that music education in China has been aligned with the shifts in the dominant Chinese political ideology. In particular, music education was a medium of political propaganda to foster resistance to Japanese aggression and support for nationalism in the 1930s and to support revolution and communism from the 1940s to the 1970s. The cultivation of correct political consciousness has sometimes become a kind of obsession in the selection and performance of music and in music education. China's open-door policy has moved the country from isolation to engagement and has intensified external pressures on China to increase its cultural interaction with the rest of the world.

Teacher education in China has entered into a new stage of development and is emerging as an essential element in improving education. The renewal of music practices and materials in school music education has also come about, due to rapid changes in Chinese society. School students are encouraged to improve their sense of musical perception and aesthetics, so that they can be more critical when listening to music, sensitive to musical creativity and have more understanding of diverse musical cultures (Law and Ho 2009; Ministry of Education 2001: 2–3; Wang 2003; Zhang *et al.* 2004; Zhu and Liao 2003: 34–41).

References

Bohr, P. R. (2000), 'Famine in China and the mission: Timothy Richard as relief administrator and advocate of national reform 1876–1884', *International Bulletin of Missionary Research*, 24, 75–80.

Cai, Y. P. (1983), *Miexue Wenxuan* (The Selected Works on Aesthetics by Cai Yuanpei). Beijing: Beijing Daxus Chubanshe.

Cai, Y. P. (1987), *Jiaoyu Lunji* (A Collection of Education Treatises by Cai Yuanpei). Hunan: Jiaoya Chubanshe.

Cao, L. (1996), *Putong Xuexiao Yinle Jiaoyuxue* (Education Method for Teaching General Schools) (2nd edn). Shanghai: Shanghai Xiaoyu Chubanshe.

Cao, L. and He, G. (2000), *Yinyue Xueke Jiaoyuxue* (The Educational Theory of Music Teaching). Beijing: Capital Normal University.

Chen, X. M. (2002), *Acting the Right Part: Political Theater and Popular Drama in Contemporary China*. Honolulu: University of Hawaii Press.

China Education Daily, 12 July 2001.

China Education and Research Network (2001), *Teacher Education in China (III): Preservice Training of Primary and Secondary School Teachers*, www.edu.cn/introduction5 _1399/20060323/t20060323_4028.shtml.

CNN News (1999), 'Reformer with an iron fist: Deng Xiaoping (1904–1997)', www. cnn.com/SPECIALS/1999/china.50/inside.china/profiles/deng.xiaoping/.

Dual, P. A. and Cheng, L. L. (1990), 'Education and projected manpower needs of Mainland China', in B. Lin and L. Fan (eds), *Education in Mainland China: Review and Evaluation*. Taipei: Institute of International Relations, National Chengchi University, pp. 254–71.

Feng, Z. P. (2008), 'The textual research about the institution of Royal Court Music in the Tang Dynasty and the function of its music education', *Kashi Shifanxueyuan Xuebao* (Journal of Kashgar Teachers College), 29, (2), 45–8.

Gild, G. (1998), 'Dreams of renewal inspired by Japan and the west: early 20th century reforms in Chinese music', *Chime*, 12–13, 116–23.

Gong, H. Y. (2004), 'Western classical music in China from Matteo Ricci to Li Delun', *Musicology in China*, 4, 138–40.

Guo, S. J. (2005), *Yishu Jiaoyulun* (Discussion on Arts Education) (3rd edn). Shanghai: Shanghai Educational Publisher.

Ho, W. C. (2003), 'Westernization and social transformation in Chinese music education, 1895–1949', *History of Education*, 32, (3), 289–301.

Ho, W. C. (2004), 'A comparative study of music education in Shanghai and Taipei: westernization and nationalization', *Compare*, 34, (2), 231–49.

Ho, W. C. (2006), 'Social change and nationalism in China's popular songs', *Social History*, 31, (4), 435–53.

Ho, W. C. (2007), 'Students' experiences with and preferences for using information technology in music learning in Shanghai's secondary schools', *British Journal of Educational Technology*, 38, (4), 699–714.

Huang, R. (1988), *China, A Macro History*. Armonk, NY: M. E. Sharpe.

Hung, C. T. (1996), 'The politics of songs: myths and symbols in the Chinese Communist war music, 1937–1949', *Modern Asian Studies*, 30, (4), Special Issue: War in modern China, 901–929.

Jin, Y. Q. (1989), 'Zhongdeng shifan jiaoyu zhuanye kecheng gaige jiyi' (Urgent comments on the reform of educational studies in the normal school curriculum), *Jiaoyu Yanjiu*, 5, 44–6.

Jin, Y. W. (2003), *Chuzhong Yinyue Xin Kecheng Jiaoxuefa* (Early Secondary School New Music Curriculum Teaching Methods). Beijing: Higher Education Publisher.

Kau, M. Y. M. and Marsh, S. H. (eds) (1993), *China in the Era of Deng Xiaoping: A Decade of Reform*. Armonk: M. E. Sharpe.

Kwok, T. J. (1987), *Zheng: A Chinese Zither and Its Music*. Michigan: University Microfilms International.

Lau, D. C. (1979), *Confucius: The Analects*. London: Penguin.

Law, W. W. (1999), 'New rules of the game in education in the People's Republic of China: education laws and regulations' (guest editor's introduction), *Chinese Education and Society*, 32, (3), 3–8.

Law, W. W. (2007), 'Legislation and educational changes: the struggle for social justice and quality in China's compulsory schooling', *Education and Law*, 19, (3/4), 177–99.

Law, W. W. and Ho, W. C. (2009), 'A review of values education in China's school music education: from nationalism to globalization', *Journal of Curriculum Studies*, 41, (4), 501–520

Legge, J. (1971), *Confucius: Confucian Analects: The Great Learning & the Doctrine of the Mean*. New York: Dover.

Liang, M. Y. (1985), *Music of the Billion: An Introduction to Chinese Musical Culture*. New York: Heinrichshofen Edition.

Lindorff, J. (2004), 'Missionaries, keyboards and musical exchange in the Ming and Qing Courts', *Early Music*, 32, (3), 403–414.

Liu, C. C. (ed.) (1990), *History of New Music in China 1946–1976: Collected Essays*, Hong Kong: University of Hong Kong.

Liu, C. C. (1998), *Zhongguo Xin Yinyue Shilun* (Historical Record of New China Music), vol. 1. Taipei: Yaowen Shiye Co.

Lu, M. D. (ed.) (1999), *Xiandai Zhongxiaoxue Yishu Xiaoyue Lun* (Education in Modern Arts Education in Primary and Secondary Schools). Nanjing: Jiangsu Educational Publisher.

Luo, C. K. (1991), 'Double cultural contact: diffusion and reformation of Japanese school songs in China', in Y. Tokumaru, M. Ohmiya, M. Kanazawa, O. Yamaguti, T. Tukitani, A. Takamatu *et al.* (eds), *Tradition and Its Future in Music: Report of SIMS 1990*. Osaka, Tokyo: Mita Press, pp. 11–14.

Ma, D. (2002), *Ershi Shiji Zhongguo Xueshao Yinyue Jiaoyue* (Chinese School Music Education of the 20th Century). Shanghai: Shanghai Educational Publisher.

Ma, D. (2005), *Yinyue Xiaoyu Kexue Yanjiu Fangfa* (The Scientific Research Method in Music Education). Shanghai: Shanghai Music Chubanshe.

Manuel, P. (1988), *Popular Music of the Non-Western World: An Introductory Survey*. New York and Oxford: Oxford University Press.

Mao, Y. R. (1991), 'Music under Mao, its background and aftermath', *Asian Music*, XXII, (2), 97–125.

Ministry of Education, The People's Republic of China (2001), *Quanri Zhi Yiwu Jiaoyu: Yinyue Kecheng Biaozhun (Shiyan Gao)* (Full-time Voluntary Education: Standard of Music Curriculum (Experimental Version). Beijing: Beijing Normal University Publisher.

Rao, K. V. S. (1985), 'Education in China, Maoist and Dengist Models', *China Report*, 21, 415–25.

Reed, G. G. (1995), 'Moral/political education in the People's Republic of China: learning through role models', *Journal of Moral Education*, 24, (2), 99–111.

Roberts, J. A. G. (2006), *A History of China* (2nd edn). New York: Palgrave Macmillan.

Scott, A. C. (1963), *Literature & the Arts in Twentieth Century China*. Garden City, NY: Doubleday.

Shen, J. P. (1994), 'Educational policy in the People's Republic of China: a political influence perspective', *Journal of Education Policy*, 9, (1), 1–13.

Song, J. (2007), 'How does a music teacher face the education of the new century', *Journal of Xichang College*, 21, (2), 101–103, 110.

Southcott, J. E. (2004), 'The first tonic sol-fa missionary: Reverend Robert Toy in Madagascar', *Research Studies in Music Education*, 23, 3–17.

Southcott, J. E. and Lee, A. H. C. (2008), 'Missionaries and tonic sol-fa music pedagogy in 19th-century China', *International Journal of Music Education*, 26, (3), 213–28.

Stevens, R. S. (2007), 'Tonic sol-fa in Asia-Pacific countries – the missionary legacy', *Asia-Pacific Journal for Arts Education*, 5, (1), 52–76.

Teaching Resources Editing Group for High School Teachers (2001), *Zhongxue Yinyue Jiaoxuelun Jiaocheng* (Theory of Secondary School Music Education) (2nd edn). Beijing: People's Music Publishing Company.

Thomas, K. T. (ed.) (1981), *Confucius*. Oxford: Oxford University Press.

Wang, J. J. (2008), 'On the music teaching and the reforms of music teaching in the teachers' universities', *Journal of Hebei Normal University* (Educational Science Edition), 10, (3), 86–9.

Wang, Y. K. (2003), *Quanri Zhi Yiwu Jiaoyu: Yishu Kecheng Biaozhun Jiaoshi Duben* (Full-time Voluntary Education: Standard of Arts Curriculum, Teacher's Copy). Wu Han: Hua Chung Normal University Chubanshe.

Wang, Y. W. (2004), 'The ethical power of music: Ancient Greek and Chinese thoughts', *Journal of Aesthetic Education*, 38, (1), 89–104.

Wiant, B. (1966), *The Music of China*. Hong Kong: Chung Chi College, the Chinese University of Hong Kong.

Wong, I. K. F. (1984), 'Geming gequ: songs for the education of the masses', in B. S. McDougall (ed.), *Popular Chinese Literature and Performing*. London: University of California Press, pp. 112–43.

Xiu, H. L. (1998), 'Modern music education and Cai Yuanpei's views on Chinese and western culture', *Musical Performance*, 21, (2), 15–17.

Xu, D. (1998), 'Reports on the seventh national music education symposium', *People's Music*, December, 2–6.

Yao, S. Y. (1989), 'On the construction and development of China schools' musical education', *People Music* (Renmin Yinyue), 10, 24–7.

Yao, S. Y. (2000), *Zhongguo Dangdai Xuexiao Xinyue Jiaoyu Wenxuan* (Selected Papers for School Music Education in Contemporary China). Shanghai: Shanghai Educational Publisher.

Zhang, D. K., Tan, T. J. and Chang, Y. H. (2004), *Zhongxiao Xue Inyue Xin Kecheng Jiaoxue Fa* (The New Teaching Method for the Primary and Secondary School Music Education). Beijing: Capital Normal University Press.

Zhang, J. R. (1990), 'The development and investigation of contemporary China music education', in C. C. Liu (ed.), *History of New Music in China 1946–1976: Collected Essays*. Hong Kong: University of Hong Kong, pp. 439–56.

Zhang, L. Z. (2000), 'Cai Yuanpei (1868–1940)', *Prospects*, XXIII, (1/2), 147–157.

Zhang, Q. (1991), 'The history and future of the reception of western music by China in the 20th Century', in Y. Tokumaru, M. Ohmiya, M. Kanazawa, O. Yamaguti, T. Tukitani, A. Takamatu *et al.* (eds), *Tradition and Its Future in Music: Report of SIMS 1990 Osaka*. Tokyo: Mita Press, pp. 407–412.

Zheng, L. and Jin, Y. M. (2004), *Music Education: New Vision*. Beijing: Higher Education Press.

Zhu, Z. P. and Liao, Y. W. (2003), *Quanri Zhi Yiwu Jiaoyu: Yinyue Kecheng Biaozhun Jiaoshi Duben* (Full-time Voluntary Education: Standard of Music Curriculum Teacher's Copy). Wu Han: Hua Chung Normal University Chubanshe.

Zhuang, Z. L. (2005), *Xuetang Chunqiu* (Schools and Colleges in Old Shanghai). Shanghai: Shanghai Cultural Publishing House.

14

Japan: Music as a tool for moral education?

Masafumi Ogawa

It may perhaps be surprising to the outsider that in 2008 the school music curriculum in Japan does not use indigenous Japanese music as its foundation. Although Japanese music has recently been included to a greater extent in contemporary music textbooks, the curriculum in Japan is essentially centred on Western music. This means that tonal music and the Western notation system are the norm. Students sing European or American songs as well as listening to Western art music, for example, to Beethoven's Fifth Symphony. There are concert grand pianos and other Western musical instruments in most music classrooms. Japanese traditional music instruments such as *koto* or *taiko* have been increasingly introduced but are still less frequently used than Western instruments. It must, of course, be recalled that in Asian countries including Japan, Western music was inseparable from industrialization and imperialism, since it was imported and implanted along with political and economical ideologies during the nineteenth century.

In this chapter, I pose three questions:

1   Why is the Japanese school music curriculum Western-centred?
2   Should indigenous Japanese music be used as the core?
3   Is the thinking underpinning Japanese music education fundamentally flawed?

As a Japanese music educator, it is my responsibility to explain and answer these important questions. It is also my responsibility to explain the current characteristics and realities of music education in Japan. Accordingly, in this chapter, I provide a brief sketch of the most critical moments in music education history in Japan beginning with the introduction of music into schools through to the educational reforms that followed the Second World War and finally addressing the key questions mentioned previously.

The beginnings of school music education

The introduction of music into school education coincided with modernization in Japan. After a long period of *sakoku* (self-seclusion from the world) by the Tokugawa shogunate (1603–1868), a new Japanese government opened up to the world in 1868 and the Meiji period began. Accordingly, the government began reforming the nation by employing world-class scientists, engineers and scholars from abroad – this was known as *Oyatoi Gaikokujin* (invited foreign employees). The area of specialization of these overseas experts covered virtually every academic discipline including music.

In 1872 a new educational law *Gakusei* (the Fundamental Code of Education) was promulgated. This was the first educational law for establishing a school system for the entire nation. The law was based on European models, principally those of Holland and France (Kimura 1983: 9). Under the Code, music was introduced for the first time as a school subject – as *shōka* (singing) for elementary schools and *sōgaku* (performing) for middle schools. However, there was an additional note to the Code, which advised that 'for the time being it can be omitted'. Since the Code was largely ineffectual and did not match the reality at that time, *Gakusei* was abandoned and replaced by *Kyōikurei* (the Educational Law) in 1879. It should be noted that music was an optional subject in the school curriculum until 1919 when the government revised the educational law (Sawasaki 1983: 215).

Establishment of the *Ongaku torishirabe kakari* (Music Study Committee)

The implementation of school music education in Japan began with the establishment of the new institution called *Ongaku torishirabe kakari* (Music Study Committee) in 1880. This institution was created in order to implement music education according to the Fundamental Code of Education and succeeding educational laws. It was the first institution for both music research and music teacher training.

It was founded and operated by the government, and three senior officials of the Ministry of Education played key roles in its formation: Tanaka Fujimaro (1845–1909), Mekada Tanetarō (1853–1926) and Isawa Shūji (1851–1917). Tanaka was Secretary General of the Ministry of Education from 1870 to 1878 and Mekada, who had graduated from Harvard, was a supervisor of the foreign scholarship programme. Isawa, who had studied at the Bridgewater Normal School in Boston, later became the director of the institution. All three visited the United States to investigate American music education as a model for Japan and after returning, they focused on establishing and developing the new institution.

The *Ongaku torishirabe kakari* had three objectives:

1 to create new music by combining Western and Eastern musical styles
2 to educate the leaders who would create 'a national music' for the future
3 to implement music education in schools nationwide.

Luther Whiting Mason

In 1872 a mission from the Japanese government visited Eben Tourjee (1834–1891), president of the New England Conservatory of Music, as part of a mission to study Western culture (see Ogawa 1991). Tourjeè recommended to the members of the mission, his close friend Luther Whiting Mason (1817–1896) – a highly respected music educator then at the peak of his career – with the result that 8 years later, Mason was officially invited to became the first invited foreign employee for the *Ongaku torishirabe kakari*.

As one of the most significant American music educators of the nineteenth century, Luther Whiting Mason served as superintendent of the Boston public schools from 1864 until 1878, and was the author of numerous music textbooks (see Howe 1997; Ogawa 2003). He was the first to publish a graded music textbook series, entitled *The National Music Course* (Mason 1870a). His method of teaching music adopted three European music education methods – from John Curwen (England), Galin-Paris-Chevé (France) and Christian Heinrich Hohmann (Germany) (see Hohmann 1853). Mason adapted and combined these methods to evolve his own American method of singing instruction.

Mason's period in Japan was from 2 March 1880 until 14 July 1882 (Nakamura 1993: 488). During this time, he had three main duties: teaching the students of *Ongaku torishirabe kakari*, developing music materials for schools and teaching music at various schools. These duties were tightly linked with the three objectives of *Ongaku torishirabe kakari*. It is important to note that although he was given a degree of authority, he was neither the director nor the final decision maker as the institution was under the control of Isawa Shūji and the Ministry of Education.

At *Ongaku torishirabe kakari*, Mason taught singing method courses, piano, reed organ, orchestra and basic harmony. It is likely that his textbook series *The National Music Course* was used for singing method classes; the textbook for piano classes was Ferdinand Bayer's *Vorschule im Klaviaspiel*, Opus 101. Singing method classes met four times per week and piano, orchestra and harmony were scheduled for once per week. In his harmony classes, Mason was not confident enough in grading students and so he sent his students' harmony exercises to Professor Stephan A. Emery (1841–1891) of the New England Conservatory of Music for correction periodically (*ibid.*: 521).

Concerning his second duty, Mason contributed to the publication of *Shōgaku shōkashū* I–III, the first music textbook series in Japan (Ministry of Education 1881, 1883, 1884). Mason was involved in the first two volumes. *Shōgaku shō kashū* I, published in 1881, contained 33 songs for unison voices of which thirty were selected from Mason's *National Music Course* with the rest being composed by *Ongaku torishirabe kakari* staff. *Shōgaku shōkashū II* (1883) consisted of 16 songs – 15 in unison and one round – of which 13 were songs from foreign music textbooks and three were original.

In addition to Mason's work with the publication of music textbooks, he also contributed to teachers' manuals for singing instruction – *The National Music Teacher* (Mason 1870b) and *A Preparatory Course and Key to the Second Series of Music Charts and Second Music Reader* (Mason 1873) – that were partially translated into Japanese as *Ongaku shinan* and *Ongaku shōkei* by Yaichi Uchida. These translated books were used not only in *Ongaku torishirabe kakari*, but also in most teacher training schools across the nation.

To fulfil his third duty, Mason taught music at the Tokyo Normal School, the Tokyo Girl's Normal School, the elementary school and kindergarten of the Tokyo Girl's School and *Gakushūin* elementary school. Aside from training the students, Mason's teaching was also intended to test the effectiveness of new teaching materials prior to the new music textbooks being published. The results of his teaching were presented at the *dai-enshūkai* (big concert) on 30 and 31 January 1882.

In November 1881 Mason's hard work was rewarded with an extension to his contract but in June 1882 he submitted a request to leave Japan for some months in order to collect new music material for publication in future music textbooks. Mason left Japan on 14 July 1882 for Hamburg via the United States. However, in November 1882 his contract was suddenly cancelled by the Japanese government. Several reasons have been suggested for this unexpected action. First, Isawa and Mason had different approaches to developing music education and 'national music' – Isawa was particularly disappointed that Mason had not shown sufficient ability in the blending together of Japanese and Western music styles. Second, Mason's salary was exceedingly high and to continue it would have been a drain on *Ongaku torishirabe kakari's* finances. Third, Mason had achieved the initial objectives and it was felt that no further contributions were needed (Nakamura 1993: 538–41). In fact, Mason's departure represented a major change in policy at the *Ongaku torishirabe kakari*. At the time when the Japanese government cancelled the contract, they had already negotiated a new contract with a professional German composer Franz Eckert (1852–1916). From this period onward, the institution became a German-orientated professional music conservatory (*ibid*.: 542–3).

Isawa Shūji and his philosophy of music education

As one of the core members who developed the music education system in Japan, Isawa Shūji has been called 'the father of music education in Japan'. He was the director of *Ongaku torishirabe kakari* from 1880 until 1891. Isawa was a student, then a friend and colleague of Mason and published his own music textbook series, which was an outcome from his study with Mason. Although Isawa was not a musician, he understood the role and importance of music education.

Isawa provided a rationale for music education to the government at least twice during his career. The first time was in 1878 when he submitted the first letter of petition, co-authored with his superior Megata Tanetarō, to the Secretary General at the Ministry of Education in which he stated:

> [Music] refreshes the mind of school children, provides relaxation from the efforts of hard study, strengthens the lungs, promotes the health, sharpens the thinking, pleases the heart well and also forms a good character. These are its direct advantageous effects functioning in the classroom, while its corresponding indirect effects functioning with regard to society are: its capacity for providing recreation and removing it from evil, for the advance of society in civil manners, for elating the people, for praising royal virtue and for the enjoyment of peace. (Eppstein 1994: 38)

Isawa made no mention of the origins of this rationale. However, although emphasizing its functional values, he nevertheless represented music as being subsidiary to other subjects. It has been suggested that Isawa may have thought this strategy would be more effective in gaining government approval but his rationale was, in fact, similar to that of the American music educator, Lowell Mason, except for the latter's arguing for the religious effectiveness of music (Ogawa 2000: 58).

In his second statement, Isawa outlined the purpose of music education in the preface to *Shōgaku shōkashū* Vol. I (1881): 'The importance of education falls into three categories – moral, intellectual and physical. At the elementary school level, moral sense is the most important of the three' (Ministry of Education 1881 [author's translation]).

The first statement was made before the *Ongaku torishirabe kakari* was established whereas the second statement was written after the institution was established and Isawa had become its director. The emphasis on the moral sense in justifying music as a curriculum subject represented not only Isawa's opinion, but also the government's position. Henceforth, it was to become the official rationale for music education in Japan.

Later in 1883 at the Academic Jury Committee (*gakuji senmon iinkai*), Isawa made another important speech on the rationale of music education in schools. Entitled 'On the Merit of Singing and the Method of Teaching',

Isawa posited two main 'merits' for music in education – for health (*kenzenjō no eki*) and for promoting a moral sense and patriotism (*tokuiku ni shisuru eki*). Here, Isawa placed greater emphasis on the moral aspects:

> The elementary school period is the most important in education because children in these ages can easily be sensitized and influenced. Therefore, music to be used in this level should be carefully chosen, and indirect and elegant, so as to guide children towards goodness and justice. For example, the songs should praise flowers, birds, winds and the moon, so that children's minds can identify with nature and the moral sense can be developed. (Tokyo Geijutsu Daigaku 1987: 15 [author's translation])

Isawa went on to point out 11 kinds of moral sense to be educated through singing instruction (Ogawa 2000: 290). In all this, music was used as a means to an end. He believed that there was a nine-step hierarchy in music learning. The actual music curriculum could be arranged accordingly:

1 rote singing (*kōju shōka*)
2 cipher notation (*sūji renshū*)
3 scale exercises (*onkai renshū*)
4 staff notation exercises (*fuhyōno renshū*)
5 unison melody singing (*tan-on shōka*)
6 rounds (*rinshō*)
7 two-part song (*fukuin shōka*)
8 piano (*yōkin*)
9 orchestra (*kangengaku*) (Tokyo Geijutsu Daigaku 1987: 121).

It is interesting that this hierarchy of music steps was muddled in that it mixed up musical styles and genres. The first seven steps are commonly used for singing training, as exemplified in the Kodály method, but this does not necessarily mean that they are the necessary prerequisites of piano and orchestral playing. However, this is what Isawa and his contemporaries believed. Another point is that these nine steps were not only hierarchical in terms of increasing levels of difficulty, but represented ascending degrees of musical value (Ogawa 2000: 293). To Isawa, the higher steps were superior in value to the lower steps. Therefore, the orchestra was ranked as the highest form of music making.

Isawa's view of music education was also seen in later documents. In 1884 the first report of *Ongaku torishirabe kakari seiseki sinpōsho* included a short essay by Isawa entitled *Ongaku to kyōiku no kankei* (The relationship between music and education). He asserted that songs in major keys were superior to those in minor keys because 'the former are usually gallant and have a vivid mood (*yūsō kappatsu*) whereas songs in minor keys are limp and have a depressing mood (*nyūjaku yūutsu*)' (quoted in Ogawa 2000: 296). Isawa continued, 'if a person is nurtured by the major key, he or she develops a gallant and vivid mind and gains a healthy and virtuous body and soul' (*ibid.*).

Isawa cited a table in which each country was listed with the distribution of songs by major keys and minor keys. Germany ranked at the top with 98 per cent of songs in major keys, followed by Switzerland, Poland and Serbia. According to Ogawa, 'culturally advanced nations tend to have more songs in major keys than culturally unsophisticated nations' (*ibid.*: 297). This belief is still evident in Japan today with the majority of songs in music textbooks being in major keys especially in lower grades.

As one of the founders of and early decision makers about music education in Japan, Isawa's philosophy effectively represented the government's position. Accordingly his ideas and influence were reflected in classroom practice for a significant period.

Three objectives reviewed

To what extent were the three objectives of *Ongaku torishirabe kakari* achieved? The first of these was to integrate Western music and Japanese music, a genre called *wa-yō secchū*. This meant that the two different music systems would interact with one another and a new music system would evolve. Fusing two different musical cultures was not easy and so what actually occurred was merely a superficial compromise. The outcomes included transference of Japanese music to Western notation, creating Japanese texts for foreign melodies and composition of new songs in Western style by Japanese staff. The evidence for this is present in the three volumes of *Shōgaku shōkashū* (Ministry of Education 1881, 1883, 1884). For example, Japanese songs were transferred to staff notation. Japanese texts were supplied for the Scottish song 'Auld Lang Syne', retitled as *hotaru* (a firefly) and the German folksong 'Lightly Row' was recast as *chōchō* (a butterfly) and each had new texts. As for the creation of new material, the song *yamato nadeshiko* (a wild pink) was composed by one of Mason's Japanese students. These achievements were the result of efforts by Mason, Isawa and the staff of the institution. However, the transformation and fusion of Western and Japanese music did not in reality occur at that time. It took about a century to achieve these objectives until the appearance of Toru Takemitsu (Ogawa 1994: 35).

As for the second objective, the institution was successful in educating leaders. When *Ongaku torishirabe kakari* was established in 1880 it had 22 students. They included a group of court musicians who had served as professional *Gagaku* players in the emperor's palace with the remainder coming mostly from noble families. The following year, 12 students entered. The curriculum was a 4-year programme. The students studied singing, piano, *koto*, reed organ, *kokyū*, violin, harmony, theory of music, history of music and teaching methods. Despite the fact that they had no background in Western music, most of them showed remarkable progress. Three of them – Tōyama Kine, Kōda Nobu and Ue Sanemichi – became faculty members of *Tokyo ongaku gakkō* (Tokyo School of Music), the successor to *Ongaku torishirabe kakari*. Other graduates became faculty members of the normal schools throughout Japan.

The third objective was also successful. The infrastructure of the school system was organized within a short period after *Ongaku torishirabe kakari* was established. As outlined earlier, the teaching materials – *Shōgaku shōkashū* – were published and music teachers were successfully trained, so that within 5 years, music education in Japan was well established.

Reflections on the significance of the foundational period

As described, music education in Japan began under government control. Japan was forced to face a cultural transformation as it organized its educational system and it was a struggle to incorporate Western music into the existing Japanese culture. For Japan during the nineteenth century, Western music was not merely a different art form but part of a social change that included industrialization, imperialism and Christianity. In order to maintain political control over music education, censorship and compromise were inevitable.

Initially, the government was unable to create a new music system that fused Western and Eastern styles. As far as schools were concerned, Western music became the norm and Japanese traditional music was not included except for a very few songs. The government was more concerned about the texts than the musical content and as a result, school music in Japan adopted the Western music system as a tool for moral education or *tokuiku*.

Another inevitable problem was achieving the expected standard of music making in schools. Since Western music had been introduced to Japan so quickly, it inevitably took a long period of time for it to permeate Japanese education. For example, elementary school song materials were sung in unison only, although occasionally two-part song materials were used in the upper elementary and middle schools.

Western vocalization was also barely understood at that time. Singing styles differ significantly between Western classical music and Japanese traditional music. Roughly speaking, the inner mouth and throat are widely open in Western singing, whereas in Japanese singing usually the inner mouth and throat are closed. It is hard to find literature about vocalization during the early period of music education in Japan but it seems likely that the pioneers tried to avoid the issue. For example, the section of vocal exercises written by Heinrich Kotzolt was omitted when

Uchida Yaichi translated Luther Whiting Mason's book, *A Preparatory Course* (1873).

For the government, music education was a tool for moral education. The purpose of music instruction was *tokusei no kanyō* (nurturing moral minds) and *kōkokumin no ikusei* (education for citizens of the emperor). Even though there was a slight change in the education system and structure, these objectives of music education lasted until the end of the Second World War.

Music education reforms

Seventy-seven years after the Meiji restoration, another historical shift occurred. In 1945 Japan was occupied by the allied powers and the former political and social systems of Japan were abandoned with new institutions being created under the control of the United States: accordingly, the system of education was entirely renovated.

In March 1946 the first United States education mission, chaired by Dr George D. Stoddard, came to Japan to assess the Japanese education system. At the end of March the 'Report of the United States Education Mission to Japan' made various recommendations to support democracy through education. Based on this report, and following the establishment of the new Japanese constitution, *Kyōiku kihon hō* (the New Fundamental Code of Education) and *Gakkō kyōiku hō* (the School Education Law) were promulgated in March 1947 (see Hamano 1982). The new school system was a 6–3–3 model: 6 years of elementary school, 3 years of middle high school and 3 years of senior high school. Elementary and middle school attendance was mandatory and the curriculum for each school was determined by the *Gakushū sidō yōryō* (the course of study). Teachers were employed by the boards of education in each prefecture and textbooks for elementary and middle schools were distributed to students without cost. This system has remained unaltered to the present day.

Music has been a compulsory subject under the new education system in both elementary school and middle school since 1947. Because the music curriculum had to be totally restructured, an expert in music education was needed. Moroi Saburō (1903–1977), a composer and graduate of the Berliner Hochschule, was appointed as head of the Ministry of Education's department preparing the new curriculum in 1946 (Kan 2003: 770). He was entirely responsible for the philosophy, methodology and materials for music education in Japanese schools. The result was the publication in 1947 of the first course of study *Gakushū sidō yōryō*.

The first course of study

The music curriculum had over 140 pages and contained 12 chapters with appendices of suggested teaching materials. The topics included the aims of music education, music learning theories, methods of teaching, the relationship between music and other subjects, the results of research studies on children's musical abilities and detailed explanations on teaching music for each grade. It was the most comprehensive and academically based resource for music education available at that time. Although the course of study was produced as a set of guidelines, teachers were advised to follow it, but were not obliged to do so. In reality, no other curriculum resources were available at the time and therefore virtually every school in Japan began its music education programme with this curriculum.

Moroi stated that the ultimate objective of music education was, and still is, *jōsō kyōiku* (education of moral and aesthetic sentiment). However, as Mashino (1986: 18) observes:

> [T]he meaning of *jōsō kyōiku* was not correctly understood. What music education as *jōsō kyōiku* really means is to nurture high quality aesthetic sentiment and rich human character through understanding and feeling the beauty of music.
> Music is essentially an art. Therefore it should not be a means but the aim. The functional idea of art does not explain the nature of art. The explanation of music as *jōsō kyōiku* is that understanding and feeling the beauty of music is in itself education of the aesthetic sentiment. (*ibid.*)

Moroi's ideas clearly indicate what can be identified as aesthetic formalism. Given that he studied composition in Germany and was strongly influenced by Bach, Mozart and Beethoven, it is natural that Moroi's conception of music education followed along these lines.

One of the most striking statements by Moroi was that music education in Japan should be based on the European musical system. This is because the 'foundation of musical sense can only be established by one kind of music' (*ibid.*: 36). He believed that 'teaching several kinds of music simultaneously would hinder the development of children's musical sense' (*ibid.*). For him, the future direction of music education was clear and for a second time, Japan chose the Western musical system for its school music education rather than looking to its own indigenous musical styles.

Moroi also stated that major keys should mainly be adopted for song materials. This was because 'not only are major keys the most basic scale of European music, but also that children prefer major keys. It is also important for children to establish a musical sense of the major key in order to free the mind and to make them cheerful and healthy citizens' (*ibid.*: 37). Although the reasoning here is slightly different, Moroi reinforces Isawa's belief in the appropriateness of major keys for school songs.

Since 1947, the basic structure of school music education has been centred on Western music, although the proportion of Japanese music material has been increasing with subsequent curriculum revisions. The course of study became legally required in 1958 which meant that every school had to follow the curriculum or face penalties. The objectives of the course of study were changed except for the underlying objective of *jōsō kyōiku* or 'education of the aesthetic and the moral sentiments'.

Music education in the present

In 2010, 63 years after the second music education reform, how can music education in Japan be best described? The current course of study was instituted in 1998, with the main objective of music in elementary schools being 'to develop the mind for loving music and musical sensitivity through expression and listening to music, and nurture the basic ability for musical activities, and cultivating rich sentiment' (Ministry of Education 1998). The objective of music in middle high schools is similar to that of elementary schools. However, it is important to note that the ultimate purpose is no longer cultivating aesthetic sentiment.

Among the course objectives for the elementary school course of study is one which states 'have students become interested in music through joyful musical activities, and cultivate an attitude and a habit of making life cheerful and rich through musical experiences' (*ibid.*). Music is obviously a means to an end. What the authorities are concerned to achieve is that students' attitudes are influenced by music rather than that music is a study in its own right.

This notion of the functional value of music education is strengthened by other course objectives. For example, one of the objectives for singing for first and second grades is to 'to *attempt* to perform music through listening' (author's italics). The words 'to attempt' imply evaluative criteria that do not relate to achievement (Ogawa 2004: 140). The targeted outcome is for students to demonstrate positive attitudes and socially congruent behaviour (*ibid.*). Again, the course is weighed towards students' attitudes rather than their musical achievements.

Regarding Japanese musical content, *Koto* or *Shakuhachi* music is required to be included in the list of listening materials as part of the music appreciation curriculum. Indigenous folk music is also recommended for use in music classes. In middle schools, Japanese music receives much greater emphasis. The singing repertoire must include songs that have been sung in Japan for a long time, can be associated with the natural beauty of Japan and refer to and include Japanese culture and the beauty of Japanese language (Ministry of Education 1998). In addition, the national anthem of Japan – *Kimigayo* – must be taught in all grades. Japanese traditional music is also to be presented in music appreciation classes.

There are many more aspects of the current course of study that could be commented on, but it is not the intention here to explain music education in its entirety in Japan. Rather the goal is to focus on its philosophical basis. It is worth bearing in mind that the current curriculum is compulsory. Every music teacher must follow this curriculum and other curricula such as those of Kodály or Orff are not officially permitted.

One of the most serious impediments to effective music teaching practice in Japan is the issue of inadequate teacher training in music.[1] Generally speaking, elementary school teachers are not effectively trained in either music performance or music pedagogy. Music is taught by regular classroom teachers and only a few local governments have specialists teaching music. Student teachers generally possess little musical background when they enter college, which is particularly the case with the larger proportion of male students who have virtually no prior experience of music at all. These students have to teach music when they become teachers and often revert simply to playing CDs to their music classes.

As for university graduates who major in music and teach music in middle schools, the majority are well trained and have good music performance skills but, unfortunately, their skills are usually limited to Western instruments. They achieve high standards in piano performance or sing arias in *bel canto* style very well, but few are proficient with Japanese instruments. Consequently, music teachers only teach Western classical music, unless they study non-Western music after graduating from university. Therefore, even if the government encourages music teachers to teach Japanese traditional music, the structure of pre-service courses of study and the teachers' own backgrounds do not easily allow for this.

Conclusion

At the start of this chapter, three questions were posited:

1 Why is the Japanese school music curriculum Western-centred?
2 Should indigenous Japanese music be used as the core?
3 Is the thinking underpinning Japanese music education fundamentally flawed?

In the early periods of music education in Japan, Western music had to be adopted for the music curriculum because the educational system was based on Westernization and a rapid change in the socio-industrial environment. The initial intention of fusing Western and Japanese musical styles failed and as a compromise, the introduced system of Western music was maintained but the philosophy and the texts were strictly controlled within a strongly nationalistic context. Immediately after the Second World War, another opportunity was presented for Japan to revise the school curriculum. However, Western music was once again chosen as the focus of the curriculum. When the course of study became the national curriculum in 1958, Western music retained a dominant role.

As far as the second question is concerned, over the 100 years since its introduction, Western music has become an integral part of Japanese culture. Despite the fact that most Japanese people perceive music to be of Western origin, I strongly support the current impetus to increase the proportion of Japanese music, but recognize that it is unrealistic to place it as the core of the curriculum.

Regarding the third question, I believe that music education has not been implemented properly and is flawed from a philosophical viewpoint. As we have seen, music education was introduced as a means of effecting a moral education for young people. This stance continued until the end of the Second World War, after which there was a chance of changing the rationale for music education. Although *tokusei no kanyō* (nurturing the moral heart) was replaced by *jōsō kyōiku* (cultivating rich sentiment), the goals remained essentially the same – music continued as a tool for a moral education. Most recently, on 28 March 2008, the Japanese Ministry of Education announced the eighth version of the new course of study effective until 2011. The music curriculum contains a new clause that even more overtly supports the status quo: 'based on the objectives of moral education, and considering the relationship to ethics, teachers should teach the topics of moral subjects appropriately, according to the characteristics of music' (see Ministry of Education 2008a, 2008b, 2008c, 2008d). This striking statement clearly suggests that music education should be related to moral education which from my perspective seems a retrograde step.

In conclusion, music education in Japan has existed primarily as a means to an end since its inception. The main goal has been to cultivate morality whereas passing on the indigenous musical culture, acquiring musical skills and accepting multicultural values have not been regarded as important functions of school music education. Is it possible that, sometime in the future, music education may disappear if it is no longer considered to be a tool for moral education?[2]

Notes

[1] For a fuller discussion of contemporary issues associated with the training of teachers in music in Japan, see Ogawa (2004).

[2] The following references provide useful supplementary information on the history of music education in Japan: Chiba (2007), Iwai (1988), Iwai *et al.* (2003), Kawaguchi (1991, 1996), Nakayama (1983), Nomura and Nakayama (1995), Sawasaki *et al.* (2003a, 2003b), Suzuki (2006), Takeshi (1996), Zdzinski *et al.* (2007).

References

Chiba, Y. (2007), *Doremi wo eranda nihon jin* (The Japanese choose the do-re-mi system). Tokyo: Ongaku no tomo sha.

Eppstein, U. (1994), *The Beginnings of Western Music in Meiji Era Japan*. Lewiston, NY: Edward Mellen Press.

Hamano,M, (1982), *Sengo ongaku kyōiku wa nani wo shitaka* (What were the achievements of music education after World War II?). Tokyo: Ongaku no tomo sha.

Hohmann, C H. (1853), *Praktischer Lehrgang des Gesang-Unterrichts in Volksschulen I-IV*. Nordlingen: Christian Beck'schen Buchhandlung.

Howe, S. W. (1997), *Luther Whiting Mason: International Music Educator*. Warren, MN: Harmonie Park Press.

Isawa, S. (1884), *Ongaku torishirabe kakari seiseki shinpōsho* (Extracts from the report of Isawa Shūji). Tokyo: Ongaku torishirabe kakari.

Iwai, M. (1988), *Kodomo no uta no bunka shi* (A history of children's songs). Tokyo: Daiichi shobō.

Iwai, M., Takeuchi, M., Sawasaki, M., Tsuda, M., Nakayama, Y. and Shimada, Y. (2003), 'Meiji kōki' (Music education in the late Meiji period), in F. Yamamoto (ed.), *Nihon ongaku kyōiku jiten* (Encyclopedia of music education). Tokyo: Ongaku no tomo sha, pp. 743–51.

Kan, M. (2003), 'Moroi Saburō', in F. Yamamoto (ed.), *Nihon ongaku kyoiku jiten* (Encyclopedia of music education). Tokyo: Ongaku no tomo sha, pp. 769–71.

Kawaguchi, M. (1991), *Ongaku kyōiku no riron to rekishi* (Theory and history of music education). Tokyo: Ongaku no tomo sha.

Kawaguchi, M. (1996), *Kindai ongaku kyōiku seiritsushi kenkyū* (A study of the development of modern music education). Tokyo: Ongaku no tomo sha.

Kimura, N. (1983), 'Nihon no kindaika to kyōiku' (Modernization of education in Japan), in F. Yamamoto (ed.), *Nihon ongaku kyōiku jiten* (Encyclopedia of music education). Tokyo: Ongaku no tomo sha, pp. 8–15.

Mashino, S. (1986), *Ongaku kyōiku yonjūnenshi* (A history of four decades of music education). Tokyo: Tōyōkan.

Mason, L. W. (1870a), *The National Music Course: Four Series of Forty Charts*. Boston, MA: Ginn.

Mason, L. W. (1870b), *The National Music Teacher*. Boston, MA: New England Conservatory of Music.

Mason, L. W. (1873), *A Preparatory Course and Key to the Second Series of Music Charts and Second Music Reader*. Boston, MA: Ginn.

Ministry of Education (1881, 1883, 1884), *Shōgaku shōkashū daiippen* (A collection of songs for elementary schools, vols 1, 2, 3). Tokyo: Ministry of Education.

Ministry of Education, Science and Culture (1998), *Gakushū shidō yōryō shōgakkō* (The course of study in the elementary school).

Ministry of Education, Science and Culture (2008a), *Gakushū shidō yōryō shōgakkō* (The course of study in the elementary school), www.mext.go.jp/b_menu/shuppan/sonota/990301/03122601/007.htm.

Ministry of Education, Science and Culture (2008b), *Gakushū shidō yōryō chūgakkō* (The course of study in the middle school), www.mext.go.jp/b_menu/shuppan/sonota/990301/03122602/006.htm.

Ministry of Education, Science and Culture (2008c), *Gakushū shidō yōryō shōgakkō* (A draft of the new course of study in the elementary school), www.mext.go.jp/a_menu/shotou/new-cs/news/080216/002.pdf.

Ministry of Education, Science and Culture (2008d), *Ongaku kyōin yōsei no rekishi* (A draft of the new course of studying the junior high school), www.mext.go.jp/a_menu/shotou/new-cs/news/080216/003.pdf.

Nakamura, R. (1993), *Yōgaku dōnyūsha no kiseki* (A history of the introduction of Western music into Japan). Tokyo: Tōsui shobō.

Nakayama, Y. (1983), 'Ongaku kyōin yōsei no rekishi' (A brief history of music teacher education in Japan), in M. Kawaguchi (ed.), *Ongaku kyōiku no rekishi* (A brief history of music education in Japan). Tokyo: Ongaku no tomo sha, pp. 143–54.

Nomura, K. and Nakayama, Y. (eds) (1995), *Ongaku kyōiku wo yomu* (Source readings in music education). Tokyo: Ongaku no tomo sha.

Ogawa, M. (1991), 'American contributions to the beginning of public music education in Japan', *Bulletin of Historical Research in Music Education*, XII, (2), 113–28.

Ogawa, M. (1994), 'Japanese traditional music and school music education', *Philosophy of Music Education Review*, 2, (1), 25–36.

Ogawa, M. (2000), 'Early nineteenth century American influences on the beginning of Japanese public music education: an analysis and comparison of selected music textbooks published in Japan and the United States' (unpublished DME thesis, Indiana University).

Ogawa, M. (2003), 'Luther Whiting Mason', in F. Yamamoto (ed.), *Nihon ongaku kyōiku jiten* (Encyclopedia of music education). Tokyo: Ongaku no tomo sha, pp. 761–5.

Ogawa, M. (2004), 'Music teacher education in Japan', *Philosophy of Music Education Review*, 12, (2), 139–53.

Sawasaki, M. (1983), 'Nihon ongaku kyōiku jiten' (A chronological table of music education in Japan), in M. Kawaguchi (ed.), *Ongaku kyōiku no rekishi* (History of music education). Tokyo: Ongaku no tomo sha, pp. 198–238.

Sawasaki, M., Nakahara, A. Takeshi, K. Tsuda, M. Yagi, S. and Yoshida, T. (2003a), 'Shōwa kōki' (Music education in the late Shōwa period), in F. Yamamoto (ed.), *Nihon ongaku kyōiku jiten* (Encyclopedia of music education). Tokyo: Ongaku no tomo sha, pp. 480–488.

Sawasaki, M., Tanabe, T., Tsuda, M., Kawazoe, K. and Hirata, Y. (2003b), 'Shōwa zenki' (Music education in the early Shōwa period, in F. Yamamoto (ed.), *Nihon ongaku kyōiku jiten* (Encyclopedia of music education). Tokyo: Ongaku no tomo sha, pp. 488–96.

Suzuki, S. (2006), 'Shōwa zenki no shihangakkō ni okeru kyōiku jissenn ni okeru shiteki kenkyū' (A historical study of music education in normal schools in the beginning of the Shōwa period) (unpublished doctoral thesis, School Education, Hyogo University of Education).

Takeshi, K. (1996), 'American educational influences on Japanese elementary music education from after World War II through the Shōwa period' (unpublished doctoral thesis, University of Illinois at Urbana-Champaign).

Tokyo Geijutsu Daigaku (1987), *Tokyo geijutsu daigaku hyakunen shi* (The centennial history of Tokyo University of Fine Arts). Tokyo: Ongaku no Tomosha.

Zdzinski, S. F., Ogawa, M., Dell, C., Yap, C. C., Adderley, C. and Dingle, R. (2007), 'Attitudes and practices of Japanese and American music teachers towards integrating music with other subjects', *International Journal of Music Education*, 25, (1), 57–73.

15

South Africa: Indigenous roots, cultural imposition and an uncertain future

Robin Stevens and Eric Akrofi

Unlike the situation in European cultures, community-based systems of education have developed over millennia in African indigenous populations to prepare children for their role as adult members in their tribal communities. In most African cultures, such a system of education has utilized 'musical arts' – singing, drumming, dancing and other forms of music – as the principal means through which both 'rites of passage' and more general life skills have been provided. Indeed, the role of music in indigenous African life, particularly within the South African context, has been an integral component of *ubuntu*. This is the notion based on the Zulu maxim *umuntu ngumuntu ngabantu* ('a person is only a person through their relationship to others') as well the Xhosa dictum, *umntu ngumntu ngabantu* ('a person is a person because of other persons') that utilizes and supports the social reciprocity inherent in music. As Herbst, de Wet and Rijsdijk (2005: 262) put it: 'Indigenous sub-Saharan African musical arts performance and education require the total involvement of individuals as they express themselves through the instruments they play and the dances they perform. All these activities take place within the context of social norms.'

This chapter draws on the three-level schema identified by several authors including Thorsén (1997) and Campbell (2008). This schema includes, respectively:

- 'informal education' that is described as 'life-long learning within families, peer groups etc, often without pronounced educational objectives' (Thorsén 1997: 3), which is synonymous with 'natural learning' that is 'enculturative, occurring naturally, non-consciously and without direct instruction of any sort' (Campbell 2008: 41)
- 'non-formal' that involves 'private or non-government educational enterprise' (Thorsén *loc. cit.*) or learning that is 'only partly guided,

occurring outside institutionalized settings through the prompting of occasional and nonconsecutive directives' (Campbell *loc. cit.*)

- 'formal' that is represented by 'the governmentally geared system from primary to tertiary education' (Thorsén *loc. cit.*) or learning that is 'occurring through a teacher's intervention in highly structured settings such as a school' (Campbell *loc. cit.*).

Despite differences in terminology and definitions, this schema allows the issue of music in compulsory schooling in South Africa – selected as perhaps the most well-documented example in the sub-Saharan African region of music in education – to be considered in a more culturally appropriate and relevant manner than considering it merely within the confines of an essentially European 'school-based' construct. In addition, this schema accommodates successive phases in the evolution of 'an education in and through music' in South Africa. Accordingly, this chapter will be arranged in three sections, which broadly speaking, incorporate this three-level schema – namely music in indigenous learning, music in mission-based schooling and music in government schooling. In all these settings, one or other forms of education were an integral part of the experience of young people and therefore all settings incorporate some measure of compulsory or at least obligatory participation in the communal learning endeavour of their immediate social environment.

The introduction and nature of compulsory school education in South Africa have varied according to the prevailing socio-political circumstances. School attendance for children of the European population became compulsory around the turn of the nineteenth century in most provinces but, as far as the indigenous population was concerned, it was not until 1994 with the coming of the 'new South Africa' that school education could be said to be both universally provided and compulsory for children of primary and lower secondary school age.

Music in indigenous learning

According to Hauptfleisch (1997: 193), the original inhabitants of South Africa were probably the San, a hunter-gatherer people who occupied a wide area of southern Africa for thousands of years. About 2,000 years ago, some San communities (calling themselves Khoikhoi) started to acquire sheep and cattle from and intermingle with the so-called Bantu-speaking black African people who were establishing themselves within the borders of present-day South Africa.

There had always been an informal education system operating among the San and the black African peoples. However, a more formal type of education took place during periods of initiation such as *ulwaluko* (circumcision) and *intonjane* (puberty rites) among the Xhosa-speaking people. Nzewi (2003, cited in Herbst, de Wet and Rijsdijk 2005) argues that, contrary to common belief, indigenous music learning has a philosophy and a systematic transmission or teaching procedure normally only associated with 'formal' training in a format different from that found in Western 'formal' institutionalized training. Although Nzewi's assertion convinced Herbst, de Wet and Rijsdijk (2005) to avoid using the terms 'formal', 'informal' and 'non-formal', the present authors have nevertheless utilized these within what is considered to be most appropriate schema with which to engage in the discourse for this chapter.

From the outset, music often formed part of schooling for children of all racial backgrounds in South Africa. Particularly in the case of indigenous schooling provided by missionary societies, the tonic sol-fa method became the mainstay of school music education especially in Cape Province. However, the introduction of European music to indigenous communities has not been without its critics. Many African scholars have identified the imposition of a foreign musical genre on the indigenous population through school education as well as through evangelizing by Christian missionaries as representing a form of 'cultural imperialism'. Primos (2003: 3, cited in Herbst, de Wet and Rijsdijk 2005: 262) points out that only hymns and other European songs were taught in schools. Thus, indigenous children attending weekday schools and Sunday schools were often denied their own indigenous music.

Mngoma (1990: 122), in asserting that the cultural history and indigenous belief systems of African people are embedded in their communal musical arts practices, laments that European culture has influenced the cultural preferences of African learners and has inhibited their growth, experience, and ability to express themselves in music, thus alienating them from their cultural heritage. Indeed, according to Herbst, de Wet and Rijsdijk (2005: 61), policymakers and many teachers prior to 1994 have often incorrectly assumed that music education in South Africa began with the arrival of the Dutch commander Jan van Riebeeck at the Cape of Good Hope in 1652 and have thus ignored the role of learning implicit in indigenous musical arts practised prior to colonization in Africa.

It is evident from these criticisms that indigenous African musical arts are still in the process of gaining full recognition within the context of South African school music education. As Akrofi (1998: 46) puts it: '[T]o place traditional African music on an equal footing with Western music in the curriculum of South African schools is an uphill task ... African music plays second fiddle to Western music in the country's school music education programme.'

Music in mission-based schooling

European settlement at the Cape of Good Hope (or Cape Colony as it was known) began in 1652 when the Dutch East India Company established Cape Town as a 'refreshment' station on the sea route to the Far East. From 1679 the Cape was a Dutch colony. It was then occupied by the British from 1795 until 1803, before becoming part of the short-lived Batavian Republic (1803–1806). The Cape Colony was reoccupied by the British in 1806 and in 1820 some 5,000 British settlers arrived. From about this time, groups of Boers, dissatisfied with British rule, migrated north across the Orange River on what became known as the 'Great Trek' (Ferguson and Immelman 1961: 7–8).

Aside from Dutch and British settlers, the other inhabitants of Cape Colony were the indigenous San (Khoikhoi) people. To the north, Transvaal became an independent Boer Republic (1852–1899) and adopted Dutch as its language. Following the two Anglo-Boer wars, the Transvaal finally became a British colony in 1907 and, in 1910, Transvaal and the other self-governing colonies of the Cape, Natal and Orange Free State became provinces of the Union of South Africa (see Figure 15.1); note that the British High Commission Territories of Basutoland (now Lesotho), Bechuanaland (now Botswana), and Swaziland were excluded from the Union of South Africa. English and Dutch (replaced later by Afrikaans) became the dual official languages in South Africa.

FIGURE 15.1 Provinces of the Union of South Africa, 1910 (Source: Grade 11 Resources, 'Boer War-South Africa 1899' at http://dt-ss.tripod.com/eleven-resources. html; adapted by the authors)

Education during the early days of Dutch colonization was based almost solely on the need for literacy in order to read the Bible. The Dutch Reformed Church established schools where new communities developed and private farm schools were frequently set up to cater for children in rural areas. With the coming of British rule, Lord Charles Somerset, Governor of Cape Colony from 1814 to 1826, established a system of free and secular education along the lines of the English elementary school system. Typically, local communities established their own schools that were subsidized and inspected by education authorities, who also prescribed the school curriculum (with English as the language of instruction). Education authorities also certificated teachers, many of whom were recruited from Scotland. When Transvaal came under British rule, the Dutch Reformed Church set up its own system of Christian national schools in which Dutch as well as English were the languages of instruction. This set the scene for the bilingual system of education in English and Afrikaans, which was adopted at the provincial level after the union (Dean, Hartmann and Katzen 1983: 23–4). Theoretically, with elementary education being free and secular, schooling was also available to the indigenous people – the Khoikhoi in the south and the Xhosa people on the east coast. However, with a colour bar effectively in operation, schools operated by missionary organizations represented the only avenue available for elementary education to non-European children.

The majority of missions established in South Africa during the nineteenth century were of either Anglican or non-conformist protestant foundations.[1] Particularly at missions established by non-conformist protestant denominations – Methodist (Wesleyan), Baptist, Presbyterian and Congregational – the tonic sol-fa method and notation were almost universally adopted as the means of promoting congregational singing. At mission schools of all denominations, music was not only employed as a means of inculcating moral and religious principles through the singing of hymns and other liturgical music, but was also formally taught as one of the 'subjects of instruction' as was frequently the case in colonial schools throughout the British Empire.

One of the first recorded instances of tonic sol-fa being introduced to mission schools was by an English dentist, Thomas Daines (1829–1880) who lived at King William's Town (Henning 1979a: 307). Before leaving England, Daines had become acquainted with tonic sol-fa and, when appointed to Grey's Hospital in King William's Town about 1860, he offered classes in sight singing and part-singing presumably to the European community. Two years later in 1862, Daines was teaching tonic sol-fa to indigenous pupils at St Matthew's Mission School and to Bantu[2] choirs in King William's Town. By 1867, Daines was conducting a Bantu choir of some 200 to 300 voices in part-songs, hymns and music by Purcell (*ibid.*).

Somewhat later, tonic sol-fa was widely used at mission stations in Basutoland, in Kaffraria[3] and around Port Elizabeth in the south (*Tonic Sol-fa Reporter* 1883: 145). One of the most prominent missions in educational work in Cape Colony was the Lovedale Missionary Institution at which tonic sol-fa was widely promoted. Lovedale Mission was founded in the 1820s by a group of clergymen from the Glasgow Missionary Society near the inland town of Alice, west-northwest of East London in what is now known as Eastern Cape Province (Shepherd 1941). Aside from religious activity, the mission's principal objective was the education of the indigenous community – the Xhosa people. A school for boys was established as the Lovedale Institution in 1841. This institution later provided higher education for young Xhosa men with the result that, during a later period, some hundreds of boys from Lovedale passed the Cape University public examinations and hundreds of Xhosa teachers were trained at the Lovedale Institution (Gandhi 1905). An important means of supporting the education of local Xhosa people – and, indeed, of indigenous South Africans generally – was the establishment at Lovedale of a printing press, which, from 1823, produced evangelical and educational publications including a Xhosa Bible, hymn books, school reading books and other Christian literature. The key figure at the Lovedale Institution during its heyday was Reverend Dr James Stewart (1831–1905) who joined Lovedale in 1867 and became its principal in 1870. The printing press at Lovedale enabled the production of music in tonic sol-fa notation and this led to the publication of music composed by indigenous South Africans including Reverend John Knox Bokwe (1855–1922) and Enoch Sontonga (d. 1904), both of whom were students at Lovedale. Akrofi (2006: 5) notes that the first generation of black South African composers of choral music – which also included Tiyo Soga, R. T. Kawa and Benjamin Tyamzashe – acquired their musical education through missionary institutions such as Lovedale where they 'were taught the rudiments of music via Tonic Sol-fa' (Hansen 1968: 3).

Although Lovedale Training Institution was a major centre for tonic sol-fa teaching, there were many other missions especially in the east of Cape Province in urban areas such as King William's Town, Fort Beaufort and Grahamstown, where the method was utilized not only in mission schools but also in the training of indigenous teachers. In urban areas where the influence of missions was less apparent, music taught principally through tonic sol-fa also assumed an important role in public and other government-supported schools.

Music in government schooling

Provision of funding for free and secular public school education by the colonial government of Cape Colony had been in place since Lord Somerset's initiatives of the 1820s. Government free schools (also known as English free schools) were generally based on Lancaster's monitorial system and the medium of instruction was English. Although free schools were originally intended to be multiracial, they essentially catered for children of European background whereas mission-based schools catered almost exclusively for indigenous children (South African History Online 1999–2008).

In the early years music in government schools was an optional subject and its introduction to the school curriculum was entirely dependent on the initiative of individual teachers who had existing knowledge and skills in music and who recognized its educational value. One of the pioneer school music teachers in South Africa was Christopher Birkett who came from Newport in Monmouth, England, to Cape Colony in about 1854. Birkett trained at the Westminster Training College with another key figure, Henry Nixon, during 1853–54 (*School Music Review* 1894: 74; hereinafter referred to as *Sch Mus Rev*). Although originally trained in Hullah's method at Westminster, they had both learned tonic sol-fa informally prior to emigrating (*Musical Herald*, 1894: 263; hereinafter referred to as *Mus Her*). In South Africa, Birkett introduced tonic sol-fa to native weekday schools and to Sunday school choirs in Grahamstown, Cradock and Healdtown (Malan 1979a: 130). Other urban school teachers using tonic sol-fa during the early 1860s included John Wedderburn and George Kidd (Henning 1979b: 104).

Another pioneer was James H. Ashley (1824–1898) who introduced tonic sol-fa to Cape Town during the 1860s (*Mus Her* 1894: 263). After some effort, Ashley and Henry Nixon were successful in having tonic sol-fa adopted for use in government schools. About 1882, the then Superintendent General of Education, Dr (later Sir) Langham Dale, introduced music to the syllabus of subjects for the public school teacher's certificate and appointed Nixon as Inspector of Music in Training Colleges and Schools for the Cape Colony (*Sch Mus Rev* 1894: 74; *Mus Her* 1894: 263). Dale was so impressed by Nixon's advocacy of tonic sol-fa that the system was put on an equal footing with staff notation for use in public schools (*Mus Her* 1894: 263).

Dale's successor as Superintendent General of Education in 1891 was Dr (later Sir) Thomas Muir – reportedly 'himself a lover of music' (*Sch Mus Rev* 1894: 74). Muir commissioned Nixon to report on the state of music in Cape schools and, as a result, two instructors – Arthur Lee and James Rodger – were appointed to teach tonic sol-fa at the male and female teacher training colleges in Cape Town (*ibid.*). All trainees were examined by Nixon and required to pass a sight singing test. For over 20 years, Nixon as inspector of school music appears to have propagated tonic sol-fa at every opportunity, including a period which he devoted to teaching singing to the Hottentot (Khoikhoi) people (*ibid.*).

By 1895 Arthur Lee, also an ardent tonic sol-fa advocate, had established a choir of 600 children from government schools in the Cape Town area. Examinations of the Tonic Sol-fa College appear to have been widely promoted in Cape Town schools as completion of the Junior Certificate examination was a prerequisite for choir membership (*Sch Mus Rev* 1895: 116). The following year, the choir numbers increased to 700 and, at its annual concert in Cape Town, the choir was accompanied by an orchestra (*Sch Mus Rev* 1896: 137). The concert included an unrehearsed programme of hand sign singing and sight reading introduced by Thomas Muir who forthrightly encouraged the adoption of tonic sol-fa in schools. In other parts of Cape Colony – for example, Uitenhage near Port Elizabeth in the east – tonic sol-fa had been introduced to the indigenous population and, partly because of this and other prejudices, the method was apparently not as popular with the European community (*Mus Her* 1896: 55–6). It may therefore be assumed that the Cape Town Schools Choir would have consisted entirely of children from the European community as it is unlikely that children of Khoikhoi or other indigenous groups would have attended government schools in Cape Town.

By 1897 Cape Colony had, for the purposes of school music at least, been divided into two 'circuits' that were inspected respectively by Frederick Farrington (eastern districts) and Arthur Lee (western districts), both of whom were tonic sol-fa advocates. Frederick Farrington (1869–1931) emigrated from North Staffordshire to South Africa in 1893 and the following year was appointed as Inspector of Music for the Cape Colony. With the division of the music inspectorate into two 'circuits', Farrington was based in the Port Elizabeth-Uitenhage area and, within a year of his arrival, over 3,500 children were being taught singing by tonic sol-fa. Also in 1898, the first examinations of the Tonic Sol-fa College were held in Port Elizabeth (Henning 1979c: 56). Farrington also introduced school choir competitions, which survived in Port Elizabeth until 1912–13 (Malan 1979b: 98). Farrington was also interested in promoting choral music among the indigenous community and, with Colonel E. Smedley-Williams, organized a Native Musical Association in East London and instituted choral singing competitions (Henning 1979c: 57).

Arthur Lee came from Birstall near Leeds, was trained as a teacher at Westminster Training College and taught for a brief period in London before emigrating to South Africa (*Mus Her* 1898: 269). He was employed as a teacher in a government school in Cape Town before being appointed as Instructor and Inspector of Singing for the Western Province. After 3 years of working in the Cape Town area, Lee extended his promotion of singing by tonic sol-fa to the whole province, undertaking extensive tours to inspect rural farm schools and mission schools as well as schools in urban centres. Like Farrington, Lee actively promoted the certificate examinations of the Tonic Sol-fa College, particularly the School Teacher's Music Certificate (*Mus Her* 1914: 206).

Farrington reported that 'the powers of the natives are astonishing' and also remarked on 'the quickness of the native children' in mission schools where 'it is not uncommon to find all the available blackboard space covered with hymns and anthems' (*Sch Mus Rev*, 1898: 23–3). Both music inspectors reported on the examinations for Tonic Sol-fa College certificates, with 498 being awarded in the eastern districts and 1,244 awarded in the western districts in 1898 (*Sch Mus Rev*, 1898: 23–3, 33). In the following year (1899) the number of Tonic Sol-fa College certificates awarded in the eastern districts increased to 736 and the number in western districts almost doubled to 2,179 (*Sch Mus Rev*, 1899: 63–4, 102).

One of the traditions in school music established in Cape Town in 1897 was the Annual School Choir Competition (for the Challenge Shield), which was organized under the auspices of Thomas Muir as Inspector-General of Education (*Sch Mus Rev*, 1898: 118–19). Although open to all schools, those competing appear initially to have been confined to 'superior' European schools such as the Normal College School, Good Hope Seminary, Trinity Public School and Rondebosch Girls' High School. Similar school choir competitions were established elsewhere in Cape Colony including the Municipal Challenge Shield at Port Elizabeth. However, at the 1898 Port Elizabeth choir competition, there were entrants from 'mixed' schools with mention being made of the typical indigenous teacher who conducts his choir, 'never looking harassed, but smilingly happy' and who has frequently composed his own songs, both music and words (*Sch Mus Rev*, 1899: 111). By 1900 a choir of coloured children from a mission school achieved second place in the Cape Town school choir competition (*Mus Her*, 1901: 15).

Thus, by the close of the nineteenth century, tonic sol-fa had had a major impact not only on music in public schools in urban areas but also in mission schools, teacher training institutions and local communities. It had enabled a high degree of musical literacy among indigenous people and, although it could be claimed that tonic sol-fa was one of the 'instruments of cultural colonization', it nevertheless contributed to the enrichment of people's lives during the nineteenth century and indeed laid a strong foundation for the later development of a fine African choral music tradition.

Colonial authorities provided for elementary education through a system of direct support of or subsidies to various types of school. The type of school was largely determined by geographic location of the pupils – government town schools catered predominantly for European children and farm schools in rural areas for the children of the European settlers, whereas school education for the indigenous population was provided almost exclusively by missionary societies. Indeed, even as late as the 1920s, the number of government schools for indigenous children was miniscule in comparison with mission schools. A case in point was in Cape Province in 1926 where there was only *one government school providing education for indigenous children* whereas there were 1,625 mission schools (Horrell 1963, cited in Hlatshwayo 2000: 36).

Also, under British colonial rule, there appears not to have been a policy of deliberate segregation of the schools according to race as there was later. For example in Natal, Lieutenant Governor Sir G. Wolseley openly expressed the view in 1875 that schools should be open equally to children of both European and non-European background (Behr and Macmillan 1971: 116). Nevertheless, particularly in larger centres, the establishment of fee-charging (although government-subsidized) private schools effectively precluded non-European pupils from attending.

Compulsory primary education was introduced to Cape Colony in 1905 by the then Superintendent of Education Sir Thomas Muir (*ibid.*: 116). In Transvaal and Orange Free State – both of which were most affected by the 1899–1902 Anglo-Boer War – compulsory primary education was introduced in 1907 and 1895 respectively (*ibid.*: 124, 136). Natal became a self-governing colony in 1893 but it was not until 1910 that primary schooling became compulsory, although it was still not free as parents were required to pay school fees (*ibid.*: 134). The compulsory nature of primary schooling at this time appears to have applied principally if not exclusively to the European population.

Nevertheless, in rural areas where there was particularly strong missionary influence, schooling at mission stations was effectively compulsory, particularly for boys. In other situations where missionary influence was weaker, compulsory attendance was impossible to achieve (Pells 1938: 79). Because of the concentration of racially dominant populations in particular areas, schools tended to cater respectively for European, coloured and black (indigenous) children. It was not until well after the coming together of the South African colonies into the Union of South Africa in 1910 that responsibility for indigenous education became increasingly centralized and separated from the European school system. With the introduction by the Afrikaans National Party of the 'apartheid' or 'own affairs' policy of segregated education in 1948, the education of the indigenous population came under the control of a single education department, the Department of Native Affairs, through the *Bantu Education Act* of 1953.

The Afrikaans National Party, while centralizing its control of education, decentralized management to racially discrete systems of administration. Education for the black, coloured and Indian communities was removed from provincial governments to the central government and separate school systems imposed on blacks in 1953, coloureds in 1963 and Indians in 1965. The establishment of the Department of National Education (DNE) in 1984 to handle 'general education affairs' continued the trend towards centralizing school education (Hauptfleisch 1997: 195).

Between 1948 and 1994 (the period of apartheid), school music education became increasingly fragmented along racial and ethnic lines for white, coloured and black South Africans. Major challenges that faced non-

European schools were that music syllabi and teaching approaches were usually Western-orientated and therefore irrelevant to a large proportion of non-white pupils. In addition, many non-white students received little or no class music tuition for a variety of reasons – a lack of a timetable allocation for classroom music, a lack of trained music teachers, a lack of facilities including musical instruments and teaching materials, a lack of career opportunities for music teachers and the low status accorded to class music in schools.

After the first democratic election in 1994 the chief policy framework for education – the Reconstruction and Development Programme (RDP) – of the African National Congress (ANC)-led Government of National Unity was put into effect. The statement in Paragraph 3.4.8 of the RDP (ANC 1994: 71) is especially significant for music education: 'Arts education should be an integral part of the national school curricula at primary, secondary and tertiary level, as well as in non-formal education. Urgent attention must be given to the creation of relevant arts curricula, teacher training, and provision of facilities for the arts within all schools' (quoted in Hauptfleisch 1997: 201).

The new Government of National Unity directed the Department of Education and the National Education and Training Forum to initiate a curriculum development programme aimed at addressing the historical crisis in South African education. As a result, 25 field and sub-field committees were formed, including an arts education field committee with subcommittees being established for each of the areas of drama, dance, music and visual arts. The music subcommittee dealt with music education both as a compulsory subject in the general class context and as an optional subject in the secondary school. The subcommittee also identified the principal impediment to the successful implementation of compulsory class music: '[T]he standard of instruction in music education was determined largely by the standard of teacher education, and the latter needed urgent attention' (quoted in Hauptfleisch 1997: 202). Curiously, the music subcommittee was not requested to address two other contentious issues relating to music education – its allocation in hours per week in the timetable and its non-examination status (the subcommittee was of the opinion that music would not be successfully implemented if it were not given 'examinable' status). Nevertheless, the music subcommittee prescribed a core syllabus, Class Music (Standard [Grade/Year] 1–10). Regarding the implementation of music as an optional subject, it noted with concern that the existing core syllabi were based exclusively on a study of Western art music. It therefore recommended that parallel core syllabi for the study of various music practices be developed.

Also during 1994 the Minister of Arts, Culture, Science and Technology appointed an Arts and Culture Task Group (ACTAG) to draw up a new arts and culture programme consistent with the new South African constitution. Among ACTAG's (1995) proposals that relate specifically to music education were:

- arts education (including music) should be an integral part of pre-school education
- in the senior primary years, learners should experience music individually and be afforded opportunities to integrate it with other arts where appropriate
- in junior secondary years, learners should be able to specialize in music
- musics from southern Africa, as well as Europe, Asia and the Americas should be included
- music curricula should have to meet local or regional resources, needs and interests
- music education should include education in, about, through and for music
- assessment and evaluation should become more important than in the past (quoted in Hauptfleisch 1997).

According to Hauptfleisch (1997: 205), ACTAG also proposed a government-sponsored nationwide research project on the value and benefits of arts education, a transformed curriculum, the offering of combined arts at primary levels, assessment and evaluation, teacher education and the development of resources, which was not done.

In summary, the new education system instituted after the fall of the apartheid system has integrated music and other subjects into an 'arts and culture learning area'. An attempt has also been made to incorporate indigenous knowledge systems into the arts and culture learning area, fostering the idea that the classroom should be an extension of the community and should therefore reflect the *ubuntu* principle (Herbst, de Wet and Rijsdijk 2005: 263). However, the majority of teachers in post-apartheid South Africa have not been exposed to this kind of teaching and learning. As Smit (2007) puts it:

> In South Africa the majority of educators who have to teach the Arts and Culture Learning Area are not trained in all four of the components, namely Music, Drama, Dance and Visual Arts. Some are trained in only one or two of these components, and many are not trained in any of them at all. This creates an overwhelming feeling of inadequacy, which also has a negative impact on the learners and on the future of the learning area. (pp. 215–16)

Implementing the new arts and culture curricula in South Africa has been difficult and will continue to be challenging due mainly to the problems faced by teachers resulting from the following historical factors identified by Herbst, de Wet and Rijsdijk (2005):

(a) the influence of colonialism on music education in sub-Saharan Africa in general and South Africa specifically; (b) the assumption that music education was only introduced to the African continent with the arrival of Western teaching ideologies and methodologies; (c) the influence of British rule on music education in South Africa, in which preference was given to singing Christian hymns and European folk tunes, learning Western European classical music, and acquiring written music literacy, to the detriment of oral literacy; (d) the influence of racial segregation on South African education generally and in music education specifically, an influence that is especially evident in the substandard teacher training at previously nonwhite teacher training colleges. (p. 264)

Furthermore, since 1994, the rationalization programme of the Department of Education has severely reduced the number of teacher training colleges in the country. Many colleges have been closed, while others have been amalgamated with universities. The remaining colleges have music departments with only one or two lecturers who are expected to implement the syllabi for arts and culture. Besides, there are still no universities in South Africa to date that award students degrees in arts and culture or specifically train teaching specialists in this area.

The two curricula that guide music and arts education in present-day South Africa – namely *Curriculum 2005* (Department of Education 2005a) (with eight arts: dance, drama, music, visual arts, media and communication, arts technology, design, and literature) and the 2005 *Revised National Curriculum Statement Grades R–9 Arts and Culture (Department of Education 2005b)* (with ten arts: dance, drama, music, visual arts, craft, design, media and communication, arts management, arts technology, and heritage) – recognize music as only one of many arts disciplines. Because these two curricula are formulated at the level of learning areas, they do not include outcomes specifically for music education. Accordingly, music is presently struggling to earn a place within the new education system. This chapter therefore concludes with the assertion that, although music has often been prominent in the school curriculum, particularly during the nineteenth century, the future of music in compulsory schooling in present-day South Africa is now uncertain. Without a major reform of the curriculum, many pupils will continue to leave school without having acquired basic musical knowledge and skills that would enable them to perform, understand and appreciate music.

Notes

1 Roman Catholic missions in Africa flourished in the French, Italian and Portuguese colonies in east, central and west Africa but not in Dutch, Boer and British colonies in southern Africa.

2 'Bantu' was a widely used generic term referring to the indigenous peoples of South Africa and more particularly to their languages.

3 Kaffraria was the area immediately to the north of the Great Fish River on the east coast, which incorporated King William's Town and East London and northwards including the area known as Transkei to the border of Natal. Kaffraria was annexed to Cape Colony in 1865.

References

African National Congress (1994), *Reconstruction and Development Programme*. Johannesburg: Umanyano.

Akrofi, E. A. (1998), 'Traditional African music education in Ghana and South Africa', *Legon Journal of the Humanities*, 11, 39–47.

Akrofi, E. A. (2006), 'Composition in tonic sol-fa: an exogenous musical practice in the Eastern Cape Province of South Africa'. Unpublished paper.

Behr, A. L. and Macmillan, R. G. (1971), *Education in South Africa* (2nd edn). Pretoria: J. L. van Schaik.

Campbell, P. S. (2008), *Musician and Teacher: An Orientation to Music Education*. New York: W. W. Norton & Company.

Dean, E., Hartman, P. and Katzen, M. (1983), *History in Black and White: An Analysis of South Africa Schools History Textbooks*. Paris: UNESCO.

Department of Education, South Africa (2005a), *Curriculum 2005*. Pretoria: Department of Education.

Department of Education, South Africa (2005b), *Revised National Curriculum Statement Grades R–9 Arts and Culture*. Pretoria: Department of Education, www.info.gov.za/otherdocs/2002/natcur.pdf (accessed 11 September 2008).

Ferguson, W. T. and Immelman, R. F. M. (1961), *Sir John Herschel and Education at the Cape, 1843–1840*. Cape Town: Oxford University Press.

Gandhi, M. K. (1905), 'Education among the Kaffirs', *Indian Opinion* (30 December 1905), in *Complete Works of Mahatma Gandhi*, Vol. 5, http://mkgandhi.org/vol5/ch045.htm.

Hansen, D. (1968), 'The life and work of Benjamin Tyamzashe: a contemporary Xhosa composer', Occasional Paper No. 11. Grahamstown: Institute of Social and Economic Research, Rhodes University.

Hauptfleisch, S. (1997), 'Transforming South African music education: a systems view' (unpublished DMus thesis, University of Pretoria).

Henning, C. G. (1979a), 'Daines, Thomas', in J. P. Malan (ed.), *South African Music Encyclopedia*, vol. I. Cape Town: Oxford University Press.

Henning, C. G. (1979b), 'Graaff Reinet', in J. P. Malan (ed.), *South African Music Encyclopedia*, vol. II. Cape Town: Oxford University Press.

Henning, C. G. (1979c), 'Farrington, Frederick', in J. P. Malan (ed.), *South African Music Encyclopedia*, vol. II. Cape Town: Oxford University Press.

Herbst, A., de Wet, J. and Rijsdijk, S. (2005), 'A survey of music education in the primary schools of South Africa's Cape Peninsula', *Journal of Research in Music Education*, 53, (3), 260–83.

Hlatshwayo, S. A. (2000), *Education and Independence: Education in South Africa, 1658–1988*. Westport, CN: Greenwood Press.

Malan, J. P. (1979a), 'Grahamstown', in J. P. Malan (ed.), *South African Music Encyclopedia*, vol. II. Cape Town: Oxford University Press.

Malan, J. P. (1979b), 'Port Elizabeth, music in (1820–1920)', in J. P. Malan (ed.), *South African Music Encyclopedia*, vol. IV. Cape Town: Oxford University Press.

Mngoma, K. (1990), 'The teaching of music in South Africa', *South African Journal of Musicology*, 10, 121–6.

Musical Herald (1892–1914). London: John Curwen & Sons.

Pells, E. G. (1938), *European, Coloured, and Native Education in South Africa, 1652–1938*. New York: AMS Press.

School Music Review (1892–1899). London: Novello & Company Limited.

Shepherd, R. H. W. (1941), *Lovedale, South Africa: The Story of a Century, 1841–1941*. Lovedale, Cape Province, South Africa: Lovedale Press.

Smit, M. (2007), 'Facilitating the formation of personal and professional identities of arts and culture educators', in E. Akrofi, M. Smit and S-M. Thorsen (eds), *Music and Identity: Transformation and Negotiation*. Stellenbosch: African Sun Media, pp. 215–31.

South African History Online (1999–2008), 'The Amersfoort legacy: a history of education in South Africa' (Timeline 1800–1899), www.sahistory.org.za/classroom/education-350years/timeline1800s.html (accessed 19 February 2009).

Thorsén, S-M. (1997), 'Music education in South Africa – striving for unity and diversity' (Swedish), *Schwedische Zeitschrift für Musikforschung (Swedish Journal for Musicology)*, 79, (1), 91–109, available in English at www.hsm.gu.se/digitalAssets/848/848801_Music_Educ_in_South_Africa_.pdf (accessed 11 September 2008).

Tonic Sol-fa Reporter (1883–1891). London: John Curwen & Sons.

Index

Aboriginal children 172
absolute pitch 33
active engagment with music making
    95–6
Adorno, T. W. 53
aesthetic education 57, 62, 94
aesthetic formalism 214
Afrikaans National Party 230
Afro-Cubans 5, 155–6
Aguayo, A. 160, 161
Aguirre, J. 143
Alberdi, J. B. 140
Alberta 109, 111
Allan, G. L. 174, 178
Alpen, H. 175, 178, 181
Alsace-Lorraine 31
Anderson, J. 114
apartheid policy 230–1
Argentina 5, 6, 7, 8, 9, 139–51
Arnaudas, M. 96
Arnold, M. 20
artistic education 148
arts and culture learning area 231–3
Arts and Culture Task Group
    (ACTAG) 231–2
Ashley, J. H. 227
Australia 4–5, 6, 7, 9, 171–87

bands
    drum and fife 178, 179, 184
    military 158–9
    see also ensembles
Barreras, G. A. 160–1
Batista regime 156, 157
Bavío, R. 146
'beautiful singing' (skjönn sang) 83–4
Behrens, J. D. 82–3

Benestad, F. 84–5
Benum, I. 86
Billings, W. 124
Binet, A. 36
Birkett, C. 227
Bismarck, O. von 5, 31, 51
black Cubans 5, 155–6
Bokwe, J. K. 226
Bologna Declaration 99
Bonal, M. D. 93
Borguñó, M. 92, 93, 94
Boston 121–2
Bousquet, J. D. 154
Breen, D. 71
Britain 6, 7, 8, 10, 15–28
    and Ireland 63, 64, 68, 73
British Columbia 111
British Committee of Council on
    Education 63
British Empire 4–5, 7

cabildos 5, 155
Cai Yuanpei 192
Calvin, J. 123
Campbell, P. S. 3
Canada 5, 7, 10, 109–20
Canadian Music Educators' Association
    (CMEA) 117, 118
Canary Islands 91
Cape Colony 224, 225, 230
Cape Town Schools Choir 227–8
Castro, F. 162–3
Catholicism 97, 109, 110, 123, 191
    Argentina 139
    Cuba 154
    Ireland 70–1
Central Music Council 93

certificate of pedagogical aptitude 98
Chailley, J. 33
charter schools 133
Chevais, M. 29, 33, 35–7
Chevé, E. 7, 32
child-centred education 24, 54, 161, 198
    Spain 99
child development 114, 142
child psychology 36–7
China 5–6, 7, 9, 189–204
choral competitions 228, 229
choral festivals 180–1
Christian Socialists 19
cipher notation 7
    France 32–3
    Germany 50
    jianpu system 7, 192
    ziffer method 7, 80, 82
civilizing influence 6, 18, 19, 62, 176–7,
    180
Clark, A. 176, 178, 181, 184
Coalition for Music Education in
    Canada 117–18
cofradías 5, 155
colonialism 4–5
    Australia 171, 172–8
    Canada 109–10
    South Africa 224–30
    USA 121–4
common school movement 124–6
Communist China 194–7
competitions
    music festivals 115, 116
    school choir competitions 228, 229
composition 87, 116
compulsory schooling 1–2
    Argentina 140–1, 147–8
    Australia 171, 173
    Britain 16
    China 197, 198
    Germany 46–7
    Ireland 61, 72, 73
    South Africa 222, 230
    Spain 91, 92, 93, 95
    USA 122, 126–9, 131, 133
concerts
    school concerts 69, 71, 181–2, 182–4
    symphony concerts for children 55
Confucian value system 6, 189–90
conservatoires/music academies 8, 9,
    10–11
    Argentina 147, 148

Cuba 154, 157, 158, 158–9, 163–4
    France 35, 38
    Germany 55
Conservatorio de Música de Buenos
    Aires 147
Conservatorio Municipal de la
    Habana 158–9
Conservatorio Municipal de Música
    Manuel de Falla 147
Conservatorio Nacional de Cuba 158
Conservatorio Nacional de Música
    (Argentina) 147
convicts 172
Corcoran, Father T. 70
Cornejo de Sánchez, M. 143
Coronado, H. 123
corruption 156–7
Crane, J. E. 129
creativity 87, 116
Cringan, A. T. 113
cross-cultural perspective 3
Cuba 5, 8, 9, 10, 153–68
Cuban Revolution 6, 162–4
cultural imperialism 223
Cultural Revolution 6, 189, 196–7
curriculum 9–10
    Argentina 148
    Australia 178–9
    Britain 24–5
    Canada 116, 117
    China 193, 197–200
    Cuba 161, 164–5
    France 30–1, 39, 40–1
    Germany 52, 54, 57
    Ireland 65, 69, 70, 72
    Japan 210, 213–15, 216–17
    Norway 83, 86–7, 87–8
    South Africa 231–3
    Spain 91, 93–6, 98, 99
Curwen, J. 5, 7, 16, 17, 112, 191

Daines, T. 225
Dale, L. 227
De Blanck, H. 157–8
Deng Xiaoping 189, 197–8
Denmark 78
Dewey, J. 84, 128, 161
Diez, G. 143
Dillner, J. 80
drill 178, 184
drum and fife bands 178, 179, 184
Dutch Reformed Church 225

Eckert, F. 208
education system
    Argentina 141
    Cuba 153, 162–4
    Germany 50–2, 58
    Ireland 61–2
    Japan 213
    South Africa 229–32
    Spain 92–3
Eidsvoll Constitution 78
Elliot, S. 125
emotional power of music 55
Empire Day 4, 110, 179, 180
Engels, E. 84
ensembles (USA) 10, 129, 130, 131, 132,
    133
Escuela de Música y Canto 140
Escuela Nacional de Artes (La ENA)
    163
Escuela Normal de Música 159
Esnaola, J. P. 140, 143, 147
eurhythmics 179
Europe 4
    see also under individual countries
extra-curricular music
    Canada 112
    Norway 85–6

Falange 97
Farnesi, J. B. de 145
Farrington, F. 228–9
fees 57, 175
festivals
    choral 180–1
    competitive 115, 116
First World War 32, 69
Fisher, J. 175, 178, 179, 181
five-stave notation 198–9
fixed-doh method 7, 16, 30, 33
folksongs 22, 82, 91
    Irish traditional music 64, 68–9,
        72–3
formal education 222
formula method 83
Fottland, I. 84–5
Fourth of May Movement 193
France 5, 7, 8, 9, 17, 29–44
Franco-Prussian War 31
Franco regime 93, 94, 98
Free Institution of Teaching 91
Friedrich Wilhelm I 51
Froebel, F. 161

Gaelic League 67
Galin-Paris-Chevé method 32–3
gender differences 8, 30
general education 51, 52–3
generalist teachers 9
    Australia 174, 175, 185
    Cuba 165
    France 34, 38
    Germany 55
Germany 5, 6, 7, 8, 9, 45–60, 83–4, 180
Glover, S. 7, 17
goldfields 176–7
gongche notation 7, 190
Goodman, P. 66, 68
Government of National Unity 231
graded schools 92, 100
'Great Trek' 224
Gruhn, W. 10
Guido d'Arezzo 7

Han dynasty 190
Hargreaves, D. J. 3
harmonium 8, 82, 143
Havana 154
Havana Municipal Band 158, 159
Henríquez, M. A. 164
hierarchy of music learning 210
higher education 99, 101
Holt, H. 113
Home and Professional School for Women
    in Madrid 92
home schooling 133
Hong Xiu-quan 191
Huang Zi 193
Hughes, G. 112–13
Hullah, J. 7, 16, 17, 19, 20
Hullah method 7, 16, 63, 64, 178
Humboldt, W. von 50–1
hymns 69, 70, 191

ideal citizen 6, 19–20
immigration 125, 127, 140–1
imperial nationalism 4–5
indigenous peoples 10, 172
    South Africa 5, 221, 222–3, 226
Indonesia 10
industrialization 32, 125, 127
informal education 221–2
instrumental teaching 8, 10, 24
    Australia 178, 179
    Canada 116
    Ireland 67, 69

instrumental teaching, *cont.*
  Norway 87
International Society for Music Education
  (ISME) 2, 3, 116–17, 118
Ireland 4, 5, 7, 61–75, 176
Isawa Shūji 6, 206, 208, 209–11
Israel 10, 58
itinerant singing masters 174, 175

Japan 6, 7, 8–9, 191, 192, 205–20
Jaques-Dalcroze, E. 36, 37, 83, 148, 179
jianpu system 7, 192
Jöde, F. 85, 89
John Adaskin Project 116
Jugendbewegung 85, 89
junior high schools 115

Kalmar Union 78
Kestenberg, L. 52–3, 58
Kilpatrick, W. H. 84
klokkeren (church officials) 79, 81, 88
Kodály method 24, 37, 53, 179, 210
Koppang, O. 83
Kuomingtang 194

Labussière, A. 37–8
Landslaget Musikk i skolen 87
language revival movement 70
Latin schools 46
Lee, A. 227, 228–9
Legge, J. 191
Lei Feng 196
Li Shutong 193
Literacy Campaign 163
London Board of Education 68
Lovedale Missionary Institution 226
Luther, M. 46

Machado regime 156, 157
Mahler, E. 164
Mainzer, J. 16
major keys 210–11, 214–15
Malaysia 10
Manby group violin teaching method 179
mandatory singing test 31
Mao Zedong 189, 194, 196
Maritime provinces, Canada 110, 114
Martí, J. 162
Marx, K. 162
Mason, Lowell 125, 126
Mason, Luther Whiting 207–8, 209
McBurney, S. 178, 182, 183

McNaught, W. G. 18, 19, 20–1, 23
Mekada Tanetarō 206, 209
Menchaca system 145–6
Menendez, M. 161–2
military bands 158–9
minor keys 210–11
mission schools 5, 223, 224–6, 229, 230
missionaries 5, 191
model schools 63, 64
model works 196–7
modernization 197–8, 206
Montessori, M. 36, 161
Montreal 113–14
Moore, T. 63, 64
moral education 6, 209–10, 213, 217
Moroi Saburō 213, 214
movable-doh system 7, 17, 33
  see also tonic sol-fa
Muir, T. 227, 228, 229, 230
music examinations 66
music inspectors 17–18
Music Manifesto 25
Music Study Committee 8–9, 206–12
'Musical Futures' 10, 25

Nägeli, H. G. 48–9, 50, 83
Natal 224, 230
national anthem, Argentinian 139, 142–3
national associations of music
  educators 11, 117, 118
National Curriculum (Britain) 24
national songs
  Britain 21–2, 26, 64
  Ireland 64, 68–9
  Japan 215–16
nationalism 4–6
  Germany 52
  Ireland 67–9
  Norway 82, 85
  see also patriotism
nature 182
Nazism 6, 53
New England colonies 121–2
New School movement 160–1
New South Wales 171, 172, 173–4, 174–5,
  176–7, 185
Newfoundland 110, 111–12
Nie Er 194
nine-step hierarchy 210
Nixon, H. 227
No Child Left Behind legislation 130
non-formal education 221–2, 224–6

Nordsjø, E. 86
North, A. 3
Norway 5, 7, 8, 77–90
  1739 decree 79–80
numeral notation *see* cipher notation

Office of Music (*Yuefu*) 190
Office of the Grand Music Master 190
Ongaku torishirabe kakari (Music Study
  Committee) 8–9, 206–12
Ontario 110–11, 113
Ontario Music Educators' Association
  (OMEA) 117
open-door policy 189, 197–8, 200
Orange Free State 224, 230
Orff method 24, 37, 53, 93–4, 97, 148, 179
organists 54, 80
Ortiz dance school 153

Panizza, J. G. 144–5
Parés, J. 154
patriotism 5–6
  Argentina 139, 141–2, 144
  Australia 179–80
  China 192–4
  France 31–2
  Germany 52
  see also nationalism
payment-by-results system 17, 18, 20, 64–6
Paynter, J. 24, 87
'pedagogical missions' 92
Pestalozzi, J. H. 48–9, 51, 111, 125
Pfeiffer, M. T. 48–9, 50
phonograph 115, 128
phonomimie 30, 36
physical education 161
Picassarri, A. 140
plain chant 71
player piano 128
Plymouth, Massachusetts 122
political independence 5–6
  Argentina 139
  Cuba 153, 156
Preston, S. H. 113
primary schools
  Cuba 160–1
  Germany 54–5, 57
  Spain 92, 93, 94, 95–6, 97–8, 99
  universal primary education 2
Primary Studies Certificate 31
printing press 226
professional music schools 163–4

Programme for International Student
  Assessment (PISA) 88, 89
progressive educational ideas 36, 114
  Norway 84–7
  Spain 92
  USA 128–9
pronunciation 142, 177
Protestantism 109–10, 191
Prussia *see* Germany
psalmodikon 7, 8, 80, 82
psalters 123

Quarton, L. 181–2
Quebec 110

racism 155–6
radio 115, 128, 165
Reconstruction and Development
  Programme (RDP) 231
refining influence 6, 18, 19, 62, 176–7, 180
Reformation 15
relative pitch 33
  see also movable-doh system; tonic sol-fa
religion 19
  Canada 109–10, 110, 111
  China 190–1
  Germany 49–50
  Ireland 62, 64, 69, 70–1
  Norway 79–80, 80–1, 85
  South Africa 223, 224–6
  USA 123
  see also Catholicism; mission schools;
    missionaries; Protestantism
repertoire *see* school music repertoire
repression 157
revolutionary music 194–7
Ricci, M. 191
Richard, T. 191
Richards, M. 182–3
Roca, J. V. 96
Roldán, A. 159
Rousseau, J. -J. 7, 80, 161
Roverud, L. 80–1
Russia 10, 163
Ryerson, E. 6, 111, 112

Salas, E. 154
Santiago Cathedral 154
Sanuy, M. 93–4
Sarmiento, D. F. 140
Saskatchewan 109, 111
Schafer, R. M. 87, 116

school choir competitions 228, 229
school concerts 69, 71, 181–2, 182–4
school music repertoire
  Argentina 139, 142–4
  Australia 179–84
  Britain 22
  Canada 114
  China 196
  France 32
  Germany 49–50, 52
  Ireland 63, 64, 68–9
  Japan 215–16
  Norway 85
secondary schools
  Germany 55, 57
  Spain 94–5, 96, 98, 99
Sefton, H. F. 111
sensory approach 35–6
Sentenat, C. P. 159
shape note system 124
Sharp, C. 22
Shen Xingong 193
Sing Up campaign 25, 26
singing at sight (by note) 6–7, 16–17, 18,
  20, 65
singing by ear (by rote) 8, 17, 18, 65, 175
  see also tonic sol-fa
singing schools 123–4
Sino-Japanese War (1937–45) 5–6, 193–4
Sistema, El 25–6
skjönn sang (beautiful singing) 83
slaves 155
Sobrequés, T. 96–7
social control 126–7, 131
Soler, M. 96
solfège 7, 30, 33, 83
solmization 6–7
  see also tonic sol-fa
Somervell, A. 6, 18, 19–20, 21, 22
Sontonga, E. 226
Søraas, L. 83–4
sound method 83
South Africa 5, 221–35
South Australia 6, 171, 172, 173, 175–6,
  177–8
Spain 6, 8, 9, 91–105, 156
specialist teachers 9
  Argentina 147
  Australia 174, 175, 185
  China 198
  Cuba 162
  Spain 94–5

staff notation 82–3, 112, 113
Stainer, J. 17, 18, 19, 20, 23
standard pitch 33
state 50–2
Statens lærerkurs 87
status of music in society 39–40, 71
Stewart, J. 226
studio teachers 154
Sturt Street School Band 184
Summers, J. 178
Swanwick, K. 11, 24
Sweden 78

'Tale of the Bellbirds' 182, 183
Tanaka Fujimaro 206
Tang dynasty 190
'teacher-kantor' 54
teacher training 8–9
  Argentina 146–7, 148
  Australia 172–6
  Britain 22–3, 25
  Canada 116
  China 192, 195–6, 198
  Cuba 159, 161–2, 164
  France 34, 38
  Germany 54–5
  Ireland 67
  Japan 211–12, 216
  Norway 81–2, 87
  South Africa 227, 229, 232, 233
  Spain 91, 96–8
  USA 129, 132
teaching materials
  Argentina 143, 144–6
  Canada 113, 114, 115, 116
  China 191, 198–200
  Cuba 162, 164, 165
  France 35–6
  Japan 207–8, 213–15
  USA 123–4, 126, 130
teaching methods 6–8
  Argentina 144–6, 148
  Australia 178
  Britain 20–2
  Canada 112–14
  Cuba 160–1
  France 32–4, 35–7
  Germany 48–9, 49–50, 53
  Hullah 7, 16, 63, 64, 178
  Ireland 63, 64
  Norway 80, 82–4
  USA 124, 126

teaching methods, *cont.*
  Wilhem 30, 63
  see also tonic sol-fa
Thousand Voices Choir 181
Tomás, G. 158–9
tonic numeral method 178
tonic sol-fa 7, 17
  Argentina 144–5
  Australia 178
  Britain 20–1
  Canada 112–14
  China 191
  Ireland 65–6, 70
  South Africa 225–6, 227–9
Tonic Sol-fa College 17, 228, 229
Torres, J. M. 142
Tourjeè, I. 207
town hall music schools 147
transfer of learning 25
Transvaal 224, 225, 230
tuition fees 57

UNESCO Conference in Brussels (1953) 2
Union of South Africa 224, 230
United Nations Millennium Development
  Goals 2, 10
United States of America (USA) 6, 8, 9,
  10, 114, 121–36
  Cuba 156
  Japan 213
universal primary education 2
urbanization 125, 127

value of music education 6, 140
  Argentina 141–2

Australia 176–8, 180
Britain 19–20
Canada 112
France 37, 38–9
Ireland 62–3, 66
Japan 209–10, 214, 215
Vélazquez, M. 154
Venezuela 25
Victoria 171, 172, 173, 174, 175, 176–7,
  185
vocal staircase 30
vocalization 212–13

Waite, J. 178
Walsh, Father J. T. 68
Walter, A. 116–17
Western music
  in China 191
  in Japan 205, 207, 211, 212–13,
    214–15, 216–17
White Garland, The 182
Wider Opportunities Scheme 25
Wilhem, G. L. B. 7, 16, 30, 63
Wilkins, W. 177, 178, 180
Williams, A. 143, 147
Woodbridge, W. 125
Wyse, Sir T. 62

Xian Xinghai 194
Xiao Yumei 192

youth culture 56

zarzuela 8, 161
ziffer notation method 7, 80, 82

Made in the USA
Lexington, KY
01 May 2012